The Pastoral Epistles and the New Perspective on Paul

The Pastoral Epistles and the New Perspective on Paul

Daniel Wayne Roberts

FOREWORD BY
Benjamin L. Merkle

WIPF & STOCK · Eugene, Oregon

THE PASTORAL EPISTLES AND THE NEW PERSPECTIVE ON PAUL

Wipf & Stock
An Imprint of Wipf and Stock Publishers
199 W. 8th Ave., Suite 3
Eugene, OR 97401

www.wipfandstock.com

PAPERBACK ISBN: 978-1-6667-1466-1
HARDCOVER ISBN: 978-1-6667-1467-8
EBOOK ISBN: 978-1-6667-1468-5

08/19/21

I dedicate this work to the God of all patience,
to the "wife of my youth," *Dodi* Leigh,
to my children, Adriana, Asher, and Levi,
and, to the children we never met, lost in this journey.

Contents

Foreword

STORIES OF LONG-LOST FAMILY members meeting for the first time are always heartwarming. In fact, TLC currently has a show called *Long Lost Family*. The show follows the reunion of children, parents, siblings, and other family members who meet after many, many years of separation. Sometimes the person has never met or has no recollection of their relative. This book presents union and interface of two areas of New Testament study that have not really met: the Pastoral Epistles and the New Perspective on Paul.

In his seminal work, *Paul and Palestinian Judaism*, E. P. Sanders never once cites or references any text from the Pastoral Epistles (according to the index). The reason for this omission is obvious: the focus of his discussion centered on Romans and Galatians. Additionally, Sanders—and many other scholars—doesn't believe Paul wrote 1 Timothy, 2 Timothy, or Titus. This pattern of omitting, ignoring, or minimizing the voice of these three epistles has persisted in discussions regarding the New Perspective on Paul. But if the Pastoral Epistles are welcomed into the New Perspective conversation, would they challenge or confirm the major tenets of the New Perspective? The answer to that question is the thrust of this present work.

Roberts skillfully addresses the major tenets of the New Perspective and tests their validity according to the teaching found in the Pastoral Epistles. The justification for bringing the epistles of 1–2 Timothy and Titus into the conversation is based on the canonical approach. Additionally, the Pastoral Epistles have been accepted as Pauline by most Christians throughout church history. Specifically, by studying select passages (1 Tim 1:6–16; 2:3–7; 2 Tim 1:3, 8–12 and Titus 3:3–7), Roberts demonstrates that although many of the tenets of the New Perspective are consistent with the data in the Pastorals, at a few places the claims of the New Perspective may need to be adjusted.

It is a joy to commend this work to you, partly because it is a joy to see the reunion of the Pastoral Epistles into the Pauline family and partly because Roberts is a great host who cordially brings both parties together.

Benjamin L. Merkle

Professor of New Testament and Greek
Editor, *Southeastern Baptist Theological Review*
Southeastern Baptist Theological Seminary, Wake Forest, NC

Acknowledgments

If C. S. Lewis speaks of himself as the "most reluctant convert," then I must speak of myself as the "most unlikely academician." And yet, through God's grace, here I am, after having finished my dissertation, publishing my first book. There are so many that have contributed to my academic journey for whom I am grateful. This journey is, in many ways, one in the same with my spiritual journey. As goes my spiritual life, so goes my academic life. I began this journey many years ago as a result of the encouragement of my grandfather, James ("Bop") Latham. I can acknowledge no one, unless I first acknowledge him. I miss him and his encouragement. I am grateful for him, and like Timothy, I am grateful for the faith of my mother (Renee) and grandmother (Marvis), and the ways in which they encouraged me in whatever pursuits I found myself engaged. I have always had a restless, excitable spirit. They embraced that spirit and helped me steer my tenacity in the right direction. I am most grateful of all people, for my wife Leigh, and my three children, Adriana, Asher, and Levi. Leigh, as a gift from God, has made me a better man—more fit to serve her, my children, and his kingdom. In many ways, God sent her to me so that I might have eyes to see.

I am grateful for, and indebted to, every church I have served and every church that has served me. The Decatur Highway Church of Christ (Gardendale, Alabama) nurtured me in my adolescence, as did the small church we attended when I was a boy, the Antioch Church of Christ (Corner, Alabama). When I think back to the roots of my faith, Antioch is there in my mind with the slow, deep bass voice of Lonnie Ingram, the preacher and our family friend. The Luverne Church of Christ (Luverne, Alabama) helped mold me as a young intern, where I lived in a small apartment attached to the church building. The Madison Park Church of Christ (Montgomery, Alabama) let me preach once per month as a young college student, which was invaluable experience for me. The Mott Church of Christ (Red

xiii

Level, Alabama) was the first church I served as the pulpit minister, while also cutting grass and working on a cotton farm. I was twenty-one. They showed me a great deal of mercy and kindness in my youthful excitement and forgave the many mistakes I made. The Central Church of Christ (Andalusia, Alabama) helped me continue to hone my skills as a teacher, orator, and servant of the kingdom. Neither they, nor the Mott church, ever (to my knowledge) let my youthfulness affect the way in which they treated me. The North Raleigh Church of Christ (Raleigh, North Carolina) helped me survive in the lean months when I lived, worked, and studied in Wake Forest. I would also like to thank the churches in Belize, with whom I have served the kingdom in various ways for twelve years. I give special thanks to the Cameron Avenue Church of Christ (Colonial Heights, Virginia) with whom I am currently serving—especially the elders (Larry Little, Jimmy Radcliffe, Gene Autry, Alan Sprowl, and Chris Strosnider) and deacons. They have supported me from the very beginning, when I first received my official acceptance letter as a PhD student. They have seen me struggle through this academic Odyssey, but I hope they have seen me grow and overcome through the grace that God supplied. Without them, I would not have been able to continue to pursue my degree. I am grateful for the challenges I receive from the church as well, both from the pulpit and in Bible study. Iron sharpens iron. During my last week of preparations before submitting this document for publication, one of our beloved sisters in the church, Wanda Meadows, passed away. These brothers and sisters in God's kingdom remind me of what is important.

I am grateful for my academic mentors Randall Bailey (my academic grandfather) and Floyd Parker, with whom I still find myself conferring on all of my academic interests and pursuits. Dr. Parker has been a true friend, and more, a father in the faith—like Paul to Timothy. In reality, my decision to pursue graduate school and a PhD is ultimately his and Dr. Bailey's doing (1 Cor 4:15).

I am indebted to the kindness and helpfulness of the library at Union Presbyterian Seminary where I did most of my studying for comprehensive exams and wrote my dissertation. Even though I was not a student at their institution, I was given the opportunity to reserve a carrel, what I have affectionally called the "dungeon," which was helpful for undistracted time to focus. In fact, they allow me to use my carrel even still. They offered a different carrel to me, but I refused because if I had a view of their beautiful campus from my carrel window, I would have found myself daydreaming instead of working. They have far surpassed their "extra mile" in order to help me. Although through my time as a PhD student I did not live on campus, the Southeastern Baptist Theological Seminary (SEBTS) library has also been extremely helpful and accommodating, making my work easier and more efficient.

I owe a debt of gratitude to Dr. Stephen Stout, SEBTS's SBL formatting reader. His kindness, timeliness, and sometimes badly needed "brutal honesty" (his words, not mine) proved invaluable in this process. I do not think I could have done this project without him. I am appreciative of my Dissertation Committee and the sharp eyes and strong minds of Dr. Miguel Echevarria and Dr. Frank Thielman. They provided valuable insight and helped me with clarity and thoroughness. I also want to thank Dr. Benjamin Merkle, my "doctor-father." He has been a perfect mentor for me. He is kind, gentle, and patient and has continually held me to the highest of standards. I had for many years wanted to write on the New Perspective on Paul, but it was he who pointed me in the direction of the Pastoral Epistles as a place that had been overlooked in Pauline studies. As I have told many, it seems that all roads led to SEBTS, even though the traveling was not always easy. I have been a full-time preacher for most of my time at SEBTS, but I was determined to continue to take traditional courses, and fortunately Cameron Avenue allowed me to do so. Every professor I had was an exemplar of excellence, and expected the same of me. This pursuit of excellence did not always come easily, but it was this pursuit that has given me the needed resilience to finish. Like Timothy, who, as a "type," bridged the gap between Jew and gentile, this project has been my stand between the church and the academy. Each week, as I wrote and studied, the congregation I serve has been a constant reminder of what is important: Christ and his church. The work I do is for him, for his church, and ultimately, all he will call to himself.

I am grateful to Paul, the apostle. I am grateful for his brilliant mind, his mission to the gentiles, and the letters and legacy he left. I am most grateful for his life, ministry, and suffering as an example of the living gospel. I feel privileged to be able to study his work.

I am grateful for all the people who have helped and encouraged me along the way: Rick and Lorna Tribby (my Indiana parents), Larry and Ginny Little, Randy and Sharon Cornelius, Byron and Erica Thomasson, Mark Applegate, Josh Collins, Gregory Lamb and Thomas Cribb (my academic comrades-in-arms), Cecil May, Martel Pace, Carl Cheatham, Don Meyers, David Stark, Tommy South, Lonnie and Kay Ingram, Mike Whisenant, Lee and Kathy Jamieson, Dale and Julie Sanders (and their son Calem), Glen Huggins, Ricky and Tricia Gibson (I cannot count the amount of times I slept on their couch or in their son, Andy's, bed as a young, traveling preacher), Andy and Jessica Gibson, Billy Gorum, Larry and Ann Foley, Lamar Foley, Kevin and Elysa Henegar, Todd and Indy

Harris, Jack and Linda Harris, Ken Chaffin, Scott and Laura Garrison, Virginia McCrory, Nick Schmahl, Paul and Shannon Holder, Chris and Kelly Hughes, Paul and Lisa Ashurst, Gary and Sherry Roberts, Debbie Blaylock, Christy Thornton (who provided encouragement before each of my tests when I was disheveled and insecure), Arny and Wanda Meadows, Chris and Janie Strosnider, Alan and Sandra Sprowl, Jimmy and Mandy Radcliffe, Gene and Tammy Autry, and many others.

I am especially grateful for the team at Wipf and Stock Publishers. I am grateful for their consideration and acceptance of my manuscript for publication. They were easy to work with, prompt, courteous, and professional. They made this process easy and enjoyable. I offer special thanks to Caleb Shupe (my copy editor and format checker), Calvin Jaffarian (my typesetter), Matthew Wimer, Emily Callihan, and George Callihan.

Finally, I give thanks to God for the gift of his Son, Christ Jesus, and for the Holy Spirit that lives in me. I am grateful for the depth of his patience, kindness, and mercy for me, a sinner.

Abbreviations

AB	Anchor Bible
ABD	The Anchor Bible Dictionary
Abib	Analecta Biblica
ACNT	Augsburg Commentary on the New Testament
ANTC	Abingdon New Testament Commentaries
AYB	The Anchor Yale Bible
BDAG	Bauer, W., W. F. Arndt, F. W. Gingrich, and F. W. Danker. *A Greek English Lexicon of the New Testament and Other Christian Literature.* 3rd edition.
BBC	Blackwell Bible Commentary
BBET	*Beiträge zur biblischen Exegese Theologie*
BJRL	*Bulletin of the John Rylands University Library of Manchester*
BNTC	Black's New Testament Commentary
BTCP	Biblical Theology for Christian Proclamation
CBC	The Cambridge Bible Commentary
CBQ	*Catholic Biblical Quarterly*
CJ	*Concordia Journal*
CP	*The Confessional Presbyterian*
CTR	*Criswell Theological Review*
DSS	Dead Sea Scrolls

EC   *Early Christianity*

ECC   The Eerdmans Critical Commentary

EDNT   *Exegetical Dictionary of the New Testament*

EDT   *Evangelical Dictionary of Theology*

ExpT   *Expository Times*

GBS   Grove Biblical Series

HBT   *Horizons in Biblical Theology*

HTR   *Harvard Theological Review*

HTS   Harvard Theological Studies

HUT   Hermeneutische Untersuchungen zur Theologie

ICC   The International Critical Commentary

Int   *Interpretation*

JBL   *Journal of Biblical Literature*

JJS   *Journal of Jewish Studies*

JPT   *Journal of Psychology and Theology*

JSNT   *Journal for the Study of the New Testament*

JSNTSup   Journal for the Study of the New Testament: Supplement Series

JTI   *Journal of Theological Interpretation*

JTS   *The Journal of Theological Studies*

LEC   Library of Early Christianity

LNTS   The Library of New Testament Studies

LPS   Library of Pauline Studies

LWC   The Living Word Commentary

MNTC   The Moffat New Testament Commentary

NIB   *The New Interpreter's Bible*

NIBC   New International Biblical Commentary

NICNT   The New International Commentary on the New Testament

NIGTC	New International Greek Testament Commentary
NPP	The New Perspective on Paul
NovT	*Novum Testamentum*
NSBT	New Studies in Biblical Theology
NTC	The New Testament in Context
NTL	The New Testament Library
NTM	New Testament Message
NTM	New Testament Monographs
NTS	*New Testament Studies*
NTT	New Testament Theology
PNTC	The Pillar New Testament Commentary
RBTR	*Reformed Baptist Theological Review*
RevBib	*Revue Biblique*
SBL	Society of Biblical Literature
SBLDS	Society of Biblical Literature Dissertation Series
SBLit	Studies in Biblical Literature
SJT	*Scottish Journal of Theology*
SNTSMS	Society of New Testament Studies Monograph Series
SNTSU	*Studien zum Neuen Testament und seiner Umwelt*
ST	*Studia Theologica*
STR	*Southeastern Theological Review*
TDNT	*Theological Dictionary of the New Testament*
Them	*Themelios*
THNTC	The Two Horizons New Testament Commentary
ThTo	*Theology Today*
TNTC	The Tyndale New Testament Commentaries
TynBul	*Tyndale Bulletin*
USQR	*Union Seminary Quarterly Review*

WBC	Word Biblical Commentary
WSJ	Wall Street Journal
WTJ	*Westminster Theological Journal*
WUNT	Wissenschaftliche Untersuchungen zum Neuen Testament
ZNW	*Zeitschrift für die neutestamentliche Wissenschaft und die Kunde der älteren Kirche*

1

The New Perspective on Paul and the Pastoral Epistles

Problem, Thesis, and Method

Introduction

THE "NEW PERSPECTIVE ON Paul,"[1] though only about forty years old, has remarkably changed the landscape of Pauline studies. Beginning with E. P. Sanders's landmark work *Paul and Palestinian Judaism* in 1977, then transitioning in various ways through the work of those like James D. G. Dunn and N. T. Wright, the NPP has become either a beacon of light or a shadow of turning to those who study it.[2] One of the major problems that the NPP has highlighted is that much of the debate is focused around early Judaism, and only consequently, on Paul.[3] What further complicates these studies is the distrust of many scholars of the NT itself with regard to accurate descriptions of Jewish belief. They feel that the polemical nature of the Gospels and Paul create a caricature rather than a properly critical, historical view of

---

1. Henceforth designated as NPP.

2. The works of Sanders, and especially that of Dunn and Wright are prolific. Some of the more specific and nuanced arguments, as well as individual contributions of these authors, will be treated more thoroughly in the next chapter. However, for now here is a small, specific sampling of some of their most influential works for quick reference: Sanders, *Paul and Palestinian Judaism*; Sanders, *Paul, the Law, and the Jewish People*; Dunn, *Theology of Paul the Apostle*; Dunn, *New Perspective on Paul*; Wright, "Paul of History and the Apostle of Faith," 61–88; Wright, *Climax of the Covenant*; Wright, *What Saint Paul Really Said*; Wright, *Paul and the Faithfulness of God*.

3. This problem can be seen in Sanders's work, who even by the estimation of Wright, does not interpret Paul well, even though Wright follows much of his thought concerning Judaism and covenantal nomism. See also the two-volume reaction against this understanding of first-century Judaism edited by D. A. Carson et al., *Justification and Variegated Nomism*.

early Judaism.[4] Because of this concern with early Judaism, then, only certain Pauline letters have contributed to the core of the NPP (Romans, Galatians, and Phil 3:1–11).[5] In other words, the letters of Paul that take up a polemic against Judaism are the letters that have stood at the fore of recent Pauline theology. The fact that Romans is one of Paul's most articulated, "full" theological treatments and considered by many to be Paul's major theology further complicates the issue because it, too, deals with the clash of Paul's theology with Judaism and the law (cf. Rom 2:12–3:9, 19–31; 7:1–23). For those like Wright, who argue that justification is not Paul's theological center[6] but that Jesus himself and the gospel is—that place is reserved for "participation in Christ" for Schweitzer and Sanders—Romans is both proof and foil. Galatians, although likely written much earlier, resembles much of the language and argumentation of Romans. However, the focus on Romans and Galatians is not new, nor is it centered around the NPP. Martin Luther himself focused his theology and study on justification, law, and grace after teaching a seminar on Romans[7] and called Galatians his Katy von Bora (his wife), insinuating "Galatians was his most treasured epistle."[8] What is different is that the overly critical methods of studying the Bible have segmented the biblical material into various "canons," with Romans, Galatians, and the other "undisputed" Pauline epistles being

4. A scholar known for arguing that Paul misrepresented the Jewish law is Heikki Räisänen. There are some who place him in the loose tradition of the NPP. However, it is hard to place Räisänen within that tradition because he argues that Paul himself is not consistent with regard to the law, even though Sanders himself may be accused of the same thing. See Räisänen, *Paul and the Law*; Räisänen, *Jesus, Paul, and Torah: Collected Essays*. For the critique of Sanders, see Dunn, *Theology of Paul the Apostle*, 339.

5. This is not to say that the NPP has not dealt with or written about other Pauline documents, but that the formation of the NPP was a result of studying undisputed Paul, with a natural emphasis on Romans and Galatians.

6. Wright is not the first to argue this thesis. William Wrede and Albert Schweitzer both notoriously argued that justification is polemical (Wrede) and a "subsidiary crater" (Schweitzer). See Wright, *Justification: God's Plan and Paul's Vision* as well Wright's *Paul in Recent Scholarship* whose title is itself reminiscent of Schweitzer's work on Pauline research. Also see Wrede, *Paulus* and Albert Schweitzer, *Paul and His Interpreters*. The oft-quoted phrase "subsidiary crater" is found in Schweitzer, *Mysticism of Paul the Apostle*, 225. Though Wright does not think justification is the center of Paul's theology, he also does not think it is purely secondary. See, Wright, *What Saint Paul Really Said*, 114.

7. J. Theodore Mueller says as much in his translation of Luther's *Commentary on Romans*. See Mueller in the Foreword to Luther, *Commentary on Romans*, vii–x. The "seminar" on Romans took three semesters to complete (November 3, 1515–September 7, 1516). Luther never taught Romans again. Mueller considers, "Had he done so, he no doubt would have revised much of what he had written at so early a time in his teaching career." Mueller, "Foreword," vii.

8. Westerholm, *Perspectives Old and New on Paul*, 22.

one such canon and the Pastoral Epistles, along with other disputed Pauline epistles, belonging to another.[9]

This focus on only a small portion of Pauline documents has led many scholars to consider what the NPP might look like if other letters were brought into the discussion. In the conclusion to his book, *Paul and the Gift*, John Barclay argues that the move from Romans (undisputed Paul) to Titus (PE) is a "contextual shift" wherein "'works' are refocused as moral achievements."[10] He cites Ephesians 2:8–10, 2 Timothy 1:9, and Titus 3:5 as examples. I. Howard Marshall and Robert Cara also make similar observations.[11] Stephen Westerholm goes so far as to say,

> No study that took Ephesians and the Pastorals into account could conclude, what proponents of the new perspective have sometimes claimed, that the Pelagian crisis or sixteenth-century controversies are the source of the 'misreading' of Paul that sees him excluding human works from salvation rather than particular works from the terms for Gentile admission into the people of God.[12]

Although this study is not able to make such a bold claim as Westerholm, his assessment segues into the second aspect of this study, the Pastoral Epistles. The Pastoral Epistles,[13] though accepted as Pauline until 1807,[14] have been considered pseudonymous by the majority of critical scholars in the last two hundred years. This relegation to a post-Pauline milieu has also reassigned the purpose of the PE with regard to Pauline theology. When once the PE were studied as part of Paul's genuine thought, now they are seen as the next development in the history of the church, from a charismatic movement to

9. For example, see Beker, *Heirs of Paul*; and Dunn, *Theology of Paul the Apostle*, 354, where he calls Ephesians and the PE, specifically 2 Tim 1:9 and Titus 3:5, "post-Pauline."

10. Barclay, *Paul and the Gift*, 571. This is similar to the argument made by John Drane and Hans Hübner, who argue that Paul developed his theology from Galatians to Romans. See Drane, *Paul, Libertine or Legalist?* and Hübner, *Das Gesetz bei Paulus*.

11. Marshall, "Faith and Works in the Pastoral Epistles," 203–18; Marshall, "Salvation, Grace, and Works in the Later Writings in the Pauline Corpus," 3–29; Cara, *Cracking the Foundation*.

12. Westerholm, *Perspectives Old and New on Paul*, 406. Although not an adherent of the NPP, Westerholm gives one of the best explanations of the history of the rise of the NPP. He deals with the major issues within the NPP and defends the Lutheran position. This work is of utmost importance if one is going to study the debates surrounding the NPP.

13. Henceforth designated PE.

14. Friedrich Scheleiermacher was the first to argue against the Pauline authorship of 1 Timothy. Schleiermacher, *Über den sogenannten ersten Brief des Paulus an den Timotheos*.

an institutionalized church—from Paul to "Paulinists."[15] And, often, this development is seen in a negative light. This shift from charismatic movement to institutionalization is not understood by most as Paul's own shift, but a shift that rose after the death of Paul, in Paul's name, though in some ways still reliant upon Paul's theology. Brevard Childs states something similar to this study's stated problem with Pauline Theology with regard to the PE: "However, often as a consequence (of non-Pauline authorship) the importance of these letters has been disregarded and they continue to be designated by many as inferior in quality."[16] In contrast to the PE's denigration, canonically speaking, the PE are Pauline documents and represent Pauline thought and should thus be considered when articulating Pauline theology. Although there may be implications concerning the authorship of the PE as a result of this study, this study is not directly concerned with authorship. Instead, what this study seeks to do is test the NPP by the theology of the Pastoral Epistles using four major characteristics of the NPP as a guide for choosing the passages to be studied.

Statement of Thesis

This project lies at the intersection of these two research trajectories.[17] The first is that of the Pastoral Epistles. For the last couple of centuries, the authorship of the PE has been a debated topic.[18] Generally speaking, the majority of critical scholars deny Pauline authorship while more conservative scholars have held to the traditional view that Paul was the author.[19]

---

15. "Paulinist" does not need to be confused with "Paulinism," and by that, this study means Paul's theological system of belief. A smattering of scholars who contend for the pseudonymous authorship of the PE, yet see continuity and development, include: Dunn, *Unity and Diversity in the New Testament*; Beker, *Heirs of Paul*, 36–47; Aageson, *Paul, the Pastoral Epistles, and the Early Church*, 1–3; Lohfink, "Paulinische Theologie in der Rezeption der Pastoralbriefe," 70–121; Trummer, *Die Paulustradition der Pastoralbrief*.

16. Childs, *Church's Guide for Reading Paul*, 70.

17. Although the project will refer to two research trajectories, these two trajectories are not mutually exclusive. However, the emergence of two disciplines in Pauline studies (the PE and the NPP) is the problem that has led to the necessity of this work.

18. See Twomey, *Pastoral Epistles through the Centuries*; Harding, *What Are They Saying About the Pastoral Epistles*, 9–27. Both of these works highlight the early acceptance of the Pastorals by the church fathers because of their Pauline connection. Since those like Friedrich Schleiermacher and F. C. Baur in the late eighteenth/early nineteenth centuries, the letters have come under more and more scrutiny, all the while maintaining some adherents to the Pauline authenticity of the letters.

19. See Johnson, *Letters to Paul's Delegates*; Mounce, *Pastoral Epistles*; and Knight,

Because the *status quo* of the secular academic community is to deny Pauline authorship, the PE are often neglected (or completely omitted) in discussions of Pauline theology and earliest church polity. Rather, many see the PE as pseudonymous, reflecting a much later, second-century depiction of the church or that the PE contain some Pauline elements, Pauline fragments, or even Pauline tradition being carried out by "Paulinists."[20] Because of the concerns of Pauline authorship, the PE have been studied as their own corpus separate from the undisputed letters of Paul and compared with "pristine" Pauline theology, which is established from the undisputed letters of Paul.[21] In recent study, the major focus of research of the Pastorals has been on church polity and women in the ministry rather than on Pauline Theology proper.[22] This is not to say that the theology of the PE has not been studied.[23] However, often, the focus of the theology of the PE is not on Pauline theology as such, but on the theology of the PE as a distinct discipline, or a theology set against proper Pauline theology found in the undisputed Pauline corpus, or even as the next development of the history of the church. It is as if the study of Paul (and, specifically for this study, the NPP) and study of the PE have been two rails of a railroad track, progressing, but not meeting.

In the meantime, study of Paul and the undisputed letters have developed dramatically over the last thirty to forty years in isolation from the PE, which introduces the second trajectory: the New Perspective on

Commentary on the Pastoral Epistles for a conservative position. In critical scholarship, pseudonymous authorship is virtually ubiquitous, with the dissident, more conservative voices being those highlighted.

20. For example, see Beker, *Heirs of Paul* who argues for "Paulinist" composition. Others opt for fragmentary works or amanuenses. See Harrison, *Problem of the Pastorals*; Miller, *Pastoral Letters as Composite Documents*; Moule, "Problem of the Pastorals: A Reappraisal," 430–52; and Wilson, *Luke and the Pastoral Epistles*. Pertinent to this work is the view of James D. G. Dunn articulated in *Unity and Diversity in the New Testament* wherein he argues (similar to F. C. Baur and Walter Bauer) that the PE are part of the "early catholic" progression of the church based in Pauline thought, but a generation removed from it.

21. Brox, *Die Pastoralbriefe*; Barnett, *Paul Becomes a Literary Influence*. Among these discussions are also the discussions concerning the PE and pseudepigraphy. For examples, see Donelson, *Pseudepigraphy and Ethical Argument in the Pastoral Epistles*; and Stanley E. Porter and Gregory P. Fewster's (eds.) collection of essays in *Paul and Pseudepigraphy*.

22. A few examples include Beker, *Heirs of Paul*; Downs, "'Early Catholicism' and Apocalypticism in the Pastoral Epistles," 641–61; Gehring, *House Church and Mission*; Harding, *Tradition and Rhetoric in the Pastoral Epistles*; Köstenberger and Schreiner, *Women in the Church*; Merkle, *Elder and Overseer*.

23. Köstenberger and Wilder, *Entrusted with the Gospel*; Towner, *Goal of Our Instruction*; Young, *Theology of the Pastoral Epistles*.

Paul (NPP), a "new" way of seeing first-century Judaism and, in turn, Paul's arguments in Romans and Galatians.[24] This "perspective" arose in the late 1970s as a result of growing dissatisfaction with the history-of-religions approach that focused on Hellenistic moorings in Paul and existentialism, rather than appreciating and accentuating the Jewish-ness of Paul.[25] The so-called "new perspective" was generated from the work of E. P. Sanders and has been more finely articulated by James D. G. Dunn and N. T. Wright.[26] Though both of these scholars have adopted portions of Sanders's program, they have critiqued it at points as well. These conversations with Sanders have caused the "new perspective on Paul" to have different manifestations in contemporary Pauline study, but it has also helped articulate some continuities and commonalities that separate the NPP hermeneutic from traditional ways of interpreting Paul.

The two aforementioned trajectories meet in this project. The NPP has focused attention on Romans and Galatians because of their similarity and undeniable Pauline pedigree, which has led much of Pauline scholarship in the same direction as scholarship responds to the NPP.[27] The PE

24. Although at this point, a rudimentary understanding of the NPP is assumed, there are two helpful introductions to thoughts concerning the NPP and some of its major tenets. First, see Yinger, *New Perspective on Paul* and, next, Thompson, *New Perspective on Paul*. It should be noted that both of these authors are sympathetic to the NPP movement, and Yinger himself has contributed a major monograph, *Paul, Judaism, and Judgment According to Deeds*. See also Meek, "New Perspective on Paul," 208–33; and McDonald, "New Perspective on Paul," 208–33. James Dunn also classifies four major tenets of the NPP similar to what has been stated by others which is (1) "a new perspective on Judaism," (2) Paul's mission to the gentiles as context for justification, (3) justification by faith versus works of law, and (4) "the whole gospel of Paul." Interestingly enough, this study is focused on the latter in incorporating the whole gospel of Paul with the inclusion of the PE. See Dunn, "New Perspective on the New Perspective on Paul," 158.

25. This began with E. P. Sanders's seminal work *Paul and Palestinian Judaism*. In a more recent work, N. T. Wright chronicles what he considers to be the inevitable rise of the NPP. See Wright, *Paul and His Recent Interpreters*, 1–131.

26. James D. G. Dunn is usually credited with this label given to the movement in his article "New Perspective on Paul," 99–120, which was originally delivered at the University of Manchester in 1982. However, N. T. Wright used similar wording ("fresh perspective") in an earlier article in 1978. See Wright, "Paul of History and the Apostle of Faith," 61–88. Also, see Dunn's collection of articles in *New Perspective on Paul* for a thorough examination and articulation of the NPP. A quick glance into this collection will demonstrate much time and space devoted to the idea of "works of law" as covenantal identifiers rather than "legalism." This argument (somewhat) maintained by Dunn and Wright stands at the center of the NPP debate. See also Wright's *What Saint Paul Really Said*; Wright, *Climax of the Covenant*; and, Wright, *Paul and the Faithfulness of God*.

27. See Wright, *Climax of the Covenant,* which focuses on Galatians in particular.

have themselves remained set apart from Pauline theology by the wider academic world and have been relegated to church polity and women's roles, or study of the theology of the PE themselves.[28] This work aims to bridge this gap between Paul and the PE by testing the validity of the NPP in the PE by way of the canonical approach. The canonical approach is the approach initiated and nuanced by Brevard Childs and, to a lesser extent, James Sanders and John Sailhamer.[29] Essentially, the canonical approach seeks to study the biblical literature as framed by the canon. The canonical approach (what this study also calls the canonical *perspective* in keeping with the nomenclature of the NPP) will help in moving beyond the impasse of Pauline authorship of the PE and bring the PE, as part of the Pauline canon, into the broader discussion of Pauline theology via the NPP. In this methodology, the PE also serve as a test case for the NPP outside the accepted undisputed Pauline parameters. So, while incorporating the PE into the larger Pauline discussion by way of the canonical perspective, this study seeks to do so using the NPP. The major question this study seeks to answer is: To what extent does the NPP make sense in the complete, canonical Pauline corpus? One suspects that this study will both vindicate as well as provide some nuanced correctives to the NPP.[30] The method for this inquiry is detailed in the section below.

James Dunn uses Romans as the template for his *Theology of Paul the Apostle*. Dunn also has commentaries on Romans and Galatians, as well as a theology of Galatians. Though N. T. Wright has not done much in the way of commentaries (other than those of his *For Everyone* Series and *Romans* for the New Interpreter's Bible Series), he has become the face of the New Perspective on Paul, even though in some cases he has rejected the label as well as his position as its spokesperson. Rebuttals from Evangelicals have proliferated, those like John Piper taking center stage through his debates and dialogue with N. T. Wright, though there are others. See Carson et al., *Justification and Variegated Nomism*; Piper, *Future of Justification*; Stuhlmacher, *Revisiting Paul's Doctrine of Justification*. Michael Bird has produced a bibliography devoted to the NPP and its opponents on *The Paul Page* (http://www.thepaulpage.com/the-new-perspective-on-paul-a-bibliographical-essay/). A look through the section that lists the commentaries that dialogue with the NPP demonstrates the overwhelming focus in Galatians and Romans. This, in itself, is proof of the general focus of the NPP. If the NPP is a viable hermeneutic through which to read Paul, then other Pauline epistles should be brought into the discussion (there are places in which Philippians is utilized, and 2 Cor 5:21 and the "righteousness of God"). The passages in the PE should also be able to be used as supplement and critique.

28. In evangelical circles, Pauline authorship has been widely held, but in mainstream academic circles there are fewer adherents. For an example of the theology of the PE see Young, *Theology of the Pastoral Epistles*.

29. Sailhamer, *Introduction to Old Testament Theology*; Sanders, *Torah and Canon*; Sanders, *Canon and Community*.

30. This thesis assumes that via the PE's placement in the canon, there is substantial

The object of this project is not to prove or disprove the NPP. For now, at least, the NPP is here to stay, a truth understood by both sides of the argument. Rather, this project is intended to fill a gap in the field of Pauline Theology. There are reasons the PE has lacked calculable contribution to "authentic" Pauline scholarship. First, the status quo of academia is that the PE are not directly Pauline documents and represent another development of church history subsequent to Paul's ministry and death. However, in recent years, relatively speaking, the PE have made their way into the Pauline discussions by tracing what Pauline elements these early Paulinists thought appropriate for their own contexts. Work by those like James Aageson, Luke Timothy Johnson, and even those like Arland Hultgren and J. Christiaan Beker have helped engage the PE.[31] Additionally, Canonical Criticism, which coincidentally originated near the same time as the NPP, also serves to merge the PE, Pauline theology, and the NPP. There are certainly some who will dismiss this project on the basis of authorship alone. However, the study hopes to engage those interested in the NPP, as well as its validity outside Romans, Galatians, and Philippians. The assumption is that if the NPP works as a system with undisputed Paul, then it should also work in the years following Paul, or in Paul's later, more institutionalized thought. If the NPP works in Paul, it ought to work in the PE. However, if the NPP cannot find resonance with the PE, what next? Is the problem with the PE? The NPP? And, a further question, which will be saved until the conclusion: Is the traditional view of Pauline theology and justification a better way of incorporating undisputed Paul with the PE?

Scope and Relevance

The NPP is a multifaceted, complex system of interpretation, which is evidenced by the writing of the three major contributors. So, in order to guide the research for this study there must be some parameters set in

---

continuity with the theology of the NT, and specifically, the Pauline tradition. This thesis also assumes, and will argue, that the Judaism of the PE and the Judaism against which Paul reacts elsewhere is similar enough to have continuity in Paul's theological reaction. The continuity of first-century Judaism found in deutero-Pauline writings is an argument posited by Robert Cara in *Cracking the Foundation of the New Perspective on Paul*. Similar to this project, he allows for pseudonymous authorship (though he himself advocates Pauline authorship), but focuses on the supposed Jewish opponents of the PE, who he argues were prone to legalism, one of, what he calls, the "three pillars" of the NPP.

31. See Hultgren, *Rise of Normative Christianity*; Aageson, *Paul, the Pastoral Epistles, and the Early Church*; Johnson, "Oikonomia Theou: The Theological Voice of 1 Timothy," 87–104; Beker, *Paul the Apostle*; Beker, *Heirs of Paul*.

place. This study has, through the help of others who have categorized some of the NPP hermeneutic, created four major categories. These categories have been set in place to sort through the material of the PE in order to find passages directly relevant to the current debate. Otherwise, this study could easily become a commentary on the entire PE. Based on these four criteria the passages included are 1 Timothy 1:6–16; 2:3–7; 2 Timothy 1:3, 8–12; and Titus 3:3–7.

These passages are not altogether perfectly correlative to these facets of the NPP, which further illustrates the need for the study. Because of the nature of the NPP's canon (undisputed Paul), some of the comparisons could be seen as artificial and contrived. Hopefully, though, the four categories together help to provide enough commonality for a proper comparison and some careful observations and conclusions.

Definition of Terms

The New Perspective on Paul:[32] For the purpose of the study, the New Perspective on Paul will refer to the specific perspective of Paul instigated by the work done by E. P. Sanders and his articulation of Judaism and "covenantal nomism." This perspective, though a loose movement, is characterized by (1) arguing that justification by faith is not Paul's central theological category, (2) that justification by faith is not in response to a "plagued conscience," (3) that the Judaism against which Paul is structuring his arguments is not "legalistic," but rather functions from a pattern of religion designated "covenantal nomism," (4) that the "works of law" described in Galatians and Romans are not merit-based works, but works that serve in a sociological sense of defining boundaries of who was in and who was out ("covenantal identifiers"), and (5) that the "righteousness of God" is God's own righteousness in fulfillment of his covenant promises. In this work, the NPP is limited to those who espouse some, or all, of these major tendencies. The major proponents are E. P. Sanders, James D. G. Dunn, and N. T. Wright. However, there are also a few others considered to be part of the NPP movement such as Richard Longenecker, Terrence Donaldson, Kent Yinger, and Don Garlington.

---

32. This perspective will be defined more fully in the next chapter. Five works detailing the connections and defining the basic beliefs of the NPP are Meek, "New Perspective on Paul," 208–33; Thompson, *New Perspective on Paul*; Yinger, *New Perspective on Paul* (both of whom are NPP proponents and/or sympathizers); Cara, *Cracking the Foundation*, whose work is primarily a polemic against the NPP; and Westerholm, *Perspectives Old and New on Paul*, whose work, though polemical, provides an impressive history of research regarding the traditional Lutheran perspective as well as the NPP.

Covenantal Nomism: This term, coined by E. P. Sanders, is defined as follows: "Briefly put, covenantal nomism is the view that one's place in God's plan is established on the basis of covenant and that the covenant requires as the proper response of man his obedience to its commandments, while providing means of atonement for transgression."[33] This definition is set in contrast to a Lutheran, systematic understanding of soteriology.[34]

Pattern of Religion: This is another term used by E. P. Sanders. He states, "A pattern of religion, defined positively, is the description of how a religion is perceived by its adherents to *function*. 'Perceived to function' has the sense not of what an adherent does on a day-to-day basis, but of *how getting in and staying in are understood*: the way in which religion is understood to admit and retain members is considered to be the way it 'functions.'"[35] For Sanders, a pattern of religion is not the same as soteriology, and this idea of "pattern of religion" is what lies at the heart of his work and, in some ways, the basis for much of NPP thought—if early Judaism was not so much concerned with otherworldly salvation by means of a proper ledger before God, then one must decide what Paul was reacting against.

Canonical Perspective:[36] The basic approach of Brevard Childs, often called the canonical approach or canonical "criticism."[37] Although defined more fully below, the canonical perspective, simply put, is the study of Scripture in the context of canon. This approach came about through study of the OT, but eventually came also to be practiced in the NT as well. Other scholars who have contributed to the articulation and practice of canonical criticism include John Sailhamer and James Sanders.[38]

33. Sanders, *Paul and Palestinian Judaism*, 75.

34. This contrast between Lutheran theology and covenantal nomism is important in the articulation of the NPP, wherein the focus is not on "salvation" from a plagued conscience so much as "justification" by faith. Works like that of Friedreich Avemarie provided corrective nuances to Sanders's view of covenantal nomism by arguing that rabbinic Judaism accepted certain tensions (like that between "election" and "salvation through good deeds") and that Judaism was more complex than Sanders allows. See Seifrid, "'New Perspective on Paul' and Its Problems," 5–6; Avemarie, *Tora und Leben*; Avemarie, "Erwählung und Vergeltung," 108–25.

35. Sanders, *Paul and Palestinian Judaism*, 17.

36. James Sanders used the term "canonical perspective" in his *Canon and Community*, 2. This study uses the term in keeping with the nomenclature of the NPP and to help define the way in which it is using the method (like Childs, this study does not want to give undue attention to the "critical").

37. This term is a moniker Childs denounced. See Childs, "Canonical Shape of the Prophetic Literature," 54.

38. Sailhamer, *Introduction to Old Testament Theology*; Sanders, *Torah and Canon*; Sanders, *Canon and Community*. Also see Thiselton, "Canon, Community, and Theological Construction," 1–30. See also Wall with Steele, *1 & 2 Timothy and Titus*, who

Historical Critical Method (HCM): Although it may be misleading to refer to "a" or "the" HCM, for the purpose of this study, HCM "refers to the specific procedures used by historical criticism; more broadly, it encompasses the underlying conception of the nature and power of historical reasoning on which historical criticism rests."[39] This reasoning entails a rejection of, or at least a momentary divorce from dogma or church tradition, replaced by a search for objective, verifiable truth.

Chapter Summaries

Chapter 1, the Introduction, will state the thesis of the study, define its terms, and set the parameters of the study in the research methodology. The study will be done from a canonical perspective in an attempt to bypass some of the often-contentious issues regarding authorship and date so that other work can be accomplished. This is not to say these issues will not be mentioned whatsoever, but, rather than reacting polemically, the canonical perspective may allow more positivity in approaching the PE as Pauline material. In this section, "canonical criticism" will be defined and articulated in regard to this project. Within this section, the study will also provide some of the major tenets of the NPP which will be the criteria for selecting the appropriate passages for the study. Rather than focusing on the entire PE, the study will sharpen focus on select passages that have relevance to the conversations surrounding the NPP. These criteria will be reviewed in the Conclusion to assess the amount of continuity or discontinuity with the NPP. The major contribution of the research methodology is setting the parameters of the study.

Chapter 2 will provide the history of research and trace the two research trajectories of the Pastorals and the NPP which meet in the present study. These trajectories are not completely distinct, and they will not be completely exhaustive. Rather, these two trajectories will trace the major issues that have led to the current state of affairs. Thus, little will be said about study done in the PE regarding church polity, women, *Haustafel,* etc.[40] As noted above, these two trajectories have come about because of the notion that Paul is not the author of the PE, and thus many see a different theology in the PE than in the undisputed letters of Paul. This chapter will highlight the inclinations of past research that have led to the *a priori* assumption of

---

use this method for the PE.

39. Soulen and Soulen, *Handbook of Biblical Criticism*, 88–89.

40. See Harding, *What Are They Saying About the Pastoral Epistles?*; and Marshall, "Pastoral Epistles in Recent Study," 268–312.

post-Pauline dating of the Pastorals and their study as separate from or, at least, in contrast to Pauline theology. The history will also chronicle the rise of the NPP in the figures of E. P. Sanders, James D. G. Dunn, and N. T. Wright (as well as a few other proponents of the NPP) focusing on the relative absence of the PE when defining and articulating the NPP. Finally, a few works will be highlighted as precursors to this project, demonstrating the need and timeliness for such a study. The focus of the chapter will be the relevance for the study in the meeting of the research trajectories.

Chapter 3 will begin to focus on the text of the PE: 1 Timothy 1:6–16 and 2:3–7. After a brief introduction to some of the issues in 1 Timothy, each of these passages will be examined in light of the NPP. These passages focus on the opponents of the letter, which may or may not be opponents similar to those found in the undisputed letters of Paul. If the opponents are different, this would certainly affect the way the author of the PE would articulate his theological positions. These passages also include insights into Paul's "conversion," which is a major subject within the NPP, as it gives insight into Paul's former way of life in Judaism. The chapter will delve into the way in which the author of the PE understood his conversion, his former life in Judaism, the new life in Christ, and his vocation as a "teacher of the Gentiles" (1 Tim 2:7).

Chapter 4 will focus on 2 Timothy 1:3 and 1:8–12. Within 1 Timothy 1:8–12, the core of the gospel is outlined in contrast to "works" which is a major contentious issue within the study of Paul. The NPP claims the "salvation/works" dichotomy is a Reformed perspective read back into Pauline Theology, much of which rests on the δικ- language of Paul. This chapter will carefully examine this passage to decipher both its original meaning and how that meaning compares to the NPP. Second Timothy 1:3 is also a key passage in that the author looks to his "forbears" with whom he shares a clear conscience. In this case, he does not seem to be critiquing them, but using them as an example of piety and faithfulness. Thus, this may again present problems to the traditional perspective concerning Judaism.

Chapter 5 will focus on Titus 3:3–7, which will most likely prove to be the most controversial of these passages with regard to the NPP. This is one of two passages mentioned by James Dunn in an article defending the NPP.[41] Rather than the usual Pauline justification-through-faith language, a similar statement is made regarding salvation through *mercy* and "justification by grace." The passage contains much Pauline terminology with slight variations in emphasis. This passage will be analyzed to find

41. The other passage is 2 Tim 1:8–9. See Dunn, "Whatever Happened to 'Works of Law'?," 391–92.

similarities, differences, or slight nuances to undisputed Pauline theology according to the NPP.

The final chapter will bring the findings of the previous chapters into some conclusions regarding the overall tenor of the PE in regard to the tenets of the NPP outlined in Chapter 1. One expects that in many ways the NPP will be vindicated and not outright dismantled on the basis of the PE. However, one also expects to see some ways in which the NPP may need to be revised or nuanced in order to account for the theology of the PE. There may also be ways in which this study will affect discussions of authorship of the PE, though this is not the primary aim of the project. This chapter will also suggest a few paths of further research.

Research Methodology

A study like this one could easily become purely polemical. Of course, with any work engaging the wider academic world, there are polemical points to be made. However, this study aims to keep polemics to a minimum. Although possibly unsatisfying to pro- and anti-NPP alike, the primary concern of this project is not the validation or invalidation of the NPP itself, but the dismissal of the PE by scholarship at large. As for this study, the NPP is not an enemy and this study is not seeking to dismantle or vindicate it. Instead, this study is an attempt to continue to push the conversation forward. Biblical studies is ever becoming more complex and variegated. This work is not an attempt to stake a claim on a side or to create yet another, new category of study. Instead, this study is an attempt to engage a provocative way of reading Paul, and test this hermeneutic in some relatively uncharted waters. Although this study cannot wholeheartedly agree that the NPP would not have come about with the inclusion of Ephesians and the PE into the Pauline corpus as stated by Westerholm, the PE—and Ephesians, for that matter—change the atmosphere of Pauline studies and provide a more textured landscape.[42] The very fact that this project is approached from a canonical perspective conveys the deeply embedded problem of authorship and what constitutes Pauline theology. Granted, this study could have stated a position regarding

---

42. Although repeated in the next chapter, one should note that both Dunn and Wright have done some work on the PE. In fact, both Dunn and Wright have written commentaries on the PE. See Dunn, "First and Second Letters," 773–880; and Wright, *Paul for Everyone*. Though mentioning that some have accepted the PE as authentic, Sanders does not provide a rebuttal as to why he does not consider them in his theology of Paul, except to say (also in regard to Colossians and Ephesians), "the soundest approach is to deal with the letters which Paul can reliably supposed to have written." Sanders, *Paul and Palestinian Judaism*, 431–32.

the authorship of the PE and moved ahead.[43] However, as an attempt to engage both sides of the debate, the canon will provide the parameters of the study, setting the authorial issues of the PE aside. One may wonder that if proponents of the NPP do not adhere to Pauline authorship of the PE, then why include the PE in a "Pauline" perspective? The answer: Canon and continuity. *Canon*, because the PE were considered Pauline until relatively recently, and *continuity*, because the compilers, and even the writer(s) of the PE, assumed continuity with the rest of Paul.

The Pastorals in Canonical Perspective

As will be demonstrated below, the debates surrounding the pedigree of the PE are complicated. For conservatives, to deny Pauline authorship and argue for pseudonymous authorship is to deny the veracity of Scripture.[44] However, from a more modernistic, liberal mindset, pseudonymous authorship provides no real problem. From this perspective, the PE simply represent a different stage in the developing church, and what better figure to use for this step other than Paul? This step, however, is not an arbitrary one, but one that assumes some continuity in Paul and the PE.

These are two major polarizing opinions and there seems to be no end to the impasse in sight. There is no presumption that this study will erase these tensions. The history of historical-critical biblical studies and the various strands of dissent these critical studies have produced cannot be removed. Nor can one erase the work that has been produced that either defends or denies Pauline authorship of the PE. However, the "canonical perspective," which is essentially the canonical approach as set out by Brevard Childs, is a path from undisputed Paul to the "Paul" of the PE. The following section focuses on defining the canonical approach and how this study utilizes the canonical approach for this project.

---

43. Luke Timothy Johnson claims that the issue of authorship absolutely affects the way in which exegesis is done. He states, "Each position has its corollaries: if regarded as authentic, the letters can be read in the same manner as Pau's other missives, that is, as real letters written to actual situations in specific communities, with literary and thematic connections possible with all the other letters; if regarded as inauthentic, they are read not as real but fictive letters, pieces of a single literary enterprise, and to be interpreted, not in the context of Paul's other letters, but with respect only to each other." Johnson, "First Timothy 1,1–20," 20.

44. See Beker's comments on this impasse in *Heirs of Paul*, 9–11.

The Impasse Among Scholarship Regarding
Authorship of the PE

The next chapter will detail the problems raised in the nineteenth century regarding the PE, specifically their authorship, so only a few words need be said here. For the sake of demonstrating the need for a canonical approach, one must realize just how ostracized the PE have been in modern NT studies. Part of the reason for this departure is that, for many, the evidence against Pauline authorship is overwhelming.[45] Keep in mind, the PE have been studied. That is not the problem. The problem is that they have been studied as a group and either separate from, part of, or as the evolution of Pauline theology. Finding agreement across these lines has proven difficult. Since there has been a canon, however, the PE have circulated as Pauline documents and for centuries were treated as such. But, after their dismissal from the Pauline canon in the academy, there have been developments of Pauline theology that have progressed without properly considering the PE, including the NPP.

This impasse regarding Pauline authorship of the PE has created a precarious position for a project like this one. Scholarship has created two Pauls, who, for this study at least, must be treated as one, if only for comparison's sake. Some continuity will connect them, even if their pedigree cannot. This continuity is the canon itself. Of course, through the early compilation of the canon, Paul was the understood author of the PE. Thus, they were considered in some way similar to the other letters attributed to Paul, even though their uniqueness is quite evident.[46] Because of these various unique features, the PE have been treated as a collection, even though the recent trend of accepting 2 Timothy as authentic proves that these letters, though similar, are not necessarily a trilogy of sorts.[47] This uniqueness exposes another of the problems with study of the PE, the nomenclature

45. For example, see Dibelius and Conzelmann, *Pastoral Epistles*, 1–5.

46. E.g., the "faithful sayings" that are found nowhere else in Pauline literature (1 Tim 1:15; 3:1; 4:9; 2 Tim 2:11; Titus 3:8).

47. There have been several works done regarding 2 Timothy that have argued for 2 Timothy's genuine Pauline pedigree. See Towner, "Portrait of Paul and the Theology of 2 Timothy," 151–70; Murphy-O'Connor, "2 Timothy Contrasted with 1 Timothy and Titus," 403–18; Prior, *Paul the Letter Writer and the Second Letter to Timothy*. N. T. Wright is "cautious" concerning 2 Timothy. However, he denies the Pauline pedigree of 1 Timothy and Titus, and he states for the purpose of his own work on Paul that these two "come in a different category, and will be used, in the opposite way to that in which a drunkard uses a lamppost, for illumination rather than support." See Wright, *Paul and the Faithfulness of God*, 61. Interestingly, even Martin Dibelius argues that 2 Timothy "best fits our accustomed picture of the Pauline letter." Dibelius and Conzelmann, *Pastoral Epistles*, 1.

and method of study, most of which follows from pseudonymous author-ship. Andreas Köstenberger argues that the group ought to be renamed "the Letters to Timothy and Titus," to remove the false impression left by the term "Pastor," as well as to help identify them as individual letters and not a collection.[48] However, this study will treat these letters both as a unit (the PE) and as individuals being careful not to let their similarities overshadow their individual uniqueness. The study, in keeping with the canonical per-spective, will also follow their canonical order.[49] In the midst of this precar-ious position of authorship, one is left with only a few options when seeking to study the PE with the rest of Paul. One can state a position on authorship, then move forward from that position, or, as this study proposes, one can allow the canon to set the parameters.

Canonical Criticism: History and Development

The canonical perspective is notoriously difficult to define. Historical criti-cism, generally speaking, is not so much concerned with continuity and canon as objectivity and inquiry. Better put for the current study, historical criticism (at least, by the above definition) is not bound by a canon set by someone else, or by who claims to have written a document. Because of this objective skepticism, and other factors like ancient pseudepigraphy, there is an inherent distrust of both the writers of individual books and letters and the compilers of the canon. So, in this regard, canonical criticism is itself, not really a critical tool, but a perspective, or more rightly, a "context."[50] Rather than "objective results of historicocritical scholarship," Childs states

---

48. Köstenberger, *1–2 Timothy and Titus*, 5–7. Often, the letters are understood as a collection circulated by the same author in the name of Paul.

49. Childs points out that the canonical order is relevant to the interpretative process. In fact, he uses Romans and the PE at each end of the canonical ordering of the Pauline corpus to set the stage for the hermeneutical process. He explains, "The structure of these books (Romans and the PE) at the beginning and end of the corpus sets the canonical context for its interpretation." See Childs, *Church's Guide for Reading Paul*, 75–78. See also Childs, *Old Testament in a Canonical Context*, 10. Others have also demonstrated the importance of canonical ordering in the Old and New Testa-ments. For example, see Emerson, "Victory, Atonement, Restoration, and Response," 177–94; Emerson, *Christ and the New Creation*, 1–37; Emerson, "Paul's Eschatological Outlook in the Pastoral Epistles," 88–92; Goswell, "Order of the Books of the Hebrew Bible," 673–88; Goswell, "Order of the Books of the Greek Old Testament," 449–66; Goswell, "Order of the Books of the New Testament," 225–41; Goswell, "Ordering of the Books of the Canon," 1–20.

50. Matthew Emerson calls it a "method." Emerson, *Christ and the New Covenant*, 4–6.

that "the status of canonicity is not an objectively demonstrable claim but a statement of Christian belief."[51] Childs maintains that the canonical perspective is resonant with this community of faith.

This approach was initiated to move beyond what Childs calls an "illustrative" use of the Bible into the "normative."[52] He states, "To do Biblical Theology within the context of the canon involves acknowledgment of the *normative* quality of the Biblical tradition."[53] He adds, "The Bible must function normatively and not merely illustratively for the church."[54] This is the first definition of the canonical approach as expressed by Childs. The implications of this approach continued after the initial definition in 1970, but the majority of the case studies and examples in the first defining years were taken from the OT.[55] However, Childs eventually also worked within the NT,[56] the most recent work being, *The Church's Guide for Reading Paul*, published in 2008.[57] Throughout Childs's career, his definition of the canonical approach became more refined and branched out from the OT and problems within biblical theology.

Childs's introduction of canonical criticism in *Biblical Theology in Crisis* was a reaction against biblical theology as characterized and defined by J. P. Gabler, called the Biblical Theology Movement.[58] In short, in Gabler's inaugural address, he argued that biblical theology was a descriptive task situated on the far side of the spectrum from systematic theology. The former was for the academy, the latter for the church.[59] Although Childs himself does not focus on Gabler's work, the dichotomy of the biblical theology of Childs's day owes its existence to Gabler's influence. Krister Stendahl, who is also part of the rise of the NPP, also followed this line of reasoning, stating, "The conviction that in the study of biblical theology we must make a definite distinction between the descriptive study of the actual theology

51. Childs, *Biblical Theology in Crisis*, 98–99.

52. Childs, *Biblical Theology in Crisis*, 100.

53. Childs, *Biblical Theology in Crisis*, 100.

54. Childs, *Biblical Theology in Crisis*, 101.

55. See Childs, *Book of Exodus*; Childs, *Introduction to the Old Testament as Scripture*; Childs, *Old Testament in a Canonical Context*.

56. Childs, *New Testament as Canon*; and Childs, *Biblical Theology of the Old and New Testaments*.

57. Childs, *Church's Guide for Reading Paul*.

58. See Childs, *Biblical Theology in Crisis*, 13–84, in which he states his case about the problems of biblical theology in the years prior to and after the Second World War.

59. For a more thorough review of Gabler's influence, see Sandys-Wunsch and Eldredge, "J. P. Gabler and the Distinction between Biblical and Dogmatic Theology," 133–80.

and theologies to be found in the Bible, and any attempt at a normative and systemic theology which could be called 'biblical.'"[60] In response to this way of thinking and the Biblical Theology Movement of Europe and America, Childs's approach is primarily reactionary, opposed to the strictly "historical-critical" methods of scholarship.[61] In other words, seeing the problems with the biblical theological method as it was, Childs began his work on canonical criticism, an attempt to bring the Bible back to its proper moorings within the church. Even though Childs's work began in the OT, Keck argues that Childs should be studied as a whole, from OT to the completion of his work in the NT.[62] Childs himself wrote a book pertaining to Paul (mentioned above), with which this project is primarily concerned. This is not a study on the development of Childs's thinking, though his program did develop from his first work to his last one. What this project is seeking to highlight is the usefulness of Childs's program for the present inquiry.[63]

The canonical perspective, although not completely ignoring historical-critical tools, sees these tools as secondary with regard to biblical theology to the context of canon. Similarly, this project seeks to approach the PE from this perspective as the last development of Pauline theology. This final development should not be understood to oppose earlier Pauline theology, such as that found in Romans or Galatians, but as Paul developing his theology in light of new problems of aberrancy from within the church, or as a prevention of foreseeable problems. Childs writes, "The historical enterprise, while fully legitimate in a certain context, is not identical with the theological enterprise of discerning the canonical shape of the material . . . . It is central to the canonical enterprise to seek to interpret the peculiar form into which the material has been rendered as the vehicle for the

---

60. Stendahl, "Method in the Study of Biblical Theology," 198–99.

61. For a more in-depth treatment, see Noble, *Canonical Approach*.

62. Keck, "Faith Seeking Canonical Understanding," 103. Keck writes primarily concerning *The Church's Guide for Reading Paul* and notes that Childs's "program" (as he calls it) was to read the PE within the framework set-up by Romans. He states, "The significance of the Pastorals in this book can hardly be overstated. They are not 'about Paul' nor do they update his thoughts. Instead, they mark a shift in the portrayal of Paul" (110).

63. John Barton stands against Childs's approach, stating this of the critical period: "And it is the 'after all' that defines the gulf—widest very often when it looks least daunting—which separates the modern critic of whatever persuasion from even the greatest of the pre-critical commentators." He identifies canon criticism with that of fundamentalism saying, "Neither could survive the demise of historical criticism, for they draw all their strength from being able to wage war on it." Barton, *Reading the Old Testament: Method in Biblical Study*, 99–100.

biblical witness."[64] In its already canonized form, what is different about the PE? And, canonically speaking, why the difference? These are questions that have already been asked by others, but as will be demonstrated in the next chapter, the answer for many was to wrest the PE from Pauline pedigree, and in that way to take away its status and veracity. Or, to put it another way: the PE are different from undisputed Paul in various unique ways, so Paul must not have written them. So, then, the "why" discussed above is not Paul's highly adaptive theology as witnessed in, say, 1 Corinthians and Romans. Instead, Paul's undisputed theology is seen as too rigid to incorporate the theology of the PE, or, on the other hand, the PE are seen as too similar to Paul, as if they are a mere collection of quotations.[65]

Even though the canonical perspective is not a historical-critical study *per se,* this approach is not without historical-critical elements. Even Childs states, "Historical criticism is here to stay."[66] He also argues, "To suggest that a new approach to the discipline of New Testament Introduction is needed is not to propose a return to traditional, pre-Enlightenment understanding of the Bible. Such an endeavor is not only wrong in concept, but impossible in practice."[67] He likens the relationship between historical criticism and NT interpretation with that of Melanchthon's view of learning Aristotle and theology, stating, "To apply this analogy, I would agree that historical criticism is an indispensable teacher."[68] From a more conservative, traditional perspective, the HCM has been used as a tool of apologetics by using these critical tools as a means to advocate Pauline authorship.[69] This effort has not been fruitless. As already stated, 2 Timothy has garnered a much greater acceptance as an authentic Pauline document because of such efforts. However, some of these studies further complicate the issue by offering yet another hypothesis regarding the authorship of the PE. With regard to the HCM, there are problems with the methods, but the major rift is the

---

64. Childs, *New Testament as Canon,* 387.

65. See Dibelius and Conzelmann, *Pastoral Epistles,* 4, wherein he states "many passages give the impression of imitation." He cites 1 Tim 1:12–16 and 2 Tim 1:3–5 in comparison with Gal 1:13–16 and Rom 1:8–11 respectively as examples.

66. Childs, *New Testament as Canon,* 45.

67. Childs, *New Testament as Canon,* 35.

68. Childs, *New Testament as Canon,* 45.

69. For example, see two secretary theories from Moule, "Problem of the Pastoral Epistles," and Wilson, *Luke and the Pastoral Epistles,* both of whom identify Luke as Paul's amanuenses. Also see Spicq, *Saint Paul, Les Epitres Pastorales*; Murphy-O'Connor, "2 Timothy Contrasted with 1 Timothy and Titus," 403–18; and Johnson, *Letters to Paul's Delegates.*

underlying assumptions—whether the PE are authentic or inauthentic. One tends to find what one is looking for.

Regarding the definition of canon, Childs explains, "At the outset it must be stressed that the term canon designates an established body of literature which the early church recognized as both authoritative and fixed in scope."[70] Childs uses the term "canon" in three ways: (1) as a fixed, normative body of literature, (2) as a "particular theological construal of the tradition which it provided to the literature by means of the shape and intertextuality it formed within the collection of writings," and (3) as modern interpretative activity.[71] The first and second are the aspects of canon this study chooses to highlight. Childs argues that while the task is descriptive it is also prescriptive.[72] He further defines his program: "What is called for is an analysis which combines both historical and theological description. It seeks to pursue not only the motives for giving the literature its peculiar shape, but also the function which the literature now performs in its special form within the smaller and larger units of the collection."[73] The shape of the canon is not an arbitrary listing of books, but also an in-depth descriptive task of why these books have become "canon."

Moving into the present inquiry, as noted earlier, Childs states concerning the PE, "However, often as a consequence (of non-Pauline authorship) the importance of these letters has been disregarded and they continue to be designated by many as inferior in quality."[74] Childs sees the PE as the final stage in the development of Pauline canon.[75] For him, the PE were necessary for the early church. But, he adds, "The decisive point to make is that the Pastorals do not reinterpret Paul for a later age."[76] Instead, the PE are seen by Childs as a "canonical move" to incorporate Paul's letters into a "normative corpus of authoritative Scripture."[77] Rather than a recontextualization of Paul for a new age, the PE are Paul's theology normalized. This is an important distinction for this study. The occasional letters such as Galatians and Romans held Paul's specific theology in opposition to certain opponents or ideas. The PE are the canonized gospel through Paul's

70. Childs, *New Testament as Canon*, 37.

71. Childs, *New Testament as Canon*, 41.

72. Childs, *New Testament as Canon*, 38.

73. Childs, *New Testament as Canon*, 38.

74. Childs, *Church's Guide for Reading Paul*, 70.

75. Childs also recognizes that the PE circulated as a group, and by that, conveys something of their purpose for and reception in the church. This is what Childs calls "canonical shaping." Childs, *Church's Guide for Reading Paul*, 49.

76. Childs, *New Testament as Canon*, 390.

77. Childs, *New Testament as Canon*, 390.

"deposit" (1 Tim 6:20; 2 Tim 1:12, 14),[78] even though they too are written in response to contemporary opponents and would-be problems. The PE react against, as well as anticipate, problems within the church and protect the church against them through the Pauline deposit, the "household of God," and church governmental structure.

An Analogy

The canonical perspective can be demonstrated in an analogy. Imagine standing in the midst of a forest with tall, dense trees all around. You can smell the pine, the dirt, and hear the wind as it sweeps through the high branches. There is no doubt you are in a forest. You walk toward the fringes. The trees are fewer and vegetation different. You begin to see in the near distance a meadow and open, rolling hills of grass, which are definitely no longer forest. In this fringe, you begin to wonder if you are any longer in the forest, but you are certainly not yet in the meadow. In this thought, you have defined the forest by its center, by its most vivid, marked characteristics. If, however, you were in the meadow, looking toward the forest, this fringe would be part of the forest, because the fringe is what has defined its borders.

This analogy represents how this study sees the canon functioning with regard to Pauline theology. Over the last two hundred years, Pauline theology has been defined, not by the canonical Paul, but by another Paul constructed by the HCM, a Paul limited to only seven epistles. We have walked into the forest's center, defined the forest, then leapt back into the meadow, ignoring the forest edge. If Romans and Galatians serve as the center of the forest, then the PE are its edge. They are not the meadow lying outside "Paul," a witness to something altogether different, but they are something else helping to define Pauline theology for a transitioning church. Although this study advocates the Pauline authorship of these letters, even if one considers them pseudonymous, they still provide a boundary for Pauline theology. As is demonstrated in the history and collection of the canon, some letters crossed that boundary and were discarded from the Pauline canon. It is with this concept in mind that this study incorporates the PE into the discussion of the NPP and Pauline theology. It will proceed with the assumption that the edge of the forest has enough in common with its center to be still considered forest, and not altogether something else. This is not a perfect analogy. However, the analogy is common enough to help make sense of the boundaries that have been set in place. There is no need

78. See Torrance, "Deposit of Faith," 1–28.

to reinvent the wheel or to state and defend a case concerning authorship, only then to be ignored by whomever does not agree with the assessment of PE authorship. So, this analogy is an attempt to incorporate all of canonical Paul into the present inquiry.

Explanatory Qualifications

Although the NPP is primarily a social-scientific and historical rendering of Pauline theology, there remains the task of appropriating that theology beyond the specific issues addressed in the undisputed letters of Paul. The canonical shape of the material takes into account the continuity and discontinuity of the Pauline tradition. Thus, there may be some difficulty in testing a primarily historical system within the rubric of a canonical, theological system. Even so, this study aims to test the historical system of the NPP within the canonical perspective, based on the belief that the canonical perspective also incorporates historical issues. Robert Wall, in his commentary on the PE written from a canonical perspective, points out that although the canonical approach is criticized for not being historical, "canonical exegesis is characterized by an interest in the human, historical element."[79]

Similarly, though the parameters of the study have been set by the NT, and specifically, Pauline canon, Childs asks, "How does the canonical approach affect actual exegesis?"[80] This is an important question to consider before progressing further into this work.[81] For the purpose of this study, the canonical approach is the canonical, consistent shaping of the Pauline corpus, read through the lens of the NPP. One of these facets has been decided already (canon), the other is up for consideration (NPP). The assumption is that the NPP hermeneutical system is inherently consistent and that consistency will be demonstrated in the PE. If not, then there is a problem with either the consistency of the canon (from authentic Paul to the PE Paul, which is the underlying assumption of most of scholarship)

---

79. Wall and Steele, *1 & 2 Timothy and Titus*, 2. Wall's thoughts regarding authorship and the canonical approach will be revisited in Chapter 2.

80. Childs, *New Testament as Canon*, 48.

81. Sanders breaks canonical criticism up into two categories: canonical process and canonical hermeneutics. Canonical process is the process by which the canon has come into being. Canonical hermeneutics is the "homegrown" and borrowed hermeneutic that shaped canonical material. For Sanders, the latter especially celebrates the pluralism found in the canon. Though this study is not in full agreement with Sanders concerning the level of plurality, his major thrust is important in that there is a process, even within the writers themselves, that canonizes the material. The plurality is accepted in unification. See Sanders, *Canon and Community*, 21–60.

or the consistency of the NPP. The method provides the parameters for the exegesis. So, "actual exegesis" in this case is comparative exegesis through the use of the NPP.

This project resembles biblical theology. Through the use of the canonical approach to the PE, this study will move in three concentric circles from the outer circle of canon, to the PE and Pauline canon, and finally into the individual letters and passages within them. What is assumed through the canonical perspective is that there is continuity found in each of these levels with one another. Also, part of this biblical theology is the operating system of the NPP and whether or not the NPP can find continuity in the canonical Pauline corpus.

The normative function of canon also plays a role in this study. Childs writes, "Because the traditions were received as religiously authoritative, they were transmitted in such a way as to maintain a normative function for subsequent generations of believers within a community of faith."[82] Though Childs speaks in this way about the Old and New Testaments generally, the same can be said of smaller bodies of literature, in this case, the Pauline corpus with the added, smaller sub-group of the PE. The PE have been set apart for their peculiarities and distinctive features. However, their reception into the canon speaks to their normative function within the larger framework of the canon. The PE were not their own corpus, but part of the growing body of literature comprising the NT. Likely, much of their reception into the canon was their connection with Paul and his apostolic authority. Although some may be wary of using the term "development," the PE are also representative of a normalizing theology, or a logical, organic follower of the Pauline theological paradigm. As the church moved from infancy to maturity, there was a natural move to provide certain parameters for orthodoxy.

Robert Wall approaches the PE from a canonical perspective arguing, "Simply put, then, the late arrival of the Pastoral letters to complete the Pauline collection is constative of a more robust Pauline witness to the Christian faith."[83] He adds, "While every detail of the process remains contested (regarding the PE) there stands one incontrovertible literary fact: the canonical form of the New Testament contains a thirteen-letter Pauline corpus."[84] The debates concerning authorship in contrast to the thirteen-letter canonical Pauline corpus are the crux of the problem. Historians of Paul are concerned with Paul and asking about his life and theology. In their questions, if Paul did not write the PE, then they may assume little can be

82. Childs, *Biblical Theology: A Proposal*, 38–39.

83. Wall, "Function of the Pastoral Letters," 28.

84. Wall, "Function of the Pastoral Epistles," 35.

learned about Paul from them. However, this assumption is not altogether true. Even if the PE are pseudonymous, they do say something about the character and influence of Paul in that the existence of the PE in the canon assumes a Pauline context.

Summation of the Canonical Perspective

To sum up, the canonical approach as defined and refined by Childs[85] provides the continuity and boundaries necessary to test the NPP in the PE, even in the current academic climate that remains skeptical regarding the Pauline pedigree of the PE. This approach is not a ploy to ignore the problems of authorship and the unique nature of the PE when compared with other Pauline documents. In fact, as noted, Childs himself did not advocate Pauline authorship of the PE, nor does Robert Wall, in that he thinks the evidence is insufficient.[86] The intention of this approach is to move beyond the discussion of authorship in order to focus on a comparison with the NPP. The main question this study seeks to answer is whether or not the PE resonate with the major tenets of the NPP. If not, where does that leave the NPP? The PE? The interpreter, instead of beginning with the where, why, how, and when of the PE (or the individual letters of the PE), begins with the broader category of canon. Then, within that framework, one begins to ask these other questions, realizing that the answer to them changes nothing about canonicity. At its most basic level, the Pauline canon includes the PE, and any discussion of Pauline theology must in some way make sense of these letters, both as a group and individually.

Criteria for the Selection of Passages

The broader history of the rise of the NPP will be traced in the next chapter. However, in order to set out properly the research methodology, four aspects of the NPP will be outlined below. These four characteristics have been adapted from those of Michael Thompson, Kent Yinger, James Meek and Robert Cara.[87] They have been adapted because they originated in study of undisputed Paul and thus do not have, in some cases, direct correlation in the PE. As has been noted by each of these scholars, and NPP scholars

85. See especially Emerson's history and definition of the canonical method, as well as his own contribution via canonical ordering in *Christ and the New Creation*, 1–37.

86. Wall and Steele, *1 & 2 Timothy and Titus*, 4–7.

87. Thompson, *New Perspective on Paul*; Yinger, *New Perspective on Paul*; Meek, "New Perspective on Paul"; and Cara, *Cracking the Foundation*, 20–25.

themselves, the NPP is not a proper collective movement, so proponents of the NPP often disagree with one another, particularly in the finer details of exegesis.[88] However, these four categories help to characterize loosely the NPP as well as to limit the passages of the PE to be studied to those that have some bearing on the major discussions in the NPP. Because the NPP is the lens through which the PE will be studied, these criteria help focus that lens on specific passages within the PE themselves. Although an attempt has been made to cover all relevant passages, there are likely some gaps left for future study. Below are four primary facets of the NPP meant to help collect the relevant passages to study from the PE. There is some overlap in the categories, but there is enough distinction to justify the inclusion of each.

Justification and Salvation

The first criteria to be considered is that of "Justification and Salvation." Justification stands as one of the pillars of Pauline theology and as one of the major areas of emphasis within the NPP, which is ironic, considering Dunn, Wright, and Sanders all argue that justification is not the center of Pauline theology.[89] It is also the subject of debate amongst Pauline scholarship.[90] Thus, this debate is a convenient place to look when trying to compare and contrast the NPP in the PE. The history of the study of justification is complex, and there are several monographs devoted to chronicling this history.[91] In fact, this one aspect of Pauline theology is so immense, that for now, only a cursory examination to highlight its significance will be attempted.[92] This section, and even this project as a whole, is not overly concerned with deciding which understanding of justification is "correct,"

88. See, for example, Wright's discussion and critique of both E. P. Sanders and James ("Jimmy") Dunn in Wright, *Paul and His Recent Interpreters*, 64–105. This is also stated by Cara, *Cracking the Foundation*, 30, and by Yinger, *New Perspective on Paul*. Cara points out that there are several "perspectives," but there are also several unifying factors as well, which is similar to this study's method of choosing which passages to cover.

89. An example from each should suffice as evidence: Wright, *Paul Debate*, 71; Dunn, *Theology of Paul the Apostle*, 335–40; Sanders, *Paul and Palestinian Judaism*, 434–42.

90. Two major, well-known works that contribute to this debate are the dueling works of John Piper and N. T. Wright. See Piper, *Future of Justification*, and Wright, *Justification*.

91. See, for example, McGrath, *Iustitia Dei*; Waters, *Justification and the New Perspectives on Paul*; Seifrid, *Justification by Faith*.

92. Chapter 5, which will examine Titus 3:3–7, will contain a more thorough review of the literature regarding justification and Pauline theology.

although, of course, some judgments must be made, especially with regard to the meaning of specific passages and their relation to the NPP. Instead, this study seeks to test the NPP's particular way of understanding Pauline justification theology within the PE.

This study has conflated these two categories—justification and salvation—because they have been conflated in many discussions of Paul and the PE, even though the NPP has historically been concerned with what they consider to be the wrongly defined sense of justification language (not salvation) by Luther and his successors.[93] Also, this study has conflated them, because of the lack of justification language in the PE and the abundance of soteriological language. To demonstrate part of the problem, justification language (i.e. the δικ- word group)[94] is not pervasive in the PE. As an example, the verb δικαιόω is used only twice (1 Tim 3:16; Titus 3:7), δίκαιος three times (1 Tim 1:9; 2 Tim 4:8; Titus 1:8), and δικαιοσύνη five times (1 Tim 6:11; 2 Tim 2:22; 3:16; 4:8; Titus 3:5) in the PE. Compare this frequency in the PE to the thirty-four times in Romans and the four times used in Galatians (2:21; 3:6, 21; 5:5), only for the word δικαιοσύνη. Despite this lack of δικ- language, some have compared passages like Titus 3:3–7 to, say, Romans 3:27–28.[95] These passages seem similar enough because they include words like ἔργων and δικαιωθέντες. However, in Titus 3:3–7, justification comes by grace (not faith) and ἔσωσεν ἡμᾶς not on the basis of ἔργων τῶν ἐν δικαιοσύνῃ ἃ ἐποιήσαμεν ἡμεῖς.

In some ways, though, justification and salvation seem to be treated as synonyms because of their correlation and proximity to the phrase "good works," "works of righteousness" (Titus 3:5), and "works of law" between Romans and Galatians and 2 Timothy 1:9 and Titus 3:5–7.[96] Though this study does not intend to make the same mistake, salvation and justification have been included together in this section because of the lack of justification language in the PE. Central to the NPP is the argument that justification is

93. N. T. Wright expresses the problem, "Theologians have spoken of the three tenses of salvation, but not always, or perhaps not clearly enough, of the three tenses of justification. (Nor are justification and salvation the same thing, despite the confusions of popular usage)." Wright, *Pauline Perspectives*, 423.

94. For a fuller discussion of this word group see Sanders, *Paul and Palestinian Judaism*, 470–71, 544–56; Irons, *Righteousness of God*; Käsemann, "Righteousness of God in Paul," 168–82; Ziesler, *Meaning of Righteousness in Paul*; Seifrid, *Christ, Our Righteousness*.

95. See Knight, *Faithful Sayings in the Pastoral Letters*, 92.

96. In fact, Robert Yarbrough states regarding what Table 31 in his commentary demonstrates, "First, being 'justified' and 'saved' can be virtually synonymous in Paul." See Yarbrough, *Letters to Timothy and Titus*, 550. Table 31 detailing Paul's usage of δικαιόω and σῴζω in the passive voice is found on pp. 548–49.

not the center of Pauline theology and that justification is not the answer to a search for a clean conscience (2 Tim 1:3) that had been soiled by sin, as stated and articulated by Luther and those with a traditional concept of justification.[97] Instead, for the NPP, justification is more a declaration from God regarding one's status of "saved," or better, as a member of God's covenantal people. Justification is less about man's righteousness and more about God's.[98] N. T. Wright explains his view of justification in this way: "In standard Christian theological language, it wasn't so much about soteriology as about ecclesiology; not so much about salvation as about the church."[99] And further, "Justification in this setting, then, is not a matter of *how someone enters the community of the true people of God,* but of *how you tell who belongs to the community.*"[100] Dunn similarly states, "In other words, salvation, and even justification, in Wright's iteration of the NPP, are aspects of God's people. The focus is more on community than on individuality."[101]

So, in this way, salvation and justification are similar: salvation is *how* one gets in, and justification is the indicator of who belongs. However, they are also distinct, especially for some proponents of the NPP who argue that justification is about who is in, who is righteous, and that salvation (or, better, *final* justification) and reward is dependent upon works.[102] Cara, while noting the disparate understandings of what justification is among proponents of the NPP, also points out the relative consensus about what justification is not, namely that it is not traditional, imputed righteousness. He concludes that for the NPP, "Justification has two components, initial and final. Initial justification primarily concerns ecclesiology, that is, who is in the covenant community, not soteriology, how does one get in. . . . Also,

97. Alister McGrath states the problem, "As the Reformation and its attendant authority figures slowly receded into the past, the difficulties associated with this way of speaking (justification as the primary category of man's reconciliation with God) became increasingly apparent." McGrath, *Iustitia Dei,* 1.

98. This idea of the "righteousness of God" will be covered more fully in the next chapter.

99. Wright, *What Saint Paul Really Said,* 119, italics original.

100. Wright, *What Saint Paul Really Said,* 119.

101. There are two articles mentioned by Michael Kruger on his website, *Canon Fodder* (https://www.michaeljkruger.com/), that draw attention to the NPP's intrigue for the modern biblical student with its focus on community over individual and how the NPP may be guilty of the sin of speaking to their own time instead of that of the NT, which, these articles point out, is the same error of which the NPP accuses Luther. See Matlock, "Almost Cultural Studies?," 433–59, and more recently, Swaim, "New Take on the Apostle Paul."

102. Yinger, *Paul, Judaism and Judgment According to Deeds.*

justification does not include the imputed righteousness of Christ—NPP is united and clear on this point!"[103]

Though they are different, the lines between justification and salvation are often blurry. It is hard to discuss justification without thinking also of salvation. Even W. D. Davies makes the mistake of conflating the two arguing in a short section on justification by faith that Paul used Genesis 15:6 and Habakkuk 2:4 to argue "that faith rather than obedience was, according to Scripture itself, the basis of salvation."[104] Neither of these passages speak about salvation. Another example is George Knight III with regard to Titus 3:8. He states, "The repudiation of works as a basis or grounds for God's saving men is a dominant theme in Paul."[105] He footnotes Romans 3:27-28, 4:2-6, 9:11 along with Galatians 2:16, Ephesians 2:9 and 2 Timothy 1:9 as proof. However, none of the references in Romans and Galatians even use the word "salvation," "saved," or any cognates.[106] Instead, these passages focus on justification. A return to justification and salvation will be made when dealing with specific passages, but the purpose here is to provide enough evidence that the change in semantics is problematic and something must be done to help situate the variant in wording within Pauline theology. There is likely a reason for Paul's shift in language, but that reason is not that justification and salvation mean the same thing. Instead, justification seems to be another metaphor under the primary subject of salvation.[107] Salvation is Paul's primary category under which justification functions.

This section cannot and does not intend to situate this issue completely. Instead, it is meant to explain the inclusion of the category, the slippery nature of the terminology, and just how similar or dissimilar Titus 3:3-7 and 2 Timothy 1:9 are to Paul's undisputed discussions of works, faith, and justification. This justification/salvation tenet of the NPP also serves to expose some of the change in semantics and argumentation between Romans and Galatians and the PE. A more thorough, comprehensive treatment will come in the following chapters. At a glance, it seems that the polemical nature of

103. Cara, *Cracking the Foundation*, 24. Though a thorough treatment of the NPP and justification, Cara's work is full of polemical, excitable, and overly exclamatory statements such as this one.

104. Davies, *Paul and Rabbinic Judaism*, 222.

105. Knight, *Faithful Sayings in the Pastoral Letters*, 92.

106. The other two references are also outside the primary discussions of the NPP, and even further prove the depth of the problem in that they also use the term "salvation," not "justification," which makes one wonder why these passages would be quoted together as proof of the "repudiation of works as a basis or grounds for God's saving men."

107. See Dunn, *Theology of Paul*, 328-33.

Romans and Galatians against Judaizers may be one of the primary reasons for the different emphasis. What can be said with some certainty is that Paul saw salvation as both an event and a process of which justification plays a major part, that justification is not a purely sequential element in salvation, but that justification is, in effect, part of the entire process.[108]

What further complicates the issue is that the verb "justified" is only part of the discussion of righteousness as a whole. The entire δικ- word group is involved. The term "righteous" (δίκαιος) in the PE often has a positive moralistic, ethical ring to it.[109] On the other hand, a passage like Titus 3:5 and the "works of righteousness" does not bear a positive tone. In fact, one could argue that the term "righteousness" is used positively in every instance, except for Titus 3:5 (cf. 1 Tim 6:11; 2 Tim 2:22; 3:16; 4:8). And, by positively, what is meant is righteousness that is to be consciously pursued and enacted (contrast Titus 3:5 with Titus 3:8). The use of the term at the end of 2 Timothy (2 Tim 4:8) is a notable exception ("the crown of righteousness"). The point of this preliminary discussion is to point out the relevance of conflating salvation and justification language as a way to engage the NPP. Even Wright points out, "To be sure, in many passages—not, perhaps, as many as some might suppose—Paul is indeed talking about salvation."[110] So, taking these two categories into consideration, the passages to be studied are 2 Timothy 1:8–12 and Titus 3:3–7.

Law and Works

There has been a tremendous amount of work done with regard to law and works in Pauline studies.[111] The NPP, primarily at the hands of James Dunn, has changed the way in which the phrase "works of law" (ἔργα νόμου) is understood. When once the phrase was understood as "works-righteousness," Dunn argues that the phrase should be understood as works that identify the Jewish covenantal relationship, works such as circumcision,

---

108. Wright makes sure to point out that if the process is considered an *ordo salutis*, then justification is "one step only within that sequence." Wright, *Pauline Perspectives*, 283.

109. For example, see 1 Tim 6:11; 2 Tim 2:22, 3:16, 4:8; Titus 3:5. Also see Ziesler, *Meaning of Righteousness in Paul*, 154–56.

110. Wright, *Paul and His Recent Interpreters*, 30.

111. A few examples include Badenas, *Christ and the End of the Law*; Cranfield, "St. Paul and the Law," 43–68; Cranfield, "'Works of the Law' in the Epistle to the Romans," 89–101; Das, *Paul, the Law, and the Covenant*; De Roo, *"Works of the Law" at Qumran and in Paul*.

food laws, and Sabbath-keeping.[112] With regard to this study, the exact phrase ἔργα νόμου is not found in the PE, or anywhere in the NT outside of Romans and Galatians. However, "works," "good works," and "works we did in righteousness" are found in the PE (e.g., 1 Tim 2:10; 4:14; 5:10, 45; 6:18; 2 Tim 1:9; Titus 1:16; 2:7; 3:5, 8, 14).

In addition to Paul's use of the word "works," one must also grapple with Paul's understanding of the law and its function. Romans 7:1–25, Galatians 3:23–24; 4:21–31, Philippians 3:1–9 and certain passages in 1 and 2 Corinthians (1 Cor 15:56; 2 Cor 3:5–6) help provide the sources for the undisputed Pauline perspective. Based on these usages and Paul's polemic against Judaism, the NPP goes so far as to say that even obedience to the law is not the problem. Instead, the NPP argues that the problem with which Paul is dealing is not one of a "plagued conscience" trying his best to obey the law (but unable to do so), but the social problem of gentile acceptance into the people of God.[113] The use of the law, and primarily its sectarian elements ("works of law"), to delineate the people of God is what Paul is combating. This study is not concerned with deconstructing or critiquing the NPP's thoughts on Paul's view of the law, though naturally, some critique will be necessary. The purpose of this study is to examine whether or not the PE use law and works in this same way.

The law, properly understood as the Mosaic law and used often that way in undisputed Paul, is mentioned only once in the PE (1 Tim 1:8–9).[114] Thus, this passage is paramount in the current study, especially considering the similarity 1 Timothy 1:8 has with Romans 7:12. Based on this tenet of the NPP, Titus 3:3–7 and 2 Timothy 1:8–12 will also be studied, because of their connection to justification/salvation, as well as "works."

Paul's View of Judaism

Along with the law comes the way in which Paul understands Judaism. Paul's pre-conversion faith and his subsequent critique of Judaism is one facet of the NPP about which not all proponents agree. E. P. Sanders famously states that the problem Paul has with Judaism is that it was not

---

112. Dunn, *New Perspective on Paul*, 98–110.

113. One example from each major contributor includes Wright, *What Saint Paul Really Said*, 113–18; Dunn, *Theology of Paul the Apostle*, 334–89; Sanders, *Paul, the Law, and the Jewish People*, 154–59. See also Stendahl, "Apostle Paul and the Introspective Conscience of the West," 199–215. This article is also found as a chapter in Stendahl's book, *Paul Among Jews and Gentiles*.

114. And possibly, Titus 3:9 (μάχας νομικὰς).

Christianity,[115] a statement that has been critiqued by Wright and Dunn alike.[116] Following the work of Krister Stendahl,[117] the NPP has noted that the Judaism of Paul's day was very much unlike the Judaism portrayed by Augustine, Martin Luther, and many Protestant scholars since. From this traditional perspective, Paul is understood to be reacting against a legalistic, merit-based Judaism. This traditional perspective can be traced back to the Augustine-Pelagian controversy of the fifth century. The question Stendahl, Sanders, and now Dunn, Wright, and others ask, is whether or not a merit-based, legalistic understanding of Judaism is a fair assessment of first-century Judaism. Sanders is well-known for arguing that the Jewish "pattern of religion" was not merit-based legalism. If Judaism was not legalistic in that way, then what was the problem Paul saw? That is what the NPP has sought to figure out. The case for Paul's polemic has already been argued by Sanders, Dunn, and Wright regarding both Galatians and Romans, though Wright takes a more nuanced position on Paul's polemic. However, does the PE offer the same polemic? How does Paul understand the Jewish enemies of Crete and Ephesus? Also, like many who believe the PE serve as a single work under the guise of three letters, are the enemies different from letter to letter within the PE themselves?

Another aspect of the characterization of first-century Judaism is Paul's own conversion. Paul was a devout Jew of the sect of the Pharisees (Phil 3:5), educated under Gamaliel (Acts 22:3), which is an impressive Jewish pedigree. But, after his encounter with Christ on the road to Damascus, there was a distinct change in his approach, not a change of religion. What was the problem? What did Christ introduce into early Judaism that forced Paul to critique and amend what it meant to be the people of God? Also, crossing over into the realm of salvation and justification, what was it about early Judaism, according to Paul, that "obviously" (Gal 3:11) could not justify one before God? Was it a plagued conscience that could not perform works well enough, or was it something else?

A discussion of Paul's view of Judaism requires, then, that the passages in the PE discussing Paul's former life (1 Tim 1:12–15; 2 Tim 1:3) be included in this study. As will be seen, there is a great deal of continuity and discontinuity between Paul and the OT. Paul's understanding of his mission to the gentiles and his thoughts on justification that emerged from

---

115. Sanders states, "In short, *this is what Paul finds wrong in Judaism: it is not Christianity.*" Sanders, *Paul and Palestinian Judaism*, 551–52, italics original.

116. See for example, Wright, *What Saint Paul Really Said*, 19; Wright, *Paul and His Recent Interpreters*, 77; Dunn, *Theology of Paul the Apostle*, 339.

117. Stendahl, "Apostle Paul and the Introspective Conscience of the West," 199–215.

this mission also play a role in the way in which he saw and understood Judaism (1 Tim 2:7; 2 Tim 1:11).

Opponents

As apostle to the gentiles, Paul's primary focus was gentile inclusion into the people of God. By that measure, Paul's natural opponents would have been Jews or Jewish Christians ("Judaizers"). At first glance, this category may seem too similar to Paul's view of Judaism. However, what Paul thought about Judaism is not necessarily the same as the thoughts and program of his opponents. In Titus, there is certainly a Jewish element to Paul's opponents (Titus 1:14), but it is a mistake to *assume* that each PE has one and the same opponent or set of opposing ideas.[118] One must come to terms with the fact that Judaism was not without factions and that the opponents of the PE may have been different, with different agendas, than those of Romans and Galatians. One must also consider that even the opponents of 1 Timothy are not necessarily the same as that of 2 Timothy, or that Judaism itself is not the enemy, but some other, strange conflation brought about by early Christianity. In other words, one cannot rightly interpret Paul in Romans, or the PE, without at least partially understanding against what Paul was reacting. One of the easiest mistakes to make is to assume that all the opponents of Paul were the same, even though they (and Paul) may have shared some similarities.

Identification and characterization of the opponents will help identify continuity and discontinuity with the NPP and the PE by assessing the position of Paul's opponents through Paul's own description of them. The assumption is that Paul's apologetic and argumentation will be consistent, yet nuanced, according to the specific problem(s) he is addressing. Having said this, Paul's opponents and polemic are different in Romans and Galatians than that of the PE as a whole. The PE are letters addressed, not only to individuals, but to individuals Paul commissions to "guard the deposit" and to those he calls his "children" (1 Tim 1:2; 6:20; 2 Tim 1:14; Titus 1:4). Thus, sometimes the "opponents" may not be specific people, as in 2 Timothy,[119] but mindsets Paul has either already seen or expects to become a problem.

118. See Michael Prior's conclusions in *Paul, the Letter Writer*, 169, wherein he states, "We hope that the evidence produced in the course of this study will encourage scholars to consider each of the Pastorals separately" which is also stated by Towner, *Letters to Timothy and Titus*, 1–3.

119. There are two individuals named in 2 Timothy (Hymenaeus and Philetus; 2 Tim 2:17), but these two individuals do not seem to be the catalyst for the sending of the letter.

Though the opponents may be different in some specific ways, there is likely also some commonality between them.

A Note Concerning the Opponents

Discussion of the opponents will be included in the introduction to each chapter of exegetical material as well as in the Conclusion. The choice to do so is due to the nature of the passages concerning opponents in the PE. First, though there may be some commonalities, the opponents of each of the PE will be treated individually. Second, these opponents will be compared and contrasted with the opponents of the undisputed Pauline epistles (primarily Romans and Galatians). Third, and most importantly with regard to this formatting matter, like Paul's epistles, the opponents are found "between the lines," so to speak. In other words, there is no one passage clearly defining who the opponents are and what they believe. Much of what we know about them is polemical and indefinite, especially with regard to 1 Timothy and Titus. It seems, at times, Paul is speaking of various warnings and opponents that already have arrived, or could arrive, rather than a well-defined specific group of people or a single person. Second Timothy is somewhat different in that specific names are given of some dissenters, deserters, and cancerous agents (cf. 2 Tim 2:16–18; 4:10, 14; also see 1 Timothy 1:20 where Alexander and Hymenaeus are named). So, instead of choosing a single passage that defines these opponents, all pertinent passages will be treated holistically in the Introduction to each chapter.

The New Perspective on Paul and the Pastoral Epistles: Reading the Pastorals as Canonical

Before advancing into the history of research and exposition, a final word must be said about the canonical perspective and this project. This perspective does not assume that all aspects of theology are unified. The use of the above defined categories is not an attempt to harmonize, or otherwise apologize, for the PE or the NPP. These criteria are in place in order to limit the scope of this study. In addition, the canonical perspective is not a tool to ignore the difficulties of authorship, but to admit that there is enough continuity by way of the shaping of the canon to study the PE through the hermeneutical lens of the NPP.

This chapter has sought to state the problem and thesis, define a few important terms, and explain the methodology of the study, which is to interpret the PE as canonical documents through the lens of the NPP to test the validity of the NPP outside undisputed Paul. This chapter also defined four of the major tenets of the NPP in an attempt to limit the scope of passages to those related to the major discussions surrounding the NPP. The next chapter will chronicle the rise of the NPP and the denial of the Pauline authorship of the PE that has led to a relative impasse regarding their pedigree. The next chapter will also chronicle the progress of some recent studies, in which there has been a rising trend to read the PE canonically and movements to engage the NPP by the PE.

2

History of Research

The New Perspective on Paul and
the Pastoral Epistles

Introduction

CHAPTER 1 OUTLINED THE methodology of this study by defining the parameters of the study (the canon) and by making a broad sketch of the NPP via the four tenets used for the selection of passages in the PE. This chapter will focus on the history of research of the two major trajectories within Pauline studies—study of the PE and the NPP. Both of these histories begin with the rise of the Historical Critical Method (HCM).[1] Without the HCM, the two trajectories would have likely remained a single trajectory—the study of Paul. However, once the PE were removed from the study of undisputed Paul (first 1 Timothy, then as a group), the split has remained in scholarship until quite recently. First, this chapter will chronicle the rise of the NPP in the movement from the Hellenistic-focused history-of-religions approach of the Tübingen School and F. C. Baur to a more Jewish-centered approach. Next, a history of the study of the PE will be attempted focusing on authorship. Though the history of the PE will be chronological, after the dismissal of the PE as Pauline, they have remained outside the Pauline corpus in most discussions of Pauline theology. The developments within study of the PE are important in the PE's relative absence from discussions surrounding Pauline theology. There has been a slight move in the direction of acceptance of the PE with studies done in 2 Timothy. However, recently, what has forced many scholars to consider

---

1. For the definition of the Historical Critical Method, see the "Definition of Terms" section in chapter 1.

the PE is the NPP and whether or not there remains any continuity with the PE, and other so-called deutero-Pauline letters.

This history seeks to do a few things: (1) It will highlight and define the major aspects of the NPP through the research of its major contributors. (2) This history chronicles the rise of the problem of the authorship of the PE and the current academic status quo of the pseudonymity of the PE. (3) This history also demonstrates the move some scholars have made in order to incorporate the PE into the greater Pauline discussion. (4) Finally, this history illustrates the NPP's relative lack of contribution to the study of Paul by not incorporating the PE, which provides the impetus for the current study.

The New Perspective on Paul: Precursors, Rise, Development, and Challenges

Breaking Fallow Ground: Precursors of the New Perspective on Paul

The NPP did not come about through the study of Paul himself. Instead, the NPP was a natural next step in the developing thoughts concerning early Judaism and, subsequently, Paul. Though most scholars had focused on other aspects of Paul, such as the centrality of justification in response to legalism, or Paul's similarity to the Greco-Roman religious world, Hellenism, and Stoicism,[2] there were those working both in early Judaism and in Paul outside the norm of the Tübingen School. F. C. Baur had placed Paul as the gentile antithesis to the Jewish Christianity of Peter and James.[3] This Hegelian method had become the standard of studying Paul, and, for some, still is.[4] However, in the years leading up to the rise of the NPP, advancements in early Jewish research and the discovery of the Dead Sea Scrolls, scholars would return to Paul's Jewish roots. This is not to say Paul had been removed from the complex matrix of the first century, but these Jewish studies did find that Paul was a Palestinian Jew (a Judaism possibly influenced

---

2. Engberg-Pederson, *Paul and the Stoics*; Bultmann, *Theology of the New Testament*, 187–89.

3. See Baur, *Paul the Apostle of Jesus Christ*. For other examples of the Jew/gentile divergent trajectories, see Bauer, *Heresy and Orthodoxy in Earliest Christianity* and Dunn, *Unity and Diversity in the New Testament*. Dunn does not see Paul himself as a Hellenistic figure in contrast to Jerusalem so much as the Paulinists who came after him (for example, the author of the PE) who ushered in what he calls "early Catholicism."

4. For example, see Crossan and Reed, *In Search of Paul*; Crossan, *Birth of Christianity*.

by Hellenism), so that reading him outside that context was bound to miss some of the genius of Paul's theology.

Though this history of research does not provide an overview of Luther's writing on the subject, one must understand that Luther's dichotomy of law and grace is what the NPP is reacting against, spearheaded by Krister Stendahl and his essay, "Paul and the Introspective Conscience of the West." This section will focus on the developments in Pauline research in concurrence with the advancing research on early Judaism. A slow consensus was coming to the fore that the Judaism of Paul's day may have been quite different than how it had become to be characterized. If Judaism had been mischaracterized by scholarship, Paul's polemic(s), understanding of the law, Judaism, and even his own "conversion" would need to be reassessed.

Justification: A "Subsidiary Crater": William Wrede and Albert Schweitzer

Though one could start, as does N. T. Wright,[5] with F. C. Baur,[6] this project will begin with the contributions of William Wrede and Albert Schweitzer. With these two figures comes a refocusing on the center of Pauline theology. Though they each have different *foci*, one thing is consistent, that Paul's doctrine of justification is *not* central to his theology, but that this doctrine is a specific polemic against Judaizing tendencies in the early church, witnessed primarily in Romans and Galatians. With regard to the NPP, this is supremely important. Though Wrede sees Paul's polemic as a caricature of Judaism, or an inconsistent way to approach his mission to the gentiles, he demonstrates that Paul's thought is not based on justification as a response to a "plagued conscience," as Krister Stendhal would later argue, but something else. That something else for Schweitzer is eschatology, or better, "being in-Christ." In Paul's eschatological thought, justification was a polemic intended to further illustrate the truth, "righteousness, in consequence of faith, through the being in-Christ."[7]

---

5. Wright, *Paul and His Recent Interpreters*, 8–16.

6. Baur is important because of his Hegelian approach to history. He argued, in essence, that gentile Christianity represented by Paul and Apollos was an antithesis to the Jewish Christianity of Peter and Christ. The synthesis of these two trajectories was "early Catholicism." He held to only four undisputed Pauline documents: Romans, Galatians, and 1 and 2 Corinthians. See Baur, *Paul the Apostle of Jesus Christ*. Something interesting to note is that James Dunn follows a similar line of historical reconstruction, taken more from Walter Bauer. See both Dunn, *Unity and Diversity*, 1–5, and Bauer, *Heresy and Orthodoxy in Earliest Christianity*.

7. Schweitzer, *Mysticism of Paul the Apostle*, 206–7.

Beginning with Wrede, one sees a move away from understanding justification as Paul's theological center. Instead, Wrede argues that Paul's theology of justification is reactionary and polemical. He states, "Die Reformation hat uns gewöhnt, diese Lehre als den Zentralpunkt bei Paulus zu betrachten. Sie ist aber nicht."[8] Instead, he argues that the doctrine is not central, but it is a reaction against Judaism. He sees Paul as having to deal with the precarious position of gentile inclusion in the gospel. From this perspective, Wrede argues from a similar point of view as the Reformers—that the law was not a way to justification (even the moralistic elements), but that grace was.[9] So, though he starts this process of moving away from justification as the theological center of Paul, he is not as far from the Lutheran position as one might imagine.[10] He takes the first steps in defining what Paul's view of justification is reacting against, but he continues to understand the natural Jewish inclination as merit-based religiosity, not only as Jewish ethnic markers. He sees the problem that the Jew/gentile dilemma is posing, and Paul's reaction to it, but he continues to characterize Judaism in the traditional way.

Schweitzer follows this line of reasoning and moves one step further in arguing that Paul "belongs to Late Judaism"[11] and that "Paulinism and Hellenism have in common their religious terminology, but in respect of ideas, nothing."[12] This was a drastic move away from the academic status quo of the time. Both of these men (Wrede and Schweitzer) noticed the paucity of justification language outside Paul's polemical discussions in Romans and Galatians. Wrede was one of the last in a long line of comparative religion interpreters from the Tübingen School following F. C. Baur. So, by this connection with the Tübingen School, he understood Paul's polemical doctrine against Judaizers as an almost entire abandonment of Judaism for the sake of his Hellenized Christianity. In *Paul and His Interpreters*, Schweitzer points out this mistake and recognizes that the comparative religions approach had the wrong questions in mind and were destined to have the wrong answers. He then recognized the need to locate Paul within, what he calls, "Late Judaism."[13] He also emphasized apocalypticism. In his

---

8. "The Reformation has accustomed us to consider this doctrine (justification) the center point of Paul. However, it is not." Wrede, *Paulus*, 72.

9. Wrede, *Paulus*, 72–79.

10. For example, he still understands the "righteousness" of Judaism to be one that is man-made and that justification in Judaism was juristic, a concept that Paul opposed. Wrede, *Paulus*, 74–75.

11. Schweitzer, *Paul and His Interpreters*, 176.

12. Schweitzer, *Paul and His Interpreters*, 238.

13. What Schweitzer called "Late Judaism" would now be called "Early Judaism"

other groundbreaking work, *The Mysticism of Paul the Apostle*, mysticism is emphasized as Paul's theological center, what he identifies as "being-in-Christ."[14] Schweitzer's position is defined in his now well-known statement concerning faith-righteousness versus works-righteousness: "The doctrine of righteousness by faith is therefore a subsidiary crater, which has formed within the rim of the main crater—the mystical doctrine of redemption through the being-in-Christ."[15] Necessary for the present work, to be highlighted later, is Schweitzer's insistence that by means of this "unnatural construction of thought . . . Paul arrives at the idea of a faith which rejects not only the works of the Law, but works in general."[16] Schweitzer argues that by Paul's connecting the doctrine of freedom to the atoning death of Christ, he effectively "closes the pathway to a theory of ethics."[17] It is in these thoughts that the NPP, particularly Wright, will part ways with Schweitzer. However, for the moment, it is important to note that Schweitzer does see a logical progression from "works of law" to "works" in general. He argues that, for Paul, righteousness by faith was simply a way for his theology of the dying and rising of Christ to be scriptural. He states, "More he does not ask of it. But those who subsequently made his doctrine of justification by faith the centre of Christian belief, have had the tragic experience of finding that they were dealing with a conception of redemption, from which no ethic could logically be derived."[18] Schweitzer argues that the traditional way of understanding justification by faith finds no place for ethics. Similarly, the NPP will address this issue with regard to justification by faith and judgment according to deeds.[19]

What these two men ushered into the main in Pauline discussion was that the doctrine of justification (or as Schweitzer put it, "righteousness by faith") was not the primary Pauline theological category. Wrede emphasized the doctrine's polemical nature in Galatians and Romans, whereas Schweitzer emphasized the mystical "being-in-Christ" element of Paul's theology that led to freedom from the law, which led to the "subsidiary crater" of righteousness by faith. For the present work, what is important to recognize are the steps being taken away from the traditional perspective of Pauline

---

or "Second Temple Judaism." For a concise explanation of the change in semantics see Collins and Harrow, *Early Judaism*, vii.

14. Schweitzer, *Mysticism of Paul*, 223.

15. Schweitzer, *Mysticism of Paul*, 225.

16. Schweitzer, *Mysticism of Paul*, 225.

17. Schweitzer, *Mysticism of Paul*, 225.

18. Schweitzer, *Mysticism of Paul*, 225.

19. See especially Yinger, *Paul, Judaism and Judgment According to Deeds*.

justification theology. The next section will focus on the Jewish elements of the argument, which Schweitzer emphasized as well. However, Schweitzer's major contributions come in the form of recognizing the secondary nature of justification in Paul's polemic, which ironically, has continued to be one of the premier topics of debate among scholars to the present day.

Paul and Judaism: Claude Montefiore, W. D. Davies, G. F. Moore, and Hans Joachim Schoeps

This section is an attempt to track some of the major shifts with regard to Paul and early Judaism from Claude Montefiore to Hans Joachim Schoeps. This track is similar to the one above in that it finds its genesis and contrasting pattern with that of Martin Luther. Luther, and those who followed, saw the works-righteousness of Judaism as Paul's primary opponent. Lack of existing rabbinic material as well as relative ignorance of what Jewish material was available led to a caricature of Judaism, not on Paul's part, but on the part of his interpreters.[20] Early in the last century, beginning with Claude Montefiore, there would be a great shift in the way in which early Judaism was understood in relation to Paul's argumentation which, in some ways, culminated in Sanders's work, *Paul and Palestinian Judaism*.

Claude Montefiore and George Foot Moore

Claude Montefiore argued that Paul was not a rabbinic Jew, that scholarship had mischaracterized rabbinic Judaism by the polemics of supposed opponents, and that Paul was, instead, a Hellenistic Jew. He argues that there were several "Judaisms" in Paul's day, including an early rabbinic (Palestinian) Judaism, but that the Judaism against which Paul reacted was a Hellenistic Judaism affected by syncretism of the Hellenistic world.[21] He argues this point by demonstrating that Paul's arguments could not stand even against the rabbinic Judaism of A. D. 300–500, much less first-century Palestinian Judaism. To a rabbinic Jew of the first century, Paul's arguments would be, as Solomon Schechter put it, "unintelligible,"[22] because his arguments fail to account for the beneficial view of the law, as well as repentance

---

20. One must keep in mind, however, that there are those who would espouse that Paul did misrepresent his Jewish opponents. For example, see Räisänen, *Paul and the Law*.

21. Montefiore, *Judaism and St. Paul*, 13.

22. Schechter, *Aspects of Rabbinic Theology*, 18.

and forgiveness common to rabbinic Judaism. Although his position did not win the day, in that it was still highly influenced by the history-of-religions approach, Montefiore nonetheless succeeded in highlighting the mistakes of previous Pauline scholarship, namely that, based on the assumption that Paul was reacting against Palestinian Judaism, that the same Judaism had been mischaracterized by Paul.

Similar to Schechter's and Montefiore's view that Paul's polemic was a misrepresentation of rabbinic Judaism, if that was indeed his opponent, Moore argued in volume 3 of his *Judaism*, which is actually a collection of notes, that "His (Paul's) thesis is that there is no salvation but by faith in the Lord and Saviour, Jesus Christ." By this, he says, Paul would hardly have convinced a Jew. Instead, Moore claims that Paul "was, in fact, not writing to convince Jews but to keep his Gentile converts from being convinced by Jewish propagandists, who insisted that faith in Christ was not sufficient to salvation apart from the observance of the law."[23] Moore is able to argue this point because, like Montefiore, if Paul was attempting to convert rabbinic Jews, his method was "inexplicable."[24]

What the work of Montefiore, Moore, and even Schechter demonstrates is the growing concern over the misrepresentation of early Judaism, especially rabbinic Judaism. They were demonstrating that Judaism itself was multifaceted and variegated, that Jews had a positive view of the law, and that they possessed a robust understanding of repentance and forgiveness. They also exposed the general ignorance of rabbinic Judaism by Pauline scholars, which had led to a misrepresentation of rabbinic Judaism, and, by that, a misunderstanding of Pauline theology.

W. D. Davies and Hans Joachim Schoeps

Davies's work is a *via media* between the Hellenistic studies of Paul done by those like Bultmann and a fully Jewish Paul as posited by Schweitzer. He takes as his starting point what was posited by Montefiore, that Paul was not part of the mainstream Judaism of the first century. What Davies offers is a rabbinic Paul. He states his thesis in contrast to Montefiore, insisting, "We shall endeavor to show that in the central points of his interpretation of the Christian dispensation Paul is grounded in an essentially rabbinic world of thought, that the Apostle was, in short, a Rabbi become Christian and was therefore primarily governed both in life and thought by Pharisaic concepts,

---

23. Moore, *Judaism*, 3:151.
24. Moore, *Judaism*, 3:151.

which he baptized 'unto Christ.'"[25] This thesis is supported by both Paul's connections with and as an aberration from rabbinic Judaism.

Interestingly, Davies aligns with both Wrede and Schweitzer in that he argues justification by faith is not the central Pauline motif. Instead, like Schweitzer, he argues that "being in Christ" is central. However, Davies also argues that polemic has pushed Paul's arguments. Regarding Colossians, Davies writes, "Polemics might lead him to speculation on creation, but he was primarily concerned with redemption."[26] He also states, "Moreover, in those contexts where the idea of Justification by Faith is central, we find that this is so only because of certain polemical necessities. It is only those Epistles, namely, Galatians and Romans, where Paul is consciously presenting the claims of his Gospel over against those of Judaism that Justification by Faith is emphasized."[27] Unlike many of the arguments that have followed, Davies does not spend much of his work discussing or defending justification by faith. So, like Wrede, because he understands justification by faith to be polemical and not central, he does not give his attention wholly to it. Subsequent writing and study, because of what he, Sanders, and the NPP have instigated, has become more and more concerned with justification by faith and its role in Pauline theological thought. E. P. Sanders called Davies's work a "water shed"[28] in the recent study of Paul up to that point, and it signified a turning point wherein, after his work, no one would be able to return to a Hellenistic background for Pauline studies.

The work of H. Joachim Schoeps illustrates the impact of Davies's work. Schoeps believed Paul to be grossly misrepresenting the Jewish position, but that Paul's primary categories of thought were not Hellenistic, but Jewish.[29] Schoeps's view is a syncretistic one. He states, "My opinion is that all the attempts at interpretation which we have studied are relatively right. The problem is only to decide correctly on their limits, to decide where and how they overlap."[30] He argues, critical of Montefiore's method and procedure, though ultimately agreeing with his conclusion, that Paul was a Hellenistic Jew, or, a Jew of the diaspora, educated under Gamaliel.[31]

---

25. Davies, *Paul and Rabbinic Judaism*, 16.

26. Davies, *Paul and Rabbinic Judaism*, 177.

27. Davies, *Paul and Rabbinic Judaism*, 222.

28. Sanders, *Paul and Palestinian Judaism*, 7.

29. Sanders explains that Davies's work marked this shift from Hellenistic backgrounds of Pauline thought to a Jewish background. Sanders, *Paul and Palestinian Judaism*, 7.

30. Schoeps, *Theology of Paul*, 47.

31. See Westerholm, *Perspectives Old and New on Paul*, 123–24; Sanders, *Paul and Palestinian Judaism*, 5–7; and Schoeps, *Theology of Paul*, 25–26. Something to note

Though Schoeps sees significant parallels between Paul and diaspora Judaism, he sees Paul greatly misrepresenting the Judaism from which he came. Thus, for him, Paul's gospel was not accepted by Jews "because from the start he misunderstood Jewish theology."[32] Schoeps's work is considered to be one of the greatest works on Paul from the last century.[33] However, his assessment that Paul misunderstood Jewish theology is ironic in that Schoeps himself seems to misunderstand Paul's theology, evidenced by his argument that Paul had reduced the law to "a matter of ethical self-justification and ritual performance."[34]

The Krister Catalyst: Krister Stendahl and the Introspective Western Conscience

As in Childs's development of the canonical perspective, Krister Stendahl is the catalyst from one perspective to another. Stendahl's contribution to the NPP is not in Judaism, or Paul for that matter, but the dichotomy he exposes between Luther, the introspective Western conscience, and Paul's own conscience. This distinction between Luther and Paul is what lies at the heart of the NPP.

In his essay, "The Apostle Paul and the Introspective Conscience of the West," first delivered at the Annual Meeting of the American Psychological Association September 3, 1961, Stendahl points out the discrepancy between the conscience of Paul and that of Martin Luther (by whom, the "West" is represented).[35] He argues that Paul had a "robust" conscience in contrast to the theology of Luther in whom "we find the problem of late medieval piety and theology."[36] He says that the early depictions of

---

in this regard is the gradual acceptance of historical reliability. For example, Rudolf Bultmann doubted whether or not Paul was ever educated by Gamliel because that did not fit into his description of the Judaism from which Paul came (Bultmann, *Theology of the New Testament*, 190). However, as the Jewish background of Paul became more and more prevalent, Paul's (and even Luke's) depiction of Paul's former life were seen to be more reliable.

32. Schoeps, *Theology of Paul*, 262. He states further, "Our conclusion is that Paul had misunderstood many things" (262).

33. Westerholm, *Perspectives Old and New on Paul*, 123.

34. Schoeps, *Theology of Paul*, 261–62. See also Sanders, *Paul and Palestinian Judaism*, 7n22.

35. The original article is Stendahl, "Apostle Paul and the Introspective Conscience of the West," 199–215. See also Stendahl, "Apostle Paul and the Introspective Conscience of the West," in *Paul Among Jews and Gentiles*, 80.

36. Stendahl, *Paul Among Jews and Gentiles*, 82.

the gospel, and justification by faith, are not responses to an introspective conscience. Instead, he draws a line from Augustine and his *Confessions* to Martin Luther, himself an Augustinian monk. Stendahl's work can be summarized as follows,

> The problem we are trying to isolate could be expressed in her-
> meneutical terms somewhat like this: The Reformers' interpre-
> tation of Paul rests on an analogism when Pauline statements
> about Faith and Works, Law and Gospel, Jews and Gentiles are
> read in the framework of late medieval piety. The Law, the To-
> rah, with its specific requirements of circumcision and food re-
> strictions becomes a general principle of "legalism" in religious
> matters. Where Paul was concerned about the possibility of
> Gentiles to be included in the Messianic community, his state-
> ments are now read as answers to the quest for assurance about
> man's salvation out of a common human predicament.[37]

Then, at the beginning of the next paragraph, he states, "This shift in the frame of reference affects the interpretation at many points."[38] It is with this "shift in frame of reference" in mind, this study moves into the rise of the NPP and the work of E. P. Sanders, whose interpretation followed from this polemic against Reformed readings of Paul.

The New Perspective on Paul:
Sanders, Dunn, and Wright

E. P. Sanders: Covenantal Nomism

All of the above studies led to the beginnings of what is now called "The New Perspective," in the work of E. P. Sanders. Wright describes the impact of Sanders's work as "an idea whose time had come."[39] Although he has pub-lished material subsequently,[40] Sanders's most influential work is *Paul and Palestinian Judaism*, published in 1977, and it is this work on which this section will focus. In this work, Sanders explains that previous research on Paul, although moving in the right direction by studying Paul's rabbinical roots, missed the patterns of religion expressed in Paul and in various forms

---

37. Stendahl, *Paul Among Jews and Gentiles*, 85–86.

38. Stendahl, *Paul Among Jews and Gentiles*, 86.

39. Wright, *Paul and His Recent Interpreters*, 66.

40. A few of his works are: Sanders, *Paul, the Law, and the Jewish People*; Sanders, *Paul*; Sanders, *Paul: The Apostle's Life, Letters, and Thought*; Sanders, "Paul's Attitude Toward the Jewish People," 175–87.

of Palestinian Judaism. He explains his purpose: "The intent, rather (as opposed to comparison between Paul and Judaism), is to answer the question of the basic relationship between Paul's religion and the forms of religion reflected in Palestinian Jewish literature. We have to go behind terminology to determine whether or not Paul and the Rabbis (for example) had the same *type* of religion."[41] Based on this *pattern of religion* Sanders coins the term "covenantal nomism," which he defines:

> (1) God has chosen Israel and (2) given the law. The law implies both (3) God's promise to maintain the election and (4) the requirements to obey. (5) God rewards obedience and punishes transgression. (6) The law provides for means of atonement, and atonement results in (7) maintenance or re-establishment of the covenantal relationship. (8) All those who are maintained in the covenant by obedience, atonement and God's mercy belong to the group which will be saved. An important interpretation of the first and last points is that election and ultimately salvation are considered to be by God's mercy rather than human achievement.[42]

This explanation and definition, essentially, still stands as the basis of NPP thought. The study of Paul did not change the Pauline landscape as much as the study of early Judaism. Sanders's work forced students of Paul to ask the question: If Judaism was a religion of grace/mercy to begin with, against what is Paul reacting? Although Dunn, and especially Wright, have nuanced and corrected much of Sanders's thoughts on Paul, Sanders's work provides the foundational element of the NPP—covenantal nomism.

Paul's Conversion: From Solution to Plight

The foundational category of covenantal nomism gave rise to what Sanders identifies as "plight versus solution." Though Dunn seems to be in general agreement with Sanders's assessment, even though he does not use the same terminology, and Wright provides a slight nuance, it is Sanders who created the category and nomenclature. He states, "It seems likely, however, that Paul's thought did not run from plight to solution but from solution to plight."[43] What he means by this is that Paul himself, while part of Palestinian Judaism, did not perceive a plight that needed a solution, or at

---

41. Sanders, *Paul and Palestinian Judaism*, 19, italics original.

42. Sanders, *Paul and Palestinian Judaism*, 422.

43. Sanders, *Paul and Palestinian Judaism*, 443.

least, a plight that existed *outside* Judaism. He argues for Paul's "solution to plight" formula in opposition to those like Bultmann, who argue that the structure and argument of Romans looks first to man's sinfulness and need for salvation.[44] This aspect of the NPP is also taken up by both Wright and Dunn, though Wright nuances the plight/solution problem differently.[45] Paul's idea of the law and "righteousness by faith" emerges from this "solution to plight" discussion, about which Sanders argues, "The contrast, in other words, is not between self-reliance and reliance on God—two kinds of self-understanding—but between belonging to Christ and not belonging to Christ."[46] This is the crux of the problem between the traditional view of the law, the human plight, and salvation in Christ in contrast to the view of Judaism and the law posited by Sanders. The traditional view argues that individuals have a plight of sinfulness from which they need salvation, the solution of which is Christ, and more specifically, justification by faith which comes by being in Christ. Sanders argues that Paul, in his conversion, saw Christ as a solution to a problem he did not know he had. It is on the basis of this unknown plight that Paul's theology emerges.

Though Sanders has received considerable critique from those for and against his basic agenda, his foundational premise of covenantal nomism (what Wright calls "covenantal narrative"[47]) has remained a steadfast tenet of the NPP in that it exposed the fallacy of assuming that the Judaism of Paul's day was merit-based, legalistic, and medieval. If the work of Sanders is to be summed up by its most salient contributions to the NPP, two primary ones are covenantal nomism and Christ as solution to an unknown plight.

Getting In and Staying In

Before moving on, one other notable aspect of Sanders's work is that within the "pattern of religion" that he calls "covenantal nomism" is the concept of

---

44. Sanders, *Paul and Palestinian Judaism*, 474–75.

45. See Wright, *Paul and the Faithfulness of God*, 743–72 for his most thorough discussion. A shorter, more concise explanation can be found in Wright, *Pauline Perspectives*, 295–97. In this article, "Redemption from the New Perspective?," originally published in 2004, he argues that Paul did have a plight, but rather than a plagued conscience, his problem was the "continuing exile" of God's people to which Jesus provided an answer. Dunn argues, in response to Zahl, that he had not taken up the plight/solution topic, stating, "it does not feature in my version of 'the new perspective.'" See Dunn, *New Perspective on Paul*, 33n133; and Zahl, "Mistakes of the New Perspective on Paul," 5–11.

46. Sanders, *Paul and Palestinian Judaism*, 482.

47. Wright, *Paul and His Recent Interpreters*, 71.

"getting in" and "staying in." Sanders states, "The debate about righteousness by faith or by works of law turns out to result from the different usage of the 'righteous' word group."[48] For some, being "righteous" was not a prerequisite to "getting in" but refers to "staying in." And thus, for Paul, the righteous status given by faith is how one gets in, but not how one maintains that relationship: "Thus when Paul says that one cannot be made righteous by works of law, he means that one cannot, by works of law, 'transfer to the body of the saved.'"[49] He argues that this is in contrast to the Jewish "pattern of religion"—that justification is how one stays in.[50] Though the jargon of this concept of "getting in" and "staying in" becomes different in Dunn and Wright, it, too, characterizes adherents to the NPP.[51]

James D. G. Dunn: ἔργα νόμου
and Paul's View of the Law

Whereas E. P. Sanders's contribution to the NPP was primarily his *Paul and Palestinian Judaism*, Dunn's writing has been more prolific and, in many ways, he has been the face of the "new perspective" proper—if there is such a thing. He is credited with naming the "new perspective,"[52] even though N. T. Wright stated he used similar terminology ("fresh perspective") several years prior.[53] Dunn's primary contribution to this development is his work done on the phrase "works of law."

48. Sanders, *Paul and Palestinian Judaism*, 544.

49. Sanders, *Paul and Palestinian Judaism*, 544.

50. Sanders, *Paul and Palestinian Judaism*, 544.

51. For example, see Dunn, *New Perspective on Paul*, 63–65; Wright, *What Saint Paul Really Said*, 119; and Wright, *Paul and His Recent Interpreters*, 80. Wright's thought concerning Sanders's categories seems to change between *What Saint Paul Really Said* and *Paul and His Recent Interpreters*. In the former, he uses Sanders's terminology, then clarifies it using theological terminology, "soteriology" and "ecclesiology." However, in *Paul and His Recent Interpreters*, 80, he explains, "I do not find these categories helpful either for Judaism or for Paul."

52. This name of the project was given on November 4, 1982 at the Manson Memorial Lecture. See *New Perspective on Paul*, 90, where Dunn writes when recounting then-recent work in Pauline studies, "In one of these cases, however, could I confidently say that I have been given (I speak personally) what amounts to a new perspective on Paul." He also writes, "What I have been pleading for in effect is a shift in perspective—from one dominated by the categories of the Reformation debates, to one properly set within the horizons of the social world of first century Judaism." Dunn, *New Perspective on Paul*, 115.

53. See Wright, "Paul of History and the Apostle of Faith," 61–88.

Dunn explains that his initiation into what would be called the "new perspective" was the work of E. P. Sanders that helped him with his own "nagging"[54] questions about Paul's polemic against Judaism. Dunn, as a student of Paul, had lingering questions regarding the traditional understanding of Paul's justification theology, with a specific interest in the "righteousness of God" and what that phrase means. Although he believed Sanders to have answered some questions about the misrepresentation of Judaism by the majority of Christian scholarship, he found that, regarding Paul, "Sanders only increased the puzzle."[55] Though Dunn has written concerning the "righteousness of God,"[56] among many other things, his most distinct (and debated) mark left on the NPP is his work on "works of law."[57] Dunn writes, "But it was obvious from any study of the key Pauline passages that his teaching on justification through faith Paul was reacting against some other teaching—'by faith *apart from works of the law*' (Rom 3:28), 'from faith in Christ and *not from works of the law*' (Gal 2:16). What was Paul reacting against? What were these 'works of the law'?"[58] Dunn contends that these "works of the law" were social boundary markers and covenantal identifiers.[59] Dunn concludes in a seminar paper titled, "Works of the Law and the curse of the Law," written in August of 1984, "Any attempt to enter sympathetically into the context of Paul's teaching on the law must take into account the social function of the law at that time. That the law served to identify the Jewish people as the people chosen by the one God for himself, and as a *boundary* to mark them off from all (other) nations, would have been a basic assumption of Jewish self-understanding."[60] In response to C.

54. Dunn, *New Perspective on Paul*, 1–3.

55. Dunn, *New Perspective on Paul*, 7.

56. See Dunn, *Theology of Paul the Apostle*, 340–46; and Dunn, *New Perspective on Paul*, 349–50.

57. A glance into the titles of the essays that make up Dunn's *New Perspective on Paul* reveals how much he has focused on the subject, much of which was written in response to criticism and to better articulate his definition. A few works written in response to Dunn's view of "works of law" are Schreiner, "'Works of Law' in Paul," 217–44; Cranfield, "'Works of the Law' in the Epistle to the Romans," 89–101; De Roo, "*Works of the Law" at Qumran and in Paul*; Lash, "New Perspective and Good Deeds"; Moo, "'Law,' 'Works of the Law,' and Legalism in Paul," 73–100; Rapa, *Meaning of "Works of the Law" in Galatians and Romans*. Dunn grants his definition of "works of law" as service to the law, not moral achievement, to Ernest Lohmeyer and J. B. Tyson. See Dunn, *New Perspective on Paul*, 116; Lohmeyer, *Probleme Paulinischer Theologie*, 33–74; Tyson, "'Works of Law' in Galatians," 423–31.

58. Dunn, *New Perspective on Paul*, 1.

59. Dunn, *New Perspective on Paul*, 112–15.

60. Dunn, *New Perspective on Paul*, 129.

E. B. Cranfield, Dunn further clarifies that "works of law" is not restricted to "circumcision, food laws, and sabbath issues."[61] He adds,

> On the contrary, as I understand the usage, "works of the law" characterize the whole mindset of "covenantal nomism"—that is, the conviction that status within the covenant (=righteousness) is maintained by doing what the law requires ("works of the law"). Circumcision and food laws in particular come into play simply(!) because they provided the test cases for most Jews of Paul's time.[62]

One final issue, also taken up by Wright, is the "inter-relationship . . . between justification by faith and judgment according to works."[63] Dunn argues, "Those who have Christ as the foundation of their lives will be saved. But, they will not be exempt from judgment. Justification by faith will not exclude judgment in accordance with the law and by reference to works done in the flesh."[64] So, for Dunn, salvation is both an initial happening (he points to Paul's use of the aorist as evidence),[65] as well as a process awaiting the final pronouncement.

Paul's Conversion and View of the Law

Dunn's work regarding Paul's conversion and Paul's retrospective view of the law is derived from his definition of "works of the law." Sanders had identified Paul's conversion as a solution to an unknown plight, and by that, saw a disjunction between Judaism and Christianity. Dunn, on the other hand, asks the question, "Should we speak of this necessary beginning as a 'conversion'?"[66] This is an important distinction to make, in that it affects the way in which Paul is read with special regard to how much—or

61. Dunn, *New Perspective on Paul*, 207–8.

62. Dunn, *New Perspective on Paul*, 207–8. This definition is what this project will continue to use when referring to the "works of law" as defined by Dunn. One of the problems faced, however, is that this specific phrase is not used outside of Romans and Galatians. So, with regard to the current project in the PE, one must ask whether or not this same polemic and mindset is present without the exact terminology.

63. Dunn, *New Perspective on Paul*, 88.

64. Dunn, *Theology of Paul the Apostle*, 491.

65. Dunn, *Theology of Paul the Apostle*, 324–26. The term "save" is a substantival participle in the aorist in 2 Tim 1:9 when referring to the God who saved Paul and Timothy ("who saved us," τοῦ σώσαντος ἡμᾶς), which says nothing about temporality. In 2 Tim 4:18, when referring to being "saved" for "his heavenly kingdom," the verb is in the future (σώσει).

66. Dunn, *Theology of Paul the Apostle*, 326.

how little—continuity Paul shares with Judaism. Paul's view, and use, of the law is used to help situate the issue.[67]

Both Dunn and Wright see more continuity in Paul's articulation of his gospel with Judaism than Sanders. As already mentioned, Sanders concluded, "In short, *this is what Paul finds wrong in Judaism: it is not Christianity.*"[68] In contrast, Dunn argues that Paul did convert from Judaism to Christianity, but from only a certain type of Judaism that was "anxious to preserve its distinctiveness from Gentile corruption."[69] In Dunn's explanation, this type of Judaism, for Paul after his encounter with Christ, was too restrictive and "zealous."[70] So, his theology of justification by faith was born to incorporate both Jews *and* gentiles, which was the continuation and culmination of God's promise to Abraham, not "works of the law" that restricted entrance into God's people to those who were distinctively Jewish. Dunn explains Paul's view of the law along similar lines. He states, "The law thus became a basic expression of Israel's *distinctiveness* as the people specially chosen by (the one) God to be his people. In sociological terms, the law functioned as an 'identity marker' and 'boundary,' reinforcing Israel's sense of distinctiveness and distinguishing Israel from the surrounding nations."[71] This definition is in contrast to the word νόμος used by Paul as a "general" law. Similarly, Wright states, "The new is in some sort of continuity with the old, as well as some sort of discontinuity."[72] Wright sums up his position that the law is both the end of Jewish nationalism, but at the same time, "this must not be taken to mean that the Torah itself was, after all, a bad thing now happily got rid of."[73] It is, for Paul, both the "law of righteousness" (Rom 9:31; 10:4) as well as the "stumbling stone" (Rom 9:30–33). The key here for the NPP's view of the law (Torah) is one of a restrictive national and ethnic "boundary," on the one side, and the law as "holy," "righteous and good" (Rom 7:12) on the other. The NPP does not interpret "law" as law in a general sense, or as a shorthand for legalism. Instead, the law was a tutor (Gal 3:24–5) meant to lead one to Christ, and that the Torah, whether as an

---

67. For example, see Gal 2:19–21; Phil 3:8–11. In both of these texts, Paul speaks of his former life in Judaism. Paul's view of his life in Judaism is especially important when dealing with 1 Tim 1:6–16 wherein Paul describes the proper use of the law which is followed by a retrospective description of his own conversion.

68. Sanders, *Paul and Palestinian Judaism*, 551–52, italics original.

69. Dunn, *New Perspective on Paul*, 358.

70. See Dunn's definition of "zealous" in Dunn, *Theology of Paul the Apostle*, 350–53. See also Wright, *What Saint Paul Really Said*, 25–29.

71. Dunn, *New Perspective on Paul*, 136, italics original.

72. Wright, *Climax of the Covenant*, 14.

73. Wright, *Climax of the Covenant*, 242.

ethical law or ceremonial law, was now dismissed on the basis of faith and the Spirit (Rom 7:1–25; 2 Cor 3:5–8). So, as far as defining Paul's "conversion," for the NPP, what Paul experienced was not a conversion from one religion to another, but from one view of law to another. The law was no longer binding in an ethical, sociological, ethnic, or even a religious sense, but, as Scripture, it was seen as that which led to Christ by defining sin (Rom 7:12–3; Gal 3:24–5; 1 Tim 1:8–9) and prophesying about the new covenant and return from exile. Thus, Paul was able to both see the positive aspects of the law as well as its deficiencies.

N. T. Wright: The Story of Israel and Justification by Faith

Wright, though attempting to dismantle the idea that the NPP is a collective movement, has become the lightning rod of the skeptical as well as the reluctant spokesperson for the NPP. However, he has also garnered the acceptance of many because he has been able to stay relatively "evangelical" as well as to soften some of the sharp edges of Dunn and Sanders.[74] Although it is hard to pinpoint his most major contribution to the development of the NPP, in keeping with the categories of the first chapter used to select passages, Wright's major contributions have been his work on the story of Israel (with a specific focus on exile), justification, and the "righteousness of God."

The Story of Israel

Wright wraps his entire hermeneutic around the story of Israel and return from exile. The thrust of this argument is set forth in his *The New Testament and the People of God*.[75] Though that particular project is focused on Jesus, the underlying element of return from exile stands also at the fore of his study of Paul. He argues in one of his early works, *Climax of the Covenant*, in some distinction from Sanders, that solution-to-plight was not the best way to articulate Paul's position. Instead, he argues Paul did not have a Lutheran or existential plight *per se*, but a different plight that focused on the "sorry state of Israel."[76] This "sorry state," he explains, could, in certain ways, encapsulate both ways of envisioning Israel's plight, in that it included individual Jewish sinfulness as well as the problem of the state of the nation as a whole.

74. For example, see Bird, *Saving Righteousness of God*, 183–93. Bird sympathizes with the worries of many evangelicals, but he also contends that Wright offers much to the Reformed, confessional church.

75. See Wright, *New Testament and the People of God*, 299–301.

76. Wright, *Climax of the Covenant*, 260–61.

Wright explains further, "But neither will do as a total or complete account. Nothing less than the framework of covenant theology will do justice to the plight perceived by Paul. It was real, indubitable, a fact of first-century life. As long as Herod or Pilate ruled over her, Israel was still under the curse of 'exile.'"[77] Later, in 1994, again Wright insists that the "good news" be understood as a return from exile, by arguing that the passages from Isaiah quoted in Second Temple Judaism still look forward to the coming kingdom.[78] He makes a similar argument in *What Saint Paul Really Said*, stating, "The 'good news' or 'glad tidings' would be the message that the long-awaited release from captivity was at hand."[79] Finally, in a more recent, massive work on Paul, he states, "All this brings us back to another point which in my view ought by now to be non-controversial but which continues to be stubbornly resisted in certain quarters. I refer, of course, to the idea of the second-Temple period as a 'continuing exile.'"[80] So, Wright has maintained that Paul sees Christ as a continuation, and ultimate climax, to God's covenant with Israel rather than in opposition to it. Within this framework of the story of Israel, Wright sees Romans 9–11 as a central passage of Paul's theology, rather than a sort of addendum or excursus after the main point of Romans 1–8.[81] This idea of continuing exile may be Wright's most original contribution to the NPP, which nevertheless finds its genesis in Paul's continuity with Israel and stems from understanding Second Temple Judaism from a sympathetic, covenantal nomistic point of view.

Justification by Faith

The focus on justification by faith has dominated the discussion of the NPP on both sides of the debate. Although Wright may have written the most on the subject, Dunn and Sanders have also contributed to the discussion.[82] As has been already pointed out, the NPP's starting point is a

---

77. Wright, *Climax of the Covenant*, 261.

78. Wright, *Pauline Perspectives*, 81–82.

79. Wright, *What Saint Paul Really Said*, 43.

80. Wright, *Paul and the Faithfulness of God*, 139–63. *Paul and the Faithfulness of God* is a collection, summation, and recapitulation of Wright's previous work on Paul all in one tome.

81. Wright argues that Romans 9–11 is about the righteousness of God, "not as an appendix to the letter but as its proper climax." See Wright, *Pauline Perspectives*, 279. See also Wright, *Climax of the Covenant*, 231–57.

82. For example, see Wright, *Justification*; Wright, *Pauline Perspectives*, 21–28, 216–22, 285–89, 422–38; Wright, *Paul and the Faithfulness of God*, 925–1042; Wright, *What Saint Paul Really Said*, 95–133; Dunn, *New Perspective on Paul*, 19–24, 63–65,

particular view of Judaism, followed by the denial of anti-Pelagian and Lutheran readings of Paul that place justification by faith as the center of Paul's theology. There are two questions, then, that must be answered for the NPP: (1) What is justification by faith? (2) If this justification by faith is not the center of Pauline theology, what is?

Although these questions have already been answered in part in previous sections, a quick survey may help. Sanders argues that justification, or better, the "righteous" word group, can have several different meanings, including "juristic" and "participatory," which Paul held, not in bifurcation, but together.[83] Dunn's identification of justification and righteousness language comes by way of a Jewish mindset in contrast to the Greek understanding of righteousness. The former is a relational concept, the latter is "an idea or ideal against which the individual and individual action can be measured."[84] Wright identifies justification in a similar way, but he draws attention to its covenantal aspect and the "law-court" imagery the Jewish understanding evokes. He insists, as well, that justification cannot be separated from eschatology. He states,

> "Justification" in the first century was not about how someone might establish a relationship with God. It was about God's eschatological definition, both future and present, of who was, in fact, a member of his people. In Sanders' terms, it was not so much about "getting in," or indeed about "staying in," as about "how you could tell who was in." In standard Christian theological language, it wasn't so much about soteriology as about ecclesiology; not so much about salvation as the church.[85]

It is this quite polemical definition, though nuanced in various ways, that defines the NPP. Justification is *not* about individual salvation from a plagued conscience (like Luther), but about the identification of God's people. In the context of Romans and Galatians, justification by faith is juxtaposed to "works of law," only one of which could properly define God's people. Wright, in this same discussion, also draws attention to the meaning of "righteousness." He argues that "it is not a moral quality which they bring into court with them; it is the legal status they carry out of court with them."[86] This is the characterization taken from undisputed Paul. However,

---

361–74; Dunn, *Theology of Paul the Apostle*, 334–89; Sanders, *Paul and Palestinian Judaism*, 470–72.

83. Sanders, *Paul and Palestinian Judaism*, 501.

84. Dunn, *New Perspective on Paul*, 363.

85. Wright, *What Saint Paul Really Said*, 119.

86. Wright, *What Saint Paul Really Said*, 119.

as demonstrated in the first chapter, the PE pose a problem in that the term "righteous" does seem to carry some moralistic tones (cf. 1 Tim 1:9, "the law was not laid down for the righteous").

The Righteousness of God

Another concept that finds its fullest definition in Wright is found in the phrase "the righteousness of God."[87] Wright argues that "Paul always uses this phrase to denote, not the status which God's people have from him or in his presence, but the righteousness of God himself."[88] He explains that the δικαιοσύνη θεοῦ ("righteousness of God") is not the same as what is found in Phil 3:9, τὴν ἐκ θεοῦ δικαιοσύνη ("righteousness from God"). In *What Saint Paul Really Said*, Wright explains that "'Righteousness' is a forensic term, that is, taken from the law court."[89] So, for Wright, the "righteousness of God" is God's own righteousness, like a judge (God) is righteous in his just acquittal of a defendant (Israel).[90] He sets this definition in opposition to Ernst Käsemann, who also says that the "righteousness of God" is God's own righteousness, but he says so from an apocalyptic, non-covenantal standpoint. For Käsemann, Paul's theology is based on the apocalyptic reality of the end of the first age, the arrival of the end time, and the "imminent expectation" (*Naherwartung*) of the triumph of God.[91]

---

87. See also Dunn's treatment in Dunn, *Theology of Paul the Apostle*, 340–46.

88. Wright, *Pauline Perspectives*, 279. In this definition, several key features of Wright's thought are found. In *Climax of the Covenant*, he puts it this way in relation to the plight/solution problem, "But what he (Paul) has done is not to invent a 'problem of the law' from scratch. The problem which underlies the problem of the law is the problem of the righteousness of God: how can God be true to the covenant, granted the present (i.e. first-century Jewish) state of things?" In this, the "righteousness of God," Paul and Israel's plight from exile, and the law all work together. Wright, *Climax of the Covenant*, 215–16.

89. Wright, *What Saint Paul Really Said*, 97.

90. Wright, *What Saint Paul Really Said*, 97–103. For Wright, the righteous status for plaintiff and defendant alike is based on the decision of the judge and the "way he handles the case" (97). In other words, "righteous" in the law-court setting has nothing to do with the moral standing of the plaintiff or defendant beforehand. He states, "No; for the plaintiff or defendant to be 'righteous' in the biblical sense *within the law-court setting* is for them to have that status *as a result of the decision of the* court" (98, italics original). He further clarifies, "If we use the language of the law court, it makes no sense whatever to say that the judge imputes, imparts, bequeaths, conveys or otherwise transfers his righteousness to either the plaintiff or the defendant" (98).

91. See Wright, *Paul and His Recent Interpreters*, 145–50; and Käsemann, "Righteousness of God in Paul," 152–82.

Other NPP Proponents and Attempts at Compromise

Although there are different ways of approaching texts and varying levels of continuity and variance with the greater lights of the NPP (Sanders, Dunn, and Wright), the definition and boundaries of the NPP have been set by them. As pointed out by others, although there is no tight-knit group of NPP scholars, there are certain elements that define that boundary, the primary one being opposition to the mischaracterization of early Judaism. For this project, "new perspective" primarily refers to the work of Sanders, Dunn, and Wright. However, others who have written on "new perspectives" in Paul have included those like J. Louis Martyn[92] and Heikki Räisänen,[93] neither of which are considered major new perspective adherents within the bounds of this project.

Terrence Donaldson and Richard Longenecker

The "lesser lights"[94] of the NPP, though not contributing as much to the fundamental definition, have nonetheless added texture to the NPP. Terrence Donaldson is placed alongside Dunn and Wright in Westerholm's eleventh chapter, "Saint Paul Against the Lutherans."[95] Donaldson takes as his starting point the paradigm shift of Sanders in contrast to "Traditional

---

92. Martyn, *Galatians*.

93. Both Guy Prentiss Waters and Stephen Westerholm justifiably place him within the NPP. See Waters, *Justification and the New Perspectives on Paul*; and Westerholm, *Perspectives Old and New on Paul*. As for Heikki Räisänen, his work certainly does come from a NPP background as to Paul's problem with his Jewish opponents and his definition of "works of law." However, his version of Paul is so convoluted and inconsistent, it is difficult to place his thoughts in the "new perspective on Paul" if Paul himself is not altogether sure what his perspective is. For example, see his conclusion that, "Paul's thought on the law is full of difficulties and inconsistencies." Räisänen, *Paul and the Law*, 264. Räisänen is sure that Paul himself was inconsistent and, at times, illogical for the purpose of making a point. He says that although he is indebted to Paul for articulating the gentile freedom from Jewish Torah observance, "I can find no fault with the Jew who says that, as a Jew, Paul should not have said much he actually said." Räisänen, *Paul and the Law*, 268. One can see even in these two passages how Räisänen utilizes some "new perspective" insights. Admittedly, Sanders himself also sees a relatively inconsistent Paul, but his work on covenantal nomism makes him an indispensable part of the NPP.

94. This term is not meant to be pejorative, but it is a way to distinguish those who have played a lesser role in the definition of the NPP, and who are less prolific in their writing.

95. Westerholm, *Perspectives Old and New*, 178–200.

Approaches."[96] Rather than a new perspective, he offers a "new paradigm," a term borrowed from the scientific community.[97] Donaldson sees Paul's theology of, and mission to, the gentiles, as one with interior tensions. On the one hand, Paul dismissed Torah observance, but on the other hand, the distinction "Jew" as an ethnicity still remained. He argues that the early church erased Paul's "commitment to natural Israel," which, he concludes, resulted in "a more consistent theology, but a consistency purchased at the price of increasingly lamentable consequences."[98] This aspect of the NPP, born from covenantal nomism, creates a more conflicted Paul than that of Dunn and Wright.[99]

Richard Longenecker, though publishing his *Paul, Apostle of Liberty*, thirteen years before Sanders's *Paul and Palestinian Judaism*, finds resonance with Sanders in the mischaracterization of early Judaism. In the foreword to the second edition, Douglas Campbell states of Longenecker, "So in a very real sense Longenecker *is* the Sanders of the evangelical tradition—or he ought to be!"[100] Longenecker himself urges, "We need not visualize every Jew under the Old Covenant as feeling frustrated, oppressed, and dissatisfied with his lot, even as we need not suppose that every minor or servant is chafing at the bit under the rule and supervision of supervisors."[101] He concludes in this regard: "It was the Person and work of Jesus Christ as the fulfillment of Israel's hopes, and not an early dissatisfaction with the Law, that made all the difference; thereby transforming the zealous Rabbi Saul into the zealous Apostle Paul."[102] So, though Longenecker may not be properly part of the NPP, he certainly saw some of the same problems with the mischaracterization of Judaism as Sanders did.

---

96. Donaldson, *Paul and the Gentiles*, 3–27.

97. Donaldson, *Paul and the Gentiles*, 3.

98. Donaldson, *Paul and the Gentiles*, 306.

99. However, worth noting is the connection to anti-Judaism espoused by Dunn and Wright because of the traditional understanding of justification by faith. The NPP dampens Paul's polemic against Judaism, in that Judaism is no longer seen as "legalistic." See Donaldson, *Jews and Anti-Judaism in the New Testament*; Dunn, *Theology of Paul the Apostle*, 336–67; Wright, *Paul and His Recent Interpreters*, 55.

100. Campbell, "Foreword," xvi.

101. Longenecker, *Paul, Apostle of Liberty*, 96.

102. Longenecker, *Paul, Apostle of Liberty*, 96.

Kent Yinger, Don Garlington, and John Ziesler

Both Kent Yinger and Don Garlington have written on the importance of obedience and how obedience fits into the NPP hermeneutic.[103] Yinger's work, *Paul, Judaism, and Judgment According to Deeds,* states, "My thesis is that Paul's use of this motif—terminologically, rhetorically, and theologically—demonstrates fundamental continuity with second Temple Jewish sources, and this in spite of notable differences."[104] It is the NPP understanding of Paul's basic continuity with Judaism as articulated by Sanders that generates this thought.[105] Similarly, Don Garlington argues, in keeping with Sanders and Dunn, the "obedience of faith" was set in contrast to the obedience of law. The problem was not legalism *per se*, but the whole law as what constitutes proper obedience. Paul says, instead, that the law was only a pedagogue (Gal 3:24–25) that brought about the obedience by faith. His focus, then, is on the continuity of Paul and Judaism regarding *obedience*, but that obedience now has come by faith. Garlington concludes, "All of the above conclusions argue in favor of the thesis, propounded most prominently by Dunn, that Paul's dispute with Israel over the law had to do not with 'grace' as opposed to 'legalism' (in the normally accepted sense of the terms) but with a more ethnically inclusive vision of God and his law as over against one which was nationalistically restrictive."[106]

John Ziesler also represents a NPP hermeneutic. In his *Pauline Christianity*, though there are few notes and attributions, he takes a more or less "new perspective" approach. He believes Paul to be a Palestinian Jew, although he admits there are some Hellenistic influences in Paul, like his quoting the LXX. He argues that Paul was, indeed, a Pharisee, and that "Paul did not become a Christian because he had come to the end of his tether as a Jew,"[107] a statement that reflects NPP assumptions. Important for the present project is that Ziesler denies the Pauline pedigree of the PE, but offers this consolation: "Curiously, non-Pauline authorship enhances rather than diminishes the letters' importance, because it means they give us a valuable glimpse of what happened to Pauline Christianity about the end of the first century."[108] Though written before Sanders's *Paul*

---

103. Garlington, *Faith, Obedience, and Perseverance*; Garlington, *An Exposition of Galatians*; Garlington, *"Obedience of Faith"*; Yinger, *Paul, Judaism, and Judgment According to Deeds.*

104. Yinger, *Paul, Judaism, and Judgment According to Deeds,* 15–16.

105. Yinger, *Paul, Judaism, and Judgment According to Deeds,* 288–91.

106. Garlington, *"Obedience of Faith,"* 265.

107. Ziesler, *Pauline Christianity,* 24.

108. Ziesler, *Pauline Christianity,* 140. The denial of Pauline authorship of the PE

and Palestinian Judaism, Ziesler also wrote a monograph *The Meaning of Righteousness in Paul.* In this work he defines "righteousness" from what he calls "Later Judaism," arguing that "righteousness" in Paul is both forensic and relational and is consistent with both the Greek and Hebrew meanings of the word (the former an ethical standing, the latter, relational).[109] Ziesler contends, "While both 'imputed' and 'imparted' approaches are inadequate and inaccurate, nevertheless both preserve one part of Paul's two-sided doctrine, and their basic affirmations must stand."[110] For Ziesler, the meaning of "righteousness" in Paul is inclusive enough to incorporate both the ethical and relational elements.

Garwood Anderson, Michael Bird, A. Andrew Das, and Brian S. Rosner

Four final voices to be heard in this section are that of Garwood Anderson, Michael Bird, A. Andrew Das, and Brian S. Rosner, all of whom provide a quasi-mediating position between the NPP and traditional Reformed theology. Garwood Anderson calls himself an NPP "God-fearer, not a proselyte,"[111] and he enters into his study highlighting the propensity of Pauline scholarship for contention, opting for "peacemaking."[112] He points out the NPP's tendency to stay within undisputed Paul, but he offers as the thesis of his work,

> Finally, we must contend with the possibility that Paul is not so much incoherent as his writings are contextually determined and that his expression of various matters developed over time. This, in fact, is the thesis of this book: as it regards his soteriology, Paul's letters show evidence of both a contextually determined diversity and also a coherent development through time.[113]

Anderson's work is important for the present study in that it highlights the diversity of Paul's soteriology, as he sees his soteriology developing to meet specific needs within the church. However, for the moment, what needs highlighting is Anderson's view that the contentious nature of Pauline

---

seems to be a trait of NPP adherents.

109. Ziesler, *Meaning of Righteousness in Paul,* 212. This work was originally published in 1972.

110. Ziesler, *Meaning of Righteousness in Paul,* 171.

111. Anderson, *Paul's New Perspective,* 37.

112. Anderson, *Paul's New Perspective,* 1–5.

113. Anderson, *Paul's New Perspective,* 6–7.

studies has prevented a proper meeting of the traditional and "new" perspectives, something the present project also contends.

Michael Bird's work, *The Saving Righteousness of God*, is similar to Anderson's work. Bird seeks to focus beyond the contention within Pauline studies between the traditional perspective and the NPP. He states, "But I have serious reservations with defining anything that is to endure in negative terms simply for the fact that one is defining oneself through criticism and not through positive exposition. If we define our self through opposition then we will loose[114] our identity when our opponents fade off the scene."[115] He insists that Paul should be studied as Paul, and not in relation to any particular perspective. He concludes by affirming much of what the NPP has defined concerning justification and righteousness, while also maintaining a traditional, Reformed perspective.[116] He adds, "Ultimately the NPP is correct in what it affirms but wrong in what it denies."[117]

A. Andrew Das, beginning with his dissertation in 1999 offers what he calls a "newer perspective" on Paul and the law that attempts to synthesize the arguments from both sides. He defends the position that Jews did believe perfect obedience was necessary,[118] and he argues,

> While first century Judaism was certainly not legalistic in its understanding of the Law, Paul's own perspective led, nevertheless, to an understanding of the works of the Mosaic Law as a merely human endeavor in contrast to God's own saving activity in Christ. In effect, the gracious framework of Judaism does not avail for salvation and has been replaced by a Christological framework. NT scholarship has not yet fully explored the consequences of a Jew abandoning "covenantal nomism" in favor of a "Christological nomism."[119]

114. This word was used by Bird. It may be a mistake in an attempt to type "lose," or that one's identity may be "loosed" or "released" once an opponent fades away.

115. Bird, *Saving Righteousness of God*, 179.

116. For example, he denies the imputation of Christ's righteousness in any explicit text, but adds, "That does not make imputation entirely redundant as imputation constitutes a cogent (and perhaps necessary) theological explanation of the mechanism thorough which union communicates righteousness to the believer." Bird, *Saving Righteousness of God*, 182.

117. Bird, *Saving Righteousness of God*, 182.

118. Das, "Beyond Covenantal Nomism," 234–52; Das, "Paul and Works of Obedience in Second Temple Judaism," 795–812.

119. Although this work is quoting from his dissertation, the same wording is found in Das, *Paul, the Law, and the Covenant*, 11. See also his dissertation, Das, "Beyond Covenantal Nomism," 16. For further work done by Das, see Das, *Paul and the Jews*.

Stephen Westerholm places Das in the "Lutheran" responses to the NPP, but this study sees some compromise with the NPP in Das's work. Das agrees that Judaism was not in its own understanding "legalistic," but once compared with the Christological framework of Paul, the law became "a merely human endeavor."[120]

Finally, Brian S. Rosner, in his *Paul and the Law: Keeping the Commandments of God*, investigates Paul's use of the law in response to the debates brought about by the NPP, finding that Paul's view cannot be identified by a single idea. He explains,

> In my view Paul does three things with the law and each one must be fully heard without prejudicing the others: (1) polemical repudiation; (2) radical replacement; and 3) whole-hearted appropriation (in two ways). These respectively correspond to treating the law as *legal code, theological motif* and *source for expounding the gospel and for doing ethics.*[121]

Most significant for this study, is his attempt "to learn something from each of these perspectives,"[122] with the NPP representing one of "these perspectives," and his inclusion of the PE (and the entire thirteen letter Pauline corpus) into the discussion of Paul and the law. One of his chapters deals with the "instruction" of the law, the title of which "written for our instruction" is taken from 2 Timothy 3:16.[123] In this chapter, he vies for Paul's use of the law as wisdom (radical replacement and appropriation, above), and how that wisdom is worked out in practice. First Timothy 1:8–10 plays a major role in Rosner's discussion of the negative use of the law ("not for the righteous"). Though he maintains that Paul's most articulated views on the law are found in the undisputed letters (particularly, Romans, Galatians, and 1 Corinthians), he contends concerning Ephesians and the PE that, "Even those scholars who work with a truncated Pauline corpus should recognize that if the law is a central concern for Paul, the pseudo-Pauline epistles provide early reflections of, or on, his views. It is a mistake to disregard such evidence, even if it is not accorded primary status."[124]

---

120. See Das's statement above.

121. Rosner, *Paul and the Law*, 39, 220–22, italics original.

122. Rosner, *Paul and the Law*, 21.

123. Rosner, *Paul and the Law*, 159–205, 219.

124. Rosner, *Paul and the Law*, 26. This comes close to the stated method of the present project regarding the inclusion of the PE into the discussion of Pauline theology, with a highly-focused view toward the NPP.

Dissenting Voices

The NPP has not been without dissenters in the years after Sanders's work. In fact, Wright describes the reaction to the "so-called" NPP as a collective movement as a "carpet bombing."[125] For this project, there is no need to exhaust the dissenting voices,[126] in that this work is not concerned with the "rightness" or "wrongness" of the NPP—at least not directly—but with whether or not the NPP is a legitimate hermeneutic for reading the PE. However, with that in mind, for the sake of a relatively complete history, some of the major dissenters will be reviewed, being mindful that a few of these voices will be reserved for the final section of this chapter that focuses on the meeting of the research trajectories.

The major collective rebuttal to the NPP is the two-volume work edited by D. A. Carson, Peter T. O'Brien, and Mark A. Seifrid, *Justification and Variegated Nomism.*[127] In the preface to the first volume, Carson explains that in the wake of Sanders's work on covenantal nomism, "what was needed was a fresh exploration of the literature of Second Temple Judaism, followed by a fresh treatment of Paul that took into account the findings of the first exploration."[128] Summarily, Carson notices that among the contributors, there is relative agreement that there are some elements of covenantal nomism found. However, there are also several points of departure as well. His concluding comments may help distill the vast, variegated material of the first volume: "Examination of Sanders's covenantal nomism leads one to the conclusion that the New Testament documents, not least Paul, must not be read against this reconstructed background—or, at least, must not be read *exclusively* against this background. It is too doctrinaire, too unsupported, by the sources themselves, too reductionistic, too monopolistic."[129] Although this volume has been lauded for the spectrum

---

125. Wright, *Pauline Perspectives*, 277. He writes about scholarship's penchant for finding new enemies just before a reference to his own carpet-bombing, saying, "Here is something called the New Perspective; it seems to be denying some of the things we have normally taught; very well, let us demonize it, lump its proponents together, and nuke them from a great height."

126. Some who have reacted against the NPP but not included in the following discussion include: Hassler, "Ethnocentric Legalism and the Justification of the Individual," 311–27; Kim, *Paul and the New Perspective*; Sprinkle, "Old Perspective on the New Perspective," 21–31; Stuhlmacher, *Revisiting Paul's Doctrine of Justification*; Venema, *Gospel of Free Acceptance in Christ*; Gathercole, *Where Is Boasting?*; Gathercole, "Doctrine of Justification and Beyond," 219–41.

127. Carson et al., *Justification and Variegated Nomism*.

128. Carson et al., *Justification and Variegated Nomism*, 1:v.

129. Carson et al., *Justification and Variegated Nomism*, 1:548, italics original.

of its study, proponents of the NPP have not been overly concerned or de-terred from proceeding. One does not have to concede that *all* of early Juda-ism functioned by covenantal nomism, only that the Judaism of which Paul was a member, and familiar with, did. Carson himself says as much: "Of course, this does not mean that the various 'new perspective' readings of Paul are wrong. It merely means that, with the increased perception of the variegated approaches to nomism represented in the literature of Second Temple Judaism, the lines adopted by new perspective interpreters enjoy less presumption of being right."[130] The essays in the second volume focus on much that has already been discussed as the staple elements of the NPP like Romans, Galatians, righteousness, "works of law," covenantal nomism, Paul's conversion, and, of course, justification by faith.

There have been other relatively extensive responses to the NPP that need to be mentioned,[131] though all of these works need not be rehearsed in detail. The sheer volume of works serves as proof of the provocative nature of the NPP hermeneutic and its supposed threat to confessional Christi-anity. John Piper wrote two monographs regarding Wright's position on justification—one in 2002, the other in 2007—to which Wright himself responded.[132] Robert Gundry warned of "synergism" within the new per-spective's hermeneutic, which Wright questions as a synergism/monergism debate not fit for the first century.[133] Although Westerholm lists Cranfield as a "Lutheran" response, Cranfield is not in direct opposition to the NPP. He simply represents the traditional perspective. However, Thomas Schreiner does oppose the NPP stating, "I believe the Reformers were profoundly cor-rect in insisting that Paul's Gospel is supremely a gospel of grace that was framed in the context of a legalistic soteriology with roots in Judaism."[134] Frank Thielman, although he does not believe Paul to have been a legalist,

---

130. Carson et al., *Justification and Variegated Nomism*, 2:v.

131. A few other works that can be reviewed responding in various ways to the NPP are Seifrid, *Justification by Faith*; Seifrid, *Christ, Our Righteousness*; Silva, "Law and Christianity," 339–53; Kruse, *Paul, the Law, and Justification*; Fesko, "Critical Examina-tion of N. T. Wright's Doctrine of Justification," 102–15; Smith, "Overview and Critique of the New Perspective on Paul's Doctrine of Justification," 188–33. Mark Seifrid's work is important because his book on justification stands in direct contrast to the NPP and its most fundamental elements (e.g., covenantal nomism and the "righteousness of God"). See especially, Seifrid, *Christ, Our Righteousness*, 13–33.

132. See Piper, *Future of Justification*; Piper, *Counted Righteous in Christ*. Wright responded in Wright, *Justification*. See also Wright, *Paul and His Recent Interpreters*, 108n8 and Wright, *Pauline Perspectives*, 422.

133. See Gundry, "Inferiority of the New Perspective on Paul," 223–24. Also, see Wright, *Paul and His Recent Interpreters*, 107n6.

134. Schreiner, *Law and Its Fulfillment*, 243.

or arguing against legalism, does see Paul arguing that "Israel has been unfaithful to the covenant, and God's future judgment will be impartial."[135] He also takes issue with Sanders, arguing that although Sanders had helped move beyond the characterization of Judaism as legalistic, he did not maintain proper continuity with Judaism with regard to the human plight.[136] For Thielman, the Jews were incapable of keeping the law, which is why the new covenant spoken of by Ezekiel and Jeremiah was brought in. He concludes, "The Old Testament looked forward to the restoration of Israel and the establishment of a new covenant, Judaism carried that hope forward into the first century, and Paul proclaimed that it had been fulfilled."[137]

The Pastoral Epistles: From Paul to Pseudonymity to . . . Paul?

When tracing the development of the NPP, the history of research followed a relatively distinct line with specific scholars, each adding bricks to a building that would become the NPP. However, the history of the PE is not so easily traced from one scholar to the next. Instead, after the PE's rejection as Pauline documents, various scholars either aided this conclusion, or other theories developed that accounted for the problems raised by the others. This section of the history of research has two primary goals: (1) to trace the various issues regarding the authorship of the PE and their rejection as authentic Pauline documents, and (2) to trace the works that have defended, and in some cases, nearly proven, the possibility of the PE being genuine Pauline documents.

From Paul to Pseudonymity

The reception of the PE in the early years of the church after Paul's death is debated among scholars, even though by the end of the second century the PE were part of the Muratorian canon, which speaks to their positive reception in the early church. Polycarp may have alluded to 1 Timothy 6:7, 10 and 2 Timothy 4:10 in his *Letter to the Philippians* 4.1, 5.2 (ca. 120–35

---

135. Thielman, *Paul and the Law*, 239. Rather than a dissenter of the NPP, Thielman represents a sort-of synthesis of the NPP. Although he does agree Paul is not combatting legalism, he does take issue with Sanders with regard to the solution/plight argument. Thielman argues from the OT and Second Temple literature that there was a "plight-solution pattern." See Thielman, *From Plight to Solution*, 118.

136. Thielman, *From Plight to Solution*, 117–22.

137. Thielman, *Paul and the Law*, 245.

C. E.)[138] and *1 Clement* 2.7, 60.4, 61.2 also contains possible allusions to the PE.[139] These early allusions are evidence that the letters were likely written before the end of the first century. In the first few lines of the Preface to *Against Heresies*, Irenaeus designates "the apostle" as the author of a quote from 1 Timothy 1:4. Clement of Alexandria quotes all three of the PE, 1 and 2 Timothy frequently.[140] Both Athenagoras and Theophilus possibly allude to 1 Timothy 2:1–2.[141] However, the earliest collection of Pauline letters, the Beatty Manuscript ($\mathfrak{P}$46), does not contain 2 Thessalonians, Philemon, and the PE. There is some debate regarding whether or not the scribe of $\mathfrak{P}$46 intended to add these letters because there were seven more leaves, but they are not in the manuscript as it is.[142] Marcion did not include the PE in his canon. He is accused by Tertullian of deliberate exclusion of the PE because they were written to individuals (though Marcion does include Philemon) and because "all treat ecclesiastical discipline."[143] Tertullian also argued that Marcion was heretical because he did not adhere to a complete Pauline canon.[144] Regardless of the date of their composition, which was likely well before Polycarp's *Letter to the Philippians* as well as the writing of Clement and Tertullian (A. D. 120–35), it seems the PE enjoyed good standing in the early composition of the canon, which is what is important for this work. It seems that though the PE held resemblance with one another, as well as proximity canonically, they were treated as individual letters to Timothy and Titus. There are problems to be considered, like their absence from $\mathfrak{P}$46, but they ultimately were adopted into the canon, because of their supposed Pauline nature.

138. This is what Philip Towner posits as allusions in Polycarp's *Letter to the Philippians*. Towner, *Letters to Timothy and Titus*, 4. Luke Timothy Johnson sees many more allusions: 1 Tim 1:1 (*Phil.* 8.1); 1 Tim 2:2 (*Phil* 12.2); 2 Tim 2:12 (*Phil.* 5.2); 2 Tim 2:11, 4:10 (*Phil.* 9.2); 3 Tim 2:25 (*Phil.* 11.3). See Johnson, *First and Second Letters to Timothy*, 20–22.

139. The possible allusions here are Titus 3:1, 1 Tim 2:7, and 1 Tim 1:17, respectively.

140. A few examples are Titus 2:11–3, 3:3–5 in *Protr.* 1; 1 Tim 5:23, 6:10, 2:9 (mistakenly attributed to Peter), 6:2 in *Paed.* 2.2, 2.3, 3.11, and 6.2 respectively.

141. Athenagoras, *Leg.* 32; Theophilus, *Autol.* 14.

142. See Johnson, *First and Second Letters to Timothy*, 17–18. Though there was more room, there were also other Pauline documents missing that the scribe may have planned to add. Some doubt there would have been enough room for all five letters. However, the scribe had been progressively fitting in more text.

143. Tertullian, *Marc.* 5.21.

144. See Tertullian, *Marc.* 5.1, 21. "That is, we shall draw our evidence from the epistles of St. Paul himself. Now, the garbled form in which we have found the heretic's Gospel will have already prepared us to expect to find the epistles also mutilated by him with like perverseness–and that even as respects their number." *Marc.* 5.1.

The PE were designated as "The Pastoral Epistles" in 1726 by Paul Anton in a series of lectures.[145] This moniker and grouping, although understandable because of their similarities, nonetheless creates a (sometimes) artificial comparison between them. Beginning in 1804,[146] then soon after, in 1807,[147] the authorship of 1 Timothy was questioned. Schmidt was the first to call the authorship of 1 Timothy into question, but the better-known rejection of Pauline authorship comes from Friedrich Schleiermacher's *Über den sogenannten ersten Brief des Paulus an den Timotheus.*[148] In 1812, Johann Gottfried Eichhorn argued that all three letters were pseudonymous for many of the same reasons Schleiermacher had rejected 1 Timothy.[149] Wilhelm M. L. De Wette rejected Pauline authorship of the PE in both his Introduction and his commentary.[150] F. C. Baur argued that the PE were late compositions intended to combat Marcion.[151] Heinrich Holtzmann may serve as the culmination of the Tübingen approach to the PE in that he states that the PE are pseudonymous, could not be fit into the life of Paul, and were written against gnostics.[152] Since Holtzmann, the majority of scholars opt for pseudonymous authorship, a compositional authorship, or an amanuensis. However, there were, even then, dissenting voices such as Henry Alford[153] and August Wiesinger.[154] Luke Timothy

145. See Spain, *Letters of Paul to Timothy and Titus*, 7.

146. Schmidt did not outright reject Pauline authorship, but he demonstrated the difficulty in placing 1 Timothy into Paul's ministry. Schmidt, *Historisch-kritische Einleitung in's Neue Testament*.

147. Schleiermacher, *Über den sogenannten ersten Brief des Paulus an den Timotheos*.

148. Although this work is not attempting to prove Pauline authorship of the PE, what is interesting is the argument of those like L. T. Johnson and Gordon Clark, who argue that Schleiermacher's attack on the authorship of 1 Timothy is rarely revisited, but the results have been accepted without objection by many "critical" scholars. See Johnson, *First and Second Letters to Timothy*, 52–54; Clark, *Pastoral Epistles*, xii; Wall and Steele, *1 & 2 Timothy and Titus*, 7.

149. See Eichhorn, *Einleitung in das Neue Testament* 3.1. The rejection of the letters, as a group, has in many ways affected the way in which the PE are received until the present day.

150. See De Wette, *Historico-Critical Introduction to the Canonical Books of the New Testament*, 298–304; De Wette, *Kurze Erklärung der Brief an Titus, Timotheus und die Hebräer*.

151. Baur argues that Marcion's work *Antitheses* is mentioned by name in 1 Timothy 6:20 (ἀντιθέσεις). See Baur, *Die sogenannten Pastoralbriefe des Apostels Paulus auf neue kritisch untersucht*, 8–39; Baur, *Paul the Apostle of Jesus Christ*.

152. Holtzmann, *Die Pastoralbriefe kritische und exegetisch untersucht*. Also see, Prior, *Paul, the Letter Writer and the Second Letter to Timothy*.

153. Alford, *Greek Testament*.

154. Wiesinger, *Biblical Commentary on St. Paul's Epistles*.

Johnson argues that even though there were, and are, a great number of commentaries that accept the Pauline authorship of the PE, those numbers can be misleading, and that most introductions and early church histories place the PE in the second century.[155] He even goes so far as to say, "The term 'debate' is surely too strong for the present situation, which is closer to a fixed academic consensus."[156]

A brief summary of issues of the authorship of the PE since F. C. Baur further demonstrates the ubiquity of the position that the PE are un-Pauline by further research in linguistics, style, and composition. P. N. Harrison, in his *The Problem of the Pastoral Epistles,* argues that because of *hapax legomena* and style that the letter belonged to the second century.[157] James Miller's literary study, *The Pastoral Letters as Composite Documents,*[158] suggests that because of the irregular nature of the language and argument of the PE, they are genuine Pauline fragments collected as an anthology of sorts by a school or community akin to that at Qumran, what, he calls, a "school for Pastors."[159] Among these discussions of various theories of composition is the resilient advocacy of pseudepigraphy and its positive, or, at least, acceptable reception in the centuries preceding and following the writing and compilation of the NT.[160] In contrast, Lewis Donelson argues in his work *Pseudepigraphy and Ethical Argument in the Pastoral Epistles,*[161] that the PE conform to the pattern of pseudepigraphy and that they were a purposeful deception and "do not employ a single device of deception or literary technique which cannot be paralleled elsewhere."[162] He also argues that the author of the PE, "appears to be a Paulinist not in theology but only in name; he is defending a man he knows mostly by reputation and legend."[163] H. C.

155. Johnson, *First and Second Letters to Timothy,* 49–53. One of the discussions surrounding the authorship of the PE is where to place them within the ministry of Paul. Some find no proper place for them, while others argue that 2 Timothy especially, is Paul's last will and testament of sorts during a second imprisonment after a short release. See Andreas Köstenberger, *Commentary on 1–2 Timothy and Titus,* 24–32.

156. Johnson, *First and Second Letters to Timothy,* 55.

157. Harrison, *Problem of the Pastoral Epistles.* Following this type of research some have argued both for and against Pauline authorship. See, in response, Kenney, *Stylometric Study of the New Testament*; and Neumann, *Authenticity of the Pauline Epistles in Light of Stylostatistical Analysis.*

158. Miller, *Pastoral Letters as Composite Documents.*

159. Miller, *Pastoral Letters as Composite Documents,* 157.

160. See also Porter and Fewster, *Paul and Pseudepigraphy*; and Brox, *Falsche Verfasserangaben.*

161. Donelson, *Pseudepigraphy and Ethical Argument.*

162. Donelson, *Pseudepigraphy and Ethical Argument,* 66.

163. Donelson, *Pseudepigraphy and Ethical Argument,* 60.

G. Moule argues that 2 Timothy was dictated by Paul to Luke in a Roman prison prior to his execution.[164] Similarly, C. F. D. Moule opts for Lukan authorship "during Paul's lifetime, at Paul's behest, and, in part (but only in part), at Paul's dictation."[165] Some work has also been done to highlight the structure of the PE, in response to the supposed "staccato" nature of the PE.[166] At any rate, the pseudepigraphical authorship of the PE (or, at least, 1 Timothy and Titus) is assumed by most of scholarship.

The PE Reconsidered: 2 Timothy

Although the majority of scholarship has moved forward from the assumption that the PE are the next developmental stage in orthodox Christianity and that they are pseudonymous, there have been some scholars that still argue for Pauline authorship, in some fashion or another, such as Moule above. Work done in 2 Timothy has been what has brought the PE under the umbrella of Pauline authorship. In *Paul, the Letter Writer*,[167] after evaluating previous positions on authorship, Michael Prior argues that Paul did not use a secretary, nor did he co-author it, because of the intimate, private nature of the letter. He also urges readers to approach each letter of the PE individually, even though they are the only three such private letters to individuals.[168]

The NPP and the PE: The Two Meet

In this section, the two trajectories traced above come together. As the NPP and the work of Sanders had its time (as Wright put it), so too, it is time for the NPP to test its hermeneutic outside the undisputed Pauline corpus. This is evidenced by (1) work that both Dunn and Wright have done in the PE as well as (2) the work done by others, and (3) the call for a proper treatment of some of the passages outside undisputed Paul that present challenges to

---

164. Moule, *Second Epistle to Timothy*, 9–10.

165. Moule, "Problem of the Pastoral Epistles," 117. Three years earlier, Stephen G. Wilson had also argued that Luke was the likely author of the PE based on style and comparison with Luke-Acts. See his conclusions in Wilson, *Luke and the Pastoral Epistles*, 136–43.

166. For example, see Van Neste, *Cohesion and Structure in the Pastoral Epistles*; Nes, *Pauline Language and the Pastoral Epistles*.

167. Prior, *Paul, the Letter Writer*. Also see the works that followed Prior's such as Towner, "Portrait of Paul and the Theology of 2 Timothy," 151–70; Murphy-O'Connor, "2 Timothy Contrasted with 1 Timothy and Titus," 403–18.

168. Worth noting, again, is Wright's "cautious" consideration of 2 Timothy. Wright, *Paul and the Faithfulness of God*, 61.

the NPP. Below are the major works that have led to the justification (and need) for this study. Though not altogether chronological, these works do illustrate a "sort-of" spiral of the NPP into the PE.

J. Christiaan Beker and James Aageson

To begin, there is the work J. Christiaan Beker and James Aageson. These works are characterized by their use of Pauline canon and continuity. Even though these writers do not adhere to authentic Pauline authorship of the PE, what they do is help bridge the gap from undisputed Paul to the Paul of the PE. In Beker's case, this is done via what he calls "coherence and contingency," in Aageson's case, it is done via the canon.

J. Christiaan Beker's work, *Heirs of Paul*,[169] will be the starting point for this shift for the present study. In this work, Beker's basic argument is as follows: "Over against those who simply contrast the 'original' Paul with the so-called misrepresentations of his later interpreters, I contend that Paul's legacy can only be evaluated correctly when the claims of the original tradition (the *traditum*) are properly balanced with the claims of the adaptations that the transmission of tradition necessitates (the *traditio*)."[170] In other words, rather than seeing a disjunction between Paul and his interpreters, Beker argues that Paul's canonical interpreters resonate with Pauline tradition. Any "adaptation" occurs through contingent circumstances. In an earlier work, Beker set forth a program focused on "contingency and coherence."[171] Concerning contingency, he states, "Paul's hermeneutic cannot be divorced from the content of his thought, because he relates the universal truth claim of the gospel directly to the particular situation in which it is addressed."[172] Coherence regards the "coherent center" of Paul's gospel.[173] This is the method he uses in *Heirs of Paul* as well, focusing not on Paul's contingent circumstances, but the contingencies Paul's successors faced. But, instead of using the terminology employed for Pauline method (contingency and coherence), *Heirs of Paul* uses *traditum* (the deposit of the tradition) and *traditio* (the process of tradition).[174] He

---

169. Beker, *Heirs of Paul.*

170. Beker, *Heirs of Paul*, 11.

171. Beker, *Paul the Apostle*, 11–19; and Beker, *Triumph of God*, 15–19. Beker focuses on the apocalyptic "triumph of God" as coherency.

172. Beker, *Paul the Apostle*, 11.

173. Beker, *Paul the Apostle*, 13.

174. Beker, *Heirs of Paul*, 102.

sees the method of comparison as unsuitable for a proper understanding of the deutero-Pauline letters. He explains,

> Therefore, a comparative method must be balanced and cor-rected by employing a tradition-historical method. The latter views Paul's adaptations by his later tradents as holistic texts in their own right, which ought not only be compared with the historical Paul, but deserve also to be evaluated in terms of the realistic demands and possibilities that their own historical lo-cation imposed on them.[175]

This statement is important for the purpose of this study. Beker saw the inef-fectiveness of comparative work with regard to the PE. He noticed what was being missed by not viewing these texts holistically in their own contexts. His method is not quite viewing the deutero-Pauline letters in their canoni-cal context, but it is inching closer in that direction.[176]

James Aageson gets one step closer to a canonical approach to the PE.[177] Though not stating that his agenda is canonically driven, he does say, "The approach of this book is to begin in Chapter 2 by assuming neither the authenticity nor pseudonymity of the Pastoral Epistles. In contrast to much scholarship of the Pastorals, the starting point for this discussion is the textual character and theological world of the respective letters."[178] This assumption of letting the PE stand on their own is a major step in incorporating the PE as part of the larger Pauline corpus. Not only does Aageson examine the letters on their own terms, he examines them as a group representing "a developing Pauline tradition."[179] He then examines them in comparison with undisputed Pauline letters, such as Philippians and Galatians. He also studies the transition of "Paul's transformation from a Jew and an apostle of Christ into a saint of the church, as well as the trans-formation of his epistles from occasional letters into authoritative texts that continued to inform the life and theology of the early church."[180]

This work is yet another incremental step to including the PE into the discussion of Pauline theology. However, the PE still stand or fall in how

---

175. Beker, *Heirs of Paul*, 97.

176. Garwood Anderson's work, focused on the NPP, has a similar methodology for incorporating the PE. See Anderson, *Paul's New Perspective*, 7–12.

177. Robert Wall does take a canonical approach to the PE. See Wall and Steele, *1 & 2 Timothy and Titus*; Wall, "Function of the Pastoral Letters within the Pauline Canon of the New Testament," 27–44; Wall and Lemcio, *New Testament as Canon*.

178. Aageson, *Paul, the Pastoral Epistles, and the Early Church*, 11.

179. Aageson, *Paul, the Pastoral Epistles, and the Early Church*, 16.

180. Aageson, *Paul, the Pastoral Epistles, and the Early Church*, 17.

they compare to undisputed Paul, or they are used to demonstrate how un-disputed Paul was utilized for the next generation of Christians after Paul's death. So, although Aageson studies them as individual letters, as well as a corpus, they still represent a post-Pauline development.

The PE incorporated into the Study of Pauline Theology

Though the NPP has been defined outside of the PE and, for the most part, has neglected to engage the PE,[181] there have been recent works seeking to incorporate the PE into the broader Pauline discussion. Some of these works are polemical, using the PE as a way to dismantle the underlying concepts of the NPP.[182] Others have considered engaging the PE in order to push the boundaries of the NPP, and question its validity outside the realm of undisputed Paul.[183] As Frances Young states, "We simply note that many of the standard comments about the Pastorals' shift of perspective on the issue of faith and works need revision in the light of the new perspective on Paul that has been emerging."[184] Now that the NPP has become another major hermeneutic for reading Paul, the standard way of regarding the PE may need to be revisited. Robert Cara, for example, does engage the NPP, but with a Reformed, traditional reading in mind and few nods to the NPP. What follows are the recent works that have engaged the NPP in the PE. Two of these works are highly polemical, seeking to dismantle some of the basic structures of the NPP, others are more inquisitive.

James Dunn and N. T. Wright

Amidst all of this work, are the studies done by Dunn and Wright them-selves. Dunn anticipates the problems that the PE (along with Ephesians and 1 Clement) present in terms of the phrase "works of law." He states, "Without the reference to the law the point being made by Paul would

181. Though the PE have been utilized, they have not been utilized from an authen-tically Pauline perspective. For example, Douglas Moo writes, "My quarrel with new perspective advocates is often not so much over what they say but about what they do not say—or, perhaps better, the overall balance that they give to certain issues." Moo, "Israel and the Law in Rom 5–11," 2:188.

182. For example, see Cara, *Cracking the Foundation of the New Perspective on Paul*; Vaughan, "Investigation of the Authenticity of the Pastoral Epistles"; Lash, *New Perspective and Good Deeds*. It is worth noting that two of the works that engage the NPP and the PE are highly polemical.

183. See Barclay, *Paul and the Gift*.

184. Young, *Theology of the Pastoral Epistles*, 30.

be lost."[185] In other words, it is the "of the law" that makes Paul's point in Galatians and Romans. For support, by way of contrast he points to Ephesians 2:8–9, 2 Timothy 1:9, and Titus 3:5, all of which simply have "works," not "works of the law." He states, "In a word, the Pastorals add little or nothing to our quest for clarification of Paul's affirmation that 'by works of the law shall no flesh be justified before God.'"[186] He also points out that in the case of the PE, the verb "saved" is in the aorist tense, which, he argues, is not done in Romans and Galatians.[187] He places all three letters in the later tradition of Paul and defines them as "a restatement of the more fundamental principle of human acceptability before God, rather than a restatement of Paul's more narrowly directed polemic."[188] Like many commentators, he also lumps all three of the PE together when discussing their theology and opponents. In short, he understands the PE (and Ephesians) to be accentuating a more "fundamental principle" than the specific polemic of Romans and Galatians, and by that, the PE and Paul's undisputed theology cannot be properly compared. With regard to his major work on Paul, *The Theology of Paul the Apostle*, the passages of the PE chosen for this project are primarily relegated to footnotes or cross-references as a tip of the hat to the misguided understanding of "traditional Protestant theology" before the new perspective.[189]

In his commentary on the PE in *The New Interpreter's Bible*, Dunn succinctly rehearses reasons against Pauline authorship and seems to deny Pauline authorship, even if not stating it outright.[190] In 1 Timothy 1:6–16, any prolonged discussion of the law and its purpose[191] and of Paul's conversion are absent. As for 2 Timothy 1:8–9, he sees echoes of earlier Paul (Rom 3:20, 28; Gal 2:16), though there has been "a shift of emphasis" from specific "works of the law" into "works" generally.[192] The discussion of Titus 3:5 is more thorough, but ultimately Dunn argues, "It is not a direct repetition of what Paul said."[193]

---

185. Dunn, *New Perspective on Paul*, 382.

186. Dunn, *New Perspective on Paul*, 53–54. There is also a reference to what he characterizes as the misinterpretation of Paul's conversion in Dunn, *New Perspective on Paul*, 361–62.

187. Dunn, *New Perspective on Paul*, 385.

188. Dunn, *New Perspective on Paul*, 385.

189. Dunn, *Theology of the Paul the Apostle*, 354.

190. Dunn, "First and Second Letters," 777–81.

191. He simply argues that the author points out the law's function as "law" and he notes the echo of Rom 7:12, 16. Dunn, "First and Second Letters," 791.

192. Dunn, "First and Second Letters," 836.

193. Dunn, "First and Second Letters," 876–77.

N. T. Wright has a less academic commentary on the PE in his *Paul for Everyone* series. This study is hesitant to use this commentary for Wright's thoughts, realizing the nature of the commentary prevents him from being thorough and engaging with matters of the academy, but it is the only place he has published anything substantial regarding the PE. In this commentary, he offers little help in understanding the place of the PE within the larger hermeneutic of the NPP. He gives no real introduction to the letters—as individual letters or as a collection. He defines the law with reference to 1 Timothy 1:8 as "a map which only marks danger"[194] and he defines the law as not only including the Pentateuch but the Ten Commandments, more specifically.[195] In Wright's discussion of 2 Timothy 1:8–12, there is no discussion of works and how these works are related to salvation. This omission, in itself, is not a real problem with the type of commentary he is writing. However, knowing how important a passage like 2 Timothy 1:9 is in the present discussions surrounding the NPP, Wright's treatment, or lack thereof, is surprising. And, again, when commenting on Titus 3:5, he states, "God's action in Christ Jesus is not a reward for good work already done. It's an act of free kindness and loving goodness. And it results, not in a pat on the back because we're the sort of people God wanted on his side, but in *washing* and *renewal.*"[196] As already noted in the last chapter, even in his massive *Paul and the Faithfulness of God*, the PE are relegated to the background and not in the primary discussion of Paul. Robert Cara points out that even in Wright's major definitions of justification, the PE are absent.[197]

John M. G. Barclay, Garwood Anderson, and Robert Cara

There are three works that deserve special mention because of their importance to the present study. The first is John Barclay's *Paul and the Gift*. John Barclay studies grace in the Greco-Roman period, early Judaism, and finally, in Paul. He outlines three major theses: (1) "'Grace' is a multi-faceted concept best approached through the category of gift."[198] Divine gift is "perfected"[199] in six ways (superabundance, singularity, priority,

---

194. Wright, *Pastoral Letters*, 8.

195. He identifies six of the ten as having some connection to the Decalogue in his list of sins. Wright, *Pastoral Letters*, 9–10.

196. Wright, *Pastoral Letters*, 160, italics original.

197. See Cara, *Cracking the Foundation*, 182–93.

198. Barclay, *Paul and the Gift*, 6.

199. He defines "perfection" as "the drawing out of a concept to an end-of-the-line extreme." See Barclay, *Paul and the Gift*, 4.

incongruity, efficacy, non-circularity). Barclay argues that the failure to disaggregate these differing perfections of grace has led to many of the disputes regarding Paul and grace. (2) "Grace is everywhere in Second Temple Judaism but not everywhere the same."[200] This concept makes up Part II of the book and provides a corrective to Sanders's standard "covenantal nomism" in that, Barclay finds that the perfections of grace within Second Temple Judaism were different and non-uniform. (3) "Paul's theology of grace characteristically perfects the *incongruity* of the Christ-gift, given without regard for worth."[201] The final portions of the book study Paul's theology of grace within Galatians and Romans.

The primary worth of this book, in the context of this study, is his engagement *between* Augustine/Luther and the NPP and how Paul's theology of grace extends beyond the early social problems with Jew and gentile and into internal issues within the early church, what he calls a "contextual shift,"[202] wherein the "missional theology is turned inward."[203] Barclay defends and critiques each view, stating,

> Thus, the reading of Paul offered in this book may be interpreted either as a recontextualization of the Augustinian-Lutheran tradition, returning the dynamic of the incongruity of grace to its original mission environment where it accompanied the formation of new communities, *or* as a reconfiguration of the "new perspective," placing its best historical and exegetical insights within the frame of Paul's theology of grace.[204]

Regarding Paul's theology of grace, he argues, "Its missionary theology is turned inward," a development traced in, what he identifies as the deutero-Pauline epistles, citing Ephesians 2:8–10, 2 Timothy 1:9, and Titus 3:5. He explains, "'Works' are refocused as moral achievements and 'boasting' indicates not the cultural confidence of the Jew in the Torah (or of the Greek in wisdom), but pride in achievement (Eph 2:9)."[205] Barclay argues, "What changes, rather, is the social context."[206]

The second work is that of Garwood P. Anderson. His study, mentioned above when discussing works aimed at compromise, or in positive dialogue, with the NPP, also incorporates the PE into the study of Paul. He

200. Barclay, *Paul and the Gift*, 6.

201. Barclay, *Paul and the Gift*, 6.

202. Barclay, *Paul and the Gift*, 571.

203. Barclay, *Paul and the Gift*, 571.

204. Barclay, *Paul and the Gift*, 573.

205. Barclay, *Paul and the Gift*, 571

206. Barclay, *Paul and the Gift*, 570.

states with regard to the method of his study, "Second, and more controversially, I ask what becomes of the contours of Pauline soteriology when the deutero-Pauline (or, as I will prefer, "disputed") letters are given a voice at the table."[207] As for the Pauline pedigree of the PE, and where they may be situated within Paul's life and ministry, he states, "There can be no final verdict as it concerns the PE."[208] He also alludes to the possibility of a canonical approach to his work, but talked himself out of it in lieu of the "historical-critical road."[209] Even so, he argues that through the development that occurs throughout Paul's letters, both the NPP and the Traditional perspective (TPP) are correct, depending on when in Paul's ministry they were written. He argues that the clearest path is seen in Paul's move from "works of the law" in Galatians, which represents the arguments of the NPP, and "works," beginning in Romans, which uses both "works" and "works of the law," into the Captivity Epistles and the PE's use of "good works."[210] He adds,

> I propose that this pattern of use, from "works of the law" to the unqualified "works," reflects a pattern of development in Paul's conception of the matters at hand, from a soteriology originally grounded in the dilemma of Gentiles inclusion to a more formal rejection of human attainment as the antithesis of grace.[211]

He traces a similar pattern of development from "justification" to "salvation" and the introduction of a "new and unprecedented metaphorical field" in "reconciliation."[212] The importance of his work for the present study is the incorporation of the PE into the Pauline trajectory and his engagement with the NPP as it relates to the PE.

The final work, also closely related to this study, is Robert Cara's *Cracking the Foundation of the New Perspective on Paul*, published in 2017. Cara's book is not as groundbreaking, or as foundation-cracking, as Barclay's work. However, Cara's work is helpful in articulating some of the major characteristics of the NPP, engaging some of the same texts that present problems for the NPP as Barclay, and demonstrating the NPP's dismissal of the PE (and Ephesians). Cara's work is a thoroughly polemical work, and one can

---

207. Anderson, *Paul's New Perspective*, 7.

208. Anderson, *Paul's New Perspective*, 221.

209. Anderson, *Paul's New Perspective*, 222. He writes, "In all candor, I have even tried to talk myself into this expedient (canonical Paul) but without success; it would save one from so many worries."

210. Along these same lines Anderson also focuses on the "pattern" of grace. Anderson, *Paul's New Perspective*, 264–80.

211. Anderson, *Paul's New Perspective*, 228.

212. Anderson, *Paul's New Perspective*, 282.

sense his passion for the Reformed position and the danger he feels the NPP poses to that position. Cara introduces his work defining the major tenets of the NPP and laying out the structure of his own work, which is primarily to counter the "covenantal nomism" of E. P. Sanders, one of the "five points of NPP."[213] He follows with a comparison of the Reformed perspective and covenantal nomism. For the purpose of this study, his most important contribution comes in dealing with Ephesians 2:8–10 and the PE, all of which he believes Paul wrote, which sets him in contrast to those of the NPP and John Barclay. He highlights three scholars (I. Howard Marshall, Michael Wolter, and John M. G. Barclay)[214] who argue that the deutero-Pauline epistles do display salvation by faith in contrast to works-righteousness. He follows with his own exegesis of three passages (Eph 2:8–10; Titus 3:4–7; 2 Tim 1:8–10) then, he gives a critique of Sanders, Dunn, and Wright in their treatment (or lack of treatment) of these passages. However, he is prone to making the same mistake of conflating salvation and justification pointed out in chapter 1 of this work. He states regarding 2 Timothy 1:9, which does not mention justification, "In context, the past tense of these two aspects of God's work relates to justification and current salvation."[215] In all, Cara's work has proven tremendously helpful in setting the stage for this study.[216] However, although Cara's work is quite similar to the current project, one can only hope to strike a more even, sympathetic tone. Cara's style, while engaging and thorough, is overly passionate and confident.[217]

History of Research: Summation

This history of research has tried to accomplish several things. (1) It has chronicled the rise of the NPP from William Wrede and Albert Schweitzer,

213. Cara, *Cracking the Foundation*, 28.

214. See Cara, *Cracking the Foundation*, 137–47; Marshall, "Salvation, Grace, and Works in the Later Writings in the Pauline Corpus," 339–58; Wolter, *Paul: An Outline of His Theology*, 398; Wolter, "Development of Pauline Christianity from a 'Religion of Conversion' to a 'Religion of Tradition,'" 49–69; Barclay, *Paul and the Gift*, 569–74.

215. Cara, *Cracking the Foundation*, 167.

216. The present study began before Cara's work was published. In that time, Cara published *Cracking the Foundation*, which helped solidify this study's validity, and helped further articulate and refine the major tenets of the NPP. His work was also quite helpful by uncovering places in which the NPP (primarily Wright) had failed to engage the PE that this study had previously missed.

217. For example, in his final footnote regarding the danger of the NPP because of their views on Titus, he writes, "Of course, another reason I am against telling the church that Paul did not write Titus is because it is not true!" Cara, *Cracking the Foundation*, 205. There are many such examples.

who represent the beginnings of the move away from F. C. Baur, the Tübingen School, and *Heilsgeschichte*. (2) It has highlighted the contributions of the three primary adherents and pioneers of the NPP (Sanders, Dunn, and Wright) in correlation with the major tenets of the NPP outlined in the methodology for choosing which passages in the PE to study. These primary characteristics are Paul's conversion, plight/solution, "works of law," Paul's view of the law, the "righteousness of God," covenantal nomism, early (rabbinic) Judaism, and justification. (3) It has reviewed the studies that rejected the PE as Pauline documents as well as later studies that have confirmed, denied, or nuanced such claims. (4) Finally, it has demonstrated the rising realization of the need to engage the PE in the works of Robert Cara, Garwood Anderson, and John Barclay. With this history in mind, the next three chapters will focus on 1 Timothy 1:6–16; 2:3–7; 2 Timothy 1:3, 8–12, and Titus 3:3–7. These passages will be studied testing the NPP hermeneutic by way of the canonical perspective, addressing one or more of the major tenets of the NPP outlined in chapter 1 and this history of research.

3

Paul, the Law, and the "Chief of Sinners"

1 Timothy 1:6–16; 2:3–7

Introduction

Having traced the two trajectories of research on Paul and the PE and how those two trajectories meet in this project, this chapter seeks to test the validity of the NPP within two passages of 1 Timothy—1 Timothy 1:6–16 and 1 Timothy 2:3–7. Each of these passages will be translated with special care given to the terminology significant to the NPP and, in comparison with, "undisputed Paul." Both passages will also be expounded in an attempt to clarify their original intent as well as to determine their level of correlation with the NPP. The primary focus of these two passages with regard to the NPP is the law, Paul's conversion, and Paul's mission to the gentiles.

As has been demonstrated, the PE themselves have been relegated to tertiary importance with regard to Pauline theology. However, even on the margins, 1 Timothy has been neglected, which is surprising, when one considers that 1 Timothy 1:6–16 and 1 Timothy 2:3–7 speaks directly to the function of the law, Paul's apostleship to the gentiles, and Paul's conversion, all of which are standard categories within Pauline studies and the NPP. The other two letters of the PE do not speak to all three of these categories. In fact, neither 2 Timothy nor Titus use the word νόμος[1] at all. Although the two passages in the following chapters are discussed by Dunn,[2] neither Dunn nor Wright, mention either of these two passages in 1 Timothy outside their respective commentaries.[3] The reason for this exclusion is likely the absence

1. However, in 2 Tim 2:5 νομίμως ("lawfully") is used and νομικός ("concerning the law") is used in Titus 3:9.

2. Dunn, *New Perspective on Paul*, 385–86.

3. These passages are referenced in a few footnotes, but there is no sustained explanation. See Dunn, *New Perspective on Paul*, 362 (1 Tim 1:15–16), 385–86 (1 Tim 1:8–9,

of justification language (which is substituted by salvation language) and other catchwords or phrases from the NPP coupled with the rejection of Pauline authorship. Nonetheless, these passages do find resonance with undisputed Paul, and some of the major Pauline categories mentioned above. The task is to examine these passages in conversation with the NPP from a canonical perspective, assuming relative Pauline continuity.[4]

1 Timothy: Timothy and Ephesus

Paul writes in 1 Tim 1:3 that Timothy was left behind in Ephesus "to instruct" (παραγγέλλω). This instruction is in opposition to certain men and their own contrary teachings.[5] As the letter progresses, other problems and instructions concerning these problems come to the fore, but it seems the primary reason for the sending of the letter is Timothy's instruction, the goal of which Paul defines as "love form a pure heart, a good conscience, and a sincere faith" (1 Tim 1:5).[6] These opponents, and/or situations, help dictate the style, tenor, and subject matter of the epistle.

---

15). See also Dunn, *Theology of the Paul the Apostle*, 799–800, where every listing in 1 Timothy in the index is found in a footnote except for 1 Tim 1:27; 2:5, 14, 24; 4:4; and 6:9. There is one reference to 1 Timothy regarding the fullest expression of "Jewish monotheism" found in Paul, even though Dunn writes, "Paul did not write the letter, but the confessions are his." Dunn, *Theology of Paul the Apostle*, 32. Wright refers only to 1 Tim 2:5 in *Climax of the Covenant* in a parenthetic reference. Wright, *Climax of the Covenant*, 160. Like Dunn, most of Wright's references to 1 Timothy are relegated to footnotes and secondary importance for "illumination rather than support." Wright, *Paul and the Faithfulness of God*, 61.

4. "Relative" is used here because all of Paul's letters, whether disputed or undisputed, carry some level of individuality and nuance, depending on the situation, opponents, and argumentation.

5. William Mounce argues that the enemies were likely men, because the two mentioned by name are men (1 Tim 1:20) and there seems to be some problem with the leadership of the church, which is made up of men (1 Tim 3:1–7). See Mounce, *Pastoral Epistles*, 18–19. Also, the "certain ones" mentioned in 1 Tim 1:3 is in the masculine (τισίν), which may not indicate gender, since most groupings are in the masculine, but it does prevent it from being only a group of women. However, it seems that some young women have also followed Satan and have given "the opposition" (ἀντικαιμένῳ) an opportunity to reproach them (cf. 1 Tim 1:10; ἀντίκειται).

6. The same phrase, "sincere faith" (πίστεως ἀνυποκίτου), is also used by Paul in 2 Tim 1:5 with a different word order (ἀνυποκρίτου πίστεως) as a description of Timothy's faith that was also present in his mother and grandmother.

First Timothy is written to Timothy, who has remained[7] in Ephesus as a teacher[8] in Paul's stead. Timothy's mother was a Jew, and his father a Greek, so he was a proper "type" representing the mission of the early church which incorporated the gentiles into the hope of Israel (Rom 11:13–15).[9] According to Acts, Paul had him circumcised because the Jews in the area knew his father was a Greek (Acts 16:1–3). Timothy was a traveling companion of Paul, as well as his delegate (1 Cor 4:17; 16:10; 1 Thess 3:2). Timothy plays a role in Acts as a companion of Paul, but he is also mentioned by Paul in several of his epistles (e.g., Rom 16:21; 2 Cor 1:1, 19; Phil 1:1; 2:19; Phlm 1). Who Timothy is, and what he has been commissioned to do, plays a significant part in the originality of this epistle. It does not seem Timothy was simply a young man in ministry in need of a mentor. Instead, in some ways, he was considered Paul's equal (Rom 16:21; 1 Cor 16:10; 2 Cor 1:19; Phil 2:19–20), his successor (1 Tim 1:20; 2 Tim 1:13; 2:2), and certainly, a representative of Paul in his absence (1 Cor 4:17).[10]

Ephesus, presumably the city in which Timothy was working (1 Tim 1:3), was a major city, estimated to have to have been smaller than only Rome and Alexandria, the population of which was about 100,000–150,000.[11] The city itself, like most urban centers, was diverse and served as

7. Mounce points out that Paul's construction is an anacoluthon, an unfinished thought (καθὼς παρεκάλεσά σε προσμεῖναι ἐν Ἐφέσῳ). He explains that some situate the issue by translating the infinitive *to remain* as a finite verb (προσμεῖναι). Mounce points out that along with Paul's quick entry into the discussion at hand without his usual thanksgivings, coupled with this anacoluthon, that the situation is urgent, and that Paul may be angry concerning those against whom he is writing. See Mounce, *Pastoral Epistles*, 15–16. See also Dibelius and Conzelmann, *Pastoral Epistles*, 15. This construction is used elsewhere by Paul (e.g., 1 Cor 1:6; Gal 3:6; Eph 1:4; Phil 1:7; 1 Thess 1:5).

8. The verb διδάσκω is used three times in 1 Timothy (2:12; 4:11; 6:2), as well as two references to ἑτεροδιδασκαλέω (1:3; 6:3) that Timothy was to combat with his own teaching that came from Paul and Timothy's "gift" (1 Tim 4:13–14). The word διδάσκαλος is used eight times (1:10: 4:1, 6, 13, 16; 5:17; 6:1, 3), compared with only two in Romans (12:7; 15:4), one in Colossians (2:22), and one in Ephesians (4:14). The other two PE have seven instances combined (2 Tim 3:10, 16; 4:3; Titus 1:9; 2:1, 7, 10).

9. Similarly, Robert Wall states that Timothy was circumcised "to personify in Timothy the restored Israel that now includes Jews and gentiles (cf. Acts 15:13–29; 1 Tim 2:7)." Wall and Steele, *1 & 2 Timothy and Titus*, 55.

10. Andreas Köstenberger explains in response to the view that often Timothy and Titus are seen as young pastors, "Rather, these men serve as Paul's apostolic delegates who are temporarily assigned to their present location in order to deal with particular problems that have arisen in their respective churches and require special attention." Köstenberger, *Commentary on 1–2 Timothy & Titus*, 8. See also Johnson, *First and Second Letters to Timothy*, 94.

11. The size of the city is taken from L. T. Johnson, who argued the city was smaller in population than only Rome and Alexandria. See Johnson, *First and Second Letters*

the νεωχόρος[12] of Artemis, the worshipers of whom Paul and the Christians there had a sharp conflict with about money lost from Paul's preaching against idols (Acts 19:22–41). So, though there were Jews within Ephesus (it was in its synagogue where Paul began his teaching and many Jews in Asia believed; Acts 18:7; 19:10), the major conflict between Christians and the population of the city was primarily financial and religious, on account of Paul's teaching against worship of gods, and specifically, the goddess, Artemis (Acts 19:22–28).[13] Other than this specific instance, Paul also must have endured other great difficulties in Ephesus. Paul offers a tearful farewell to the Ephesian elders at Miletus, even though he did not spend time in the city on this occasion (Acts 20:17). Paul knew that a visit would delay him on his way to Jerusalem (Acts 20:16), and this would happen, possibly because of trouble within the city, or with certain members of the church there (1 Tim 1:19–20).[14] He mentions some of his troubles in Ephesus, such as the plots of the Jews (Acts 20:19), and he warns them about "savage wolves" from among them (Acts 20:29–30; 1 Cor 15:32; 16:8).[15] So, Ephesus is a familiar place for Paul, apparently having just been there, and Timothy has not been sent there as a young "preacher" eager to serve his new church. Instead, Timothy, as Paul's delegate and "fellow worker"[16]

---

to Timothy, 142–43. He cites White, "Urban Development and Social Change in Imperial Ephesos," 27–79. However, Rodney Stark, following the work of Chandler and Fox, estimates the population of the city at 200,000. See Stark, Rise of Christianity, 131; Chandler and Fox, Three Thousand Years of Urban Growth. For more information about Ephesus, see also Crossan and Reed, In Search of Paul, 243–49.

12. This term means "temple-keeper." See Reicke, New Testament Era, 230.

13. The goddess played a major role for the city, and Sharon Hodgrin Gritz argues it is within this Mother Goddess culture of Ephesus that Paul speaks concerning women and teaching and exercising their authority over their husbands. See Gritz, Paul, Women Teachers, and the Mother Goddess at Ephesus.

14. The reference here to Alexander and Hymenaeus being taught "not to blaspheme," is likely a reference not to blasphemy against God, or even Christ or the Spirit, but of slander against Paul or Timothy. These men may have rejected Timothy, and in that way, had rejected Paul himself. Paul uses the same word to refer to slander in Rom 3:8, 1 Cor 10:30, and Titus 3:2. In contrast, Luke Timothy Johnson argues that Paul is connecting his "self-characterization" in 1 Tim 1:13 as formerly "a blasphemer." See Johnson, First and Second Letters to Timothy, 186–87. Philip Towner argues that their blasphemy is both "false teaching and rejection of Paul's authority" and that it is connected to Paul before his conversion. Towner, Letters to Timothy and Titus, 162.

15. Cf. 1 Cor 15:32 and the metaphorical "beasts at Ephesus" about which Paul speaks. Paul also writes in Phil 3:2, "Beware of the dogs, beware of the evil workers, beware of the false circumcision . . . ," which does not refer to actual dogs, but the opponents of "false circumcision." The wording is not identical, but the similarity is worth consideration.

16. The word "fellow worker" (συνεργός) is used also of Epaphroditus (Phil 2:25),

(Rom 16:21; 1 Thess 3:2), has remained there to provide teaching and correction as Paul departed to Macedonia.[17]

Timothy's Opponents in Ephesus

The passages from which the rough sketch of Paul's opponents will be taken are 1 Timothy 1:3–11, 19–20; 2:8–15; 4:1–3, 7; 5:19–20; 6:3–10, 17–21. First Timothy deals with matters of practice, such as the appointment of elders and deacons and the assistance of widows, but it also deals with matters of teaching. Thus, when speaking of "opponents," there may be different sets of opposing thoughts, teachings, and practices. For example, some were teaching strange doctrines that were prone to speculation, but these teachers may not be (and likely are not) the same ones who have suffered a shipwreck of faith (1 Tim 1:19–20).[18] Paul is not dealing with opponents as those outside the "household of God" (1 Tim 3:15), but struggles within the church, some of which Luke Timothy Johnson characterizes as problems within the presbytery.[19] With regard to some of this opposition, Johnson also points out that there are notable parallels between 1 Corinthians and 1 Timothy.[20]

Priscila and Aquila (Rom 16:3), Urbanus (Rom 16:9), Apollos and Cephas (1 Cor 3:9), the Corinthians (2 Cor 1:24), Titus (2 Cor 8:23), Philemon (Phlm 1), and Mark, Aristarchus, Demas, and Luke (Phlm 24).

17. The timeline for placement of the PE into the life of Paul is complex. Luke Timothy Johnson fits 2 Timothy into Paul's Roman imprisonment recorded in Acts 28:30–31. See Johnson, *Letters to Paul's Delegates*, 37. However, Johnson states of 1 Timothy, "I think it is the most difficult of the three letters to defend as authentic" (106). He also admits the plausibility of the letter being Pauline, referencing Paul's extensive travel in Asia Minor and Ephesus (105). He envisages the letter as that sent by Paul to a delegate, which granted the delegate *mandata principis* (commandments of the ruler). He points to other documents of the Greco-Roman era as examples, citing the work of Michael Wolter and Benjamin Fiore (106–7). See also the work of Wolter, *Die Pastoralbriefe als Paulustradition*; and Fiore, *Function of Personal Example in the Socratic and Pastoral Epistles*.

18. William Mounce thinks Alexander and Hymenaeus are part of this group, stating, with a reference to Moule's idiom book, that the genitive (ὧν) is partitive. Mounce, *Pastoral Epistles*, 67. See also Moule, *Idiom Book of New Testament Greek*, 42–43.

19. Johnson, *First and Second Letters to Timothy*, 143–44.

20. For example, some of these parallels include the following: Timothy is a Pauline representative (1 Tim 1:3; 4:11–14; cf. 1 Cor 4:17; 16:10–11), the phrase "handed over to Satan" (1 Tim 4:20; cf. 1 Cor 5:1–5), wealthy members and social status (1 Tim 2:9–10; cf. 1 Cor 11:17–22), discussion of slaves/ownership (1 Tim 6:1–2; cf. 1 Cor 1:11; 7:21–3), the phrase "household of God" (1 Tim 3:15 οἴκῳ θεοῦ; cf. 1 Cor 3:9 θεοῦ οἰκοδομή), knowledge (1 Tim 1:7; 6:20–1; cf. 1 Cor 1:17; 3:18–19; 8:1), lawsuits (1 Tim 5:19–20; cf. 1 Cor 6:1–5), sexuality and gender roles (1 Tim 2:8–15; 4:3; 5:13; cf. 1 Cor 7:2, 36; 11:2–16; 14:33–36), instructions for widows (1 Tim 5:3–16; cf. 1 Cor 7:8, 39), use of the word ἀρσενοκοίτης ("homosexual," only used in 1 Tim 1:10;

In order to best understand 1 Timothy, one must characterize the opponents of Paul, or at least the opposing ideas, even if the characterization must
remain vague. Paul begins by urging Timothy to instruct "certain ones not to
teach any different doctrine" (1 Tim 1:3). Referring to "certain ones," τισίν, is
not an uncommon way for Paul to refer to his opponents, even when speaking of specific, known individuals.[21] The verb ἑτεροδιδασκαλέω is used only
in 1 Timothy (1 Tim 1:3; 6:3), and it is a compound word meaning, "to teach
contrary to standard instruction."[22] Paul does say it was for this reason that
Timothy was left behind, as a vicarious Paul, or "true child," (1 Tim 1:2) combating anything that might be "different" (1 Tim 1:3, 10). Robert Wall states
that Paul wrote 1 Timothy as "an epistolary substitute for his personal presence to provide pastoral encouragement and apostolic instruction to guide
believers during his absence from him."[23] Certainly, Paul knows how easily
someone can creep in and "spy out liberty," teaching something different that
can potentially contaminate the entire group (cf. Gal 2:4; 5:9). Paul's comparison between speculation produced by what is different and the "administra-
tion of God which is by faith" (1 Tim 1:4), serve to demonstrate problems that
are posed by insiders. The speculation against which Paul speaks comes from
the study of "myths and endless genealogies." The term "myth" is only used
in the PE (1 Tim 1:4, 4:7; 2 Tim 4:4; Titus 1:14) with the exception of 2 Peter
1:16 ("cleverly devised myths"). Two of the times the word is used, there is
further explanation ("Jewish myths" and "old wives' myths," 1 Tim 4:7; Titus

---

cf. 1 Cor 6:9), eating of certain foods (1 Tim 4:3; cf. 1 Cor 8:1—10:33), and financial
support of minister/elder (1 Tim 5:17–18; cf. 1 Cor 9:1–14). There are also parallels
with Romans, such as Paul's statement about the law (1 Tim 1:8; cf. Rom 7:12, 14)
and issues involving food (1 Tim 4:3–5; cf. Rom 14:1–23). Many of these parallels
with 1 Corinthians were noticed while the author was preaching and teaching through
the PE, especially when preaching through 1 Timothy 4. For these similarities, see
also Thielman, *Paul and the Law*, 230–31. These parallels serve to demonstrate that
the problems with the Ephesian church do not have to be relegated to a much later
dispensation of Christian history, as well as to demonstrate that when 1 Timothy is
compared with another letter in the undisputed Pauline corpus rather than only the
other "Pastorals," there are remarkable similarities. See Johnson, *First and Second Letters to Timothy*, 14, who also compares 2 Timothy with Philippians (and, to a certain
degree, Philemon) and Titus to Galatians. See Johnson, *1 Timothy, 2 Timothy, Titus*,
11, 112; and Johnson, *Letters to Paul's Delegates*, 214.

21. 2 Cor 3:1; 10:12; 11:20; Gal 1:7; 2:12; Phil 1:15.

22. "ἑτεροδιδασκαλέω," BDAG, 399.

23. This characterization can be said of many of Paul's letters, but, 1 Timothy is
unique in that "rather than presenting readers with the content of his gospel, Paul gives
Timothy instructions in the organization, moral and professional practices, and working relationships that guide those responsible for forming Christian congregations into
God's household." Wall and Steele, *1 & 2 Timothy and Titus*, 57.

1:14[24]). Most commentators seem to agree that although myth is used for Greek myths in Hellenistic literature, the problem in 1 Timothy is a Hellenized "gnosticizing Judaism,"[25] and not a response to Palestinian (rabbinic) Judaism that sought to constrain acceptance into the people of God due to ethnic identity.[26] The gnosticism here is not the late Gnosticism of the second century and beyond, but the *makings* of Gnosticism or gnostic tendencies before the movement was given a proper label.

What is clear is that the problem(s) being faced in Ephesus was not the same sort of problem faced in Romans and Galatians. Both Gerhard Kittel and James Dunn point out that the myths and genealogies are not the genealogies of Abrahamic descent in the Pentateuch, but those found in writings such as 1 Enoch wherein persons from these genealogical accounts are mythologized and the accounts expanded.[27] The word νομοδιδάσκαλος ("teachers of the Law") is another compound word only found elsewhere in the NT in Luke 5:17 and Acts 5:34. These teachers of the law are likely not

24. Most commentators connect the "myths" of 1 Tim 1:4 to the "Jewish myths" of Titus 1:14. Although there may be justification for the comparison, this study is attempting to allow 1 Timothy a place on its own rather than in comparison with Titus. There may have been similar problems in both Ephesus and Crete, but, for the sake of solidarity, the similarities between them must not be overemphasized.

25. See Dibelius and Conzelmann, *Pastoral Epistles*, 16–17; Mounce, *Pastoral Epistles*, 19. "Gnosticizing" has been left uncapitalized to differentiate the opponents of 1 Timothy with later Gnosticism proper.

26. Johnson, avoiding the term "Gnosticism," in reference to the second-century Christian movement, figures the opponents "an intellectual elite that demands performance measured by law and asceticism rather than by grace and conscience." Johnson, *1 and 2 Timothy*, 146. He points out that the term "knowledge" (γνῶσις) is used extensively in Paul, and thus, need not be understood as a reference to Gnosticism in 1 Timothy (312). Although Johnson is correct concerning Paul's use of "knowledge" and that Paul is likely not combatting what we now know as "Gnosticism," the fact that there are aspects of Dualism (1 Tim 4:3) and genealogical and mythical issues involved do seem more akin to an early form of Gnosticism rather than legalism *per se*—what he calls "performance measured by law." Admittedly, Paul's examples regarding the "lawful" use of the law are problematic in that one does get the impression that there may have been a tendency of some to focus on strict adherence to the law. However, the people for whom the law is needed that Paul mentions (1 Tim 1:9–10) are not mentioned as a response to strict adherence to the law but were obviously sinful acts meant to compare with "whatever else is contrary to sound doctrine." In other words, it seems these opponents misunderstood the law through their own use of the law for myths and genealogies rather than obeying strict moral, covenantal, or ceremonial regulations. Also see Paul's discussion of true knowledge in 1 Cor 8:1–3, which has some correlation with 1 Timothy 1. Paul states, "knowledge makes arrogant, but love edifies" (1 Cor 8:1; cf. 1 Tim 1:4–5). There are other correlations of 1 Timothy with 1 Cor 8 ("God is one," 1 Cor 8:6; cf. 1 Tim 2:5; "conscience," 1 Cor 8:12; cf. 1 Tim 1:5, 19; 3:9; 4:2).

27. See Kittel, "Die γενεαλογίαι der Pastoralbriefe," 49–69; and Dunn, "First and Second Letters," 791–92.

"experts" on the law in a rabbinical sense, but "teachers of the law" espousing outlandish teachings based on scant biblical evidence.[28]

Regarding these opponents, Paul does not contrast his "gospel" with
them as much as he does his "teaching" (διδασκαλία).[29] These opponents
are changing doctrine from the inside by their *teaching*, not by presenting a
fundamentally different *gospel* of gentile exclusion (as in Galatians).[30] However, their teaching is likely essentially different in its exclusion of love, faith,
and good conscience. So, though "teaching" and "gospel" may have different
emphases, they are not mutually exclusive.[31]

Among these opponents are Hymenaeus and Alexander,[32] men who
suffered shipwreck in the faith, had been "given over to Satan," and taught
not to blaspheme. These men could have been part of the same group who
had been teaching something different and who had supposed themselves
"teachers of the law."[33] They stood in contrast to Timothy, who was to obey
the instructions of Paul by "fighting the good fight" and keeping good conscience and faith.[34] They had failed to do so (keep good conscience and

28. Paul accuses them of not understanding "what they are saying or the matters
about which they make confident assertions" (1 Tim 1:7). There may be a predilection
to compare these teachers of the law with the "teacher of the immature" (διδάσκαλον
νηπίων) in Rom 2:20. However, the problems presented in Romans and 1 Timothy
seem to be quite different. The opponents in Romans are teaching a life of piety while
not practicing their teachings (inconsistency), while those in Ephesus are using the law
to promote myths, genealogies, and forbidding marriage and eating certain foods (1
Tim 1:4; 4:3) which produce speculation and fruitless talk (incoherency).

29. In fact, the word gospel (εὐαγγέλιον) is used only once in 1 Timothy (1 Tim
1:11). Εὐαγγελίζω is not used at all in 1 Timothy (or the rest of the PE, for that matter).
It is used most often in Romans, 1 and 2 Corinthians, and Galatians (Rom 1:15; 10:15;
15:20; 1 Cor 1:17; 9:16, 18: 15:1, 2; 2 Cor 10:16; 11:7; Gal 1:8, 9, 11, 16, 23; 4:13).

30. Based on the fluid nature of these opponents, the term "heresy" may not characterize these opponents well in that the system of thought was not well-articulated or
coherent. Mounce, *Pastoral Epistles*, lxxv.

31. Though there are parallels between the opponents of Titus and 1 Timothy, they
are also distinct. For example, 1 Timothy simply mentions "myths," while Titus adds the
adjective "Jewish." One may assume from the context of 1 Timothy that Paul is referring
to Jewish myths, but he does not say so (Titus 1:14 is the only time the word "Jewish"
(Ιουδαϊκοῖς) is used in the NT). Also, as noted below, 1 Timothy has some vocabulary
only shared with 2 Timothy.

32. Hymenaeus (along with Philetus) is also mentioned in 2 Tim 2:17 as having
said the resurrection had already taken place. It is unclear whether or not this is the
same Hymenaeus of 1 Tim 1:20. The name Alexander is used several times in the NT,
but only once outside Acts and the PE (Mark 15:21; Acts 4:6; 19:33; 1 Tim 1:20; 2 Tim
4:14). Interestingly, one of the occurrences in Acts records an Alexander being brought
forward to make a defense in Ephesus with regards to Paul's teachings (Acts 19:33).

33. See Mounce, *Pastoral Epistles*, 67; Bassler, *1 Timothy, 2 Timothy, Titus*, 46.

34. Good conscience and "sincere" faith were two of the three goals of Paul's (and

faith), in whatever capacity, and by that had been "given over to Satan" (1 Tim 1:18–20).[35]

Immediately following the second major passage discussed in this chapter (1 Tim 2:3–7) is Paul's directive that men should lift holy hands, "without wrath and dispute,"[36] which is likely a reference to some of the disputes that had risen among the men which caused a different sort of hand-raising, one that probably included (at least) the threat of violence (1 Tim 2:8). An ecclesial culture in which men are prone to endless specula-tion, is a culture that will inevitably lead to conflict. Among these teach-ings/speculations are forbidding marriage and abstinence from certain foods[37] (what some have characterized as asceticism, or even Dualism).[38]

Timothy's) instruction (1 Tim 1:5).

35. This exact terminology is used again only in 1 Cor 5:5 in reference to the sexual sin of a Corinthian brother. In the first case, he was handed over so that "his spirit may be saved in the day of the Lord Jesus" (1 Cor 5:5). Even in the case of Alex-ander and Hymenaeus, they were handed over "in order that they may be taught not to blaspheme" (1 Tim 1:20). In both cases, these men were removed for the sanctity of the church as a whole.

The word βλασφημέω is used seven times by Paul (Rom 2:24; 3:8; 14:16; 1 Cor 10:30; 1 Tim 1:20; 6:1; Titus 2:5; 3:2). Sometimes it refers to blasphemy against God and/or his word (Rom 2:24; 1 Tim 6:1; Titus 2:5), but it also refers to not blaspheming the things that are good (Rom 14:16) and to slanderous speech against Paul and whoever he included with him ("we" Rom 3:8; 1 Cor 10:30; Titus 3:2). In the case of 1 Tim 6:1 the blasphemy to be avoided is that against both God and "teaching." In this case, it seems Paul does not have in view blasphemy against God directly, but blasphemy against Paul's teaching and authority and a possible careful allusion to Paul's own blasphemy from which he was saved (cf. 1 Tim 1:13, where he identifies himself as a "blasphemer").

36. The word, "dispute" (διαλογισμός), is used in a similar sense elsewhere by Paul (Rom 1:21; 1 Cor 3:20; Phil 2:14). Although this is the only time the word is used in 1 Timothy, or the PE, when coupled with the contentious and speculative talk mentioned in 1 Tim 1:3–4 and 1 Tim 6:20, one can see Paul intends to dispel the anger these disputes are creating.

37. Liberality with regard to diet is not new in Paul. In 1 Cor 8:1–13, Christians are given the freedom to eat, but not to do so while making others stumble (cf. also Rom 14:1–23; 1 Cor 10:23–33; Gal 5:13). Also, while Paul himself warns against the dangers of marriage, and encourages the Corinthians to "remain as I," he does not go so far as to forbid it (1 Cor 7:7–9, 26–28).

38. Ceslaus Spicq states that the simplest way to characterize these opponents who forbid marriage and abstinence from foods is Dualism and Gnosticism. However, Spicq argues that the Essenes, and those at Qumran, also taught abstaining from certain food and marriage. Gnosticism also taught asceticism, but as is pointed out by Spicq, many religions when seeking purification and holiness often abstained from food (or certain food) and sexual intercourse (marriage). Spicq writes in response to the "plus simple" answer, "Mais toutes ces données comparables sont très postérieures à notre épître" ("But, all these comparable data are much later than our epistle"). See Spicq, *Saint Paul, Les Epitres Pastorales*, 497–98.

The prohibition of food does not necessitate Jewish opponents. Paul takes the time to argue this point, stating, "everything created by God is good" (1 Tim 4:4). Because Christianity was dependent upon Judaism in some ways, ignorant adherents could have easily read the Torah and assumed the food laws were still in effect.[39]

It seems that Paul was not anticipating a possible threat, but instead he was speaking from his own experience and knowledge.[40] Paul reacts both to what is taught, as well as ways of living that were inconsistent with his teaching.[41] He gives instructions regarding widows who may have been taking advantage of the church's support rather than looking to their families or marrying.[42] The qualifications for elders and deacons may also have been given in response to some men unqualified for the position, or who had become so. He also urges Timothy to beware of the rich, riches, and the troubles it brings (1 Tim 6:3–10).[43] When identifying the "opponents," for the sake of comparison with the NPP, what is important is understanding the opponents who have misunderstood the law, those who have been influenced by "myths and endless genealogies," and those teaching asceticism, which may also reflect *some* Jewish influence.

39. Eating unclean food was addressed by the early church (Mark 7:18–19; Acts 10:10–16; Rom 14:20). There were also foods to be avoided listed by the Jerusalem Council (Acts 15:20, 29; 21:25). The cleanness of all foods also represents and reflects the universal nature of the gospel (Acts 10:28; Rom 14:16–23).

40. Paul may have been combating an early form of "Gnosticism," but it is unlikely it was anything like fully-formed Gnosticism. However, more likely, when Paul speaks of "what is falsely called knowledge" (1 Tim 6:20), he is referring to the same "teachers of the law" who thought they knew what they were talking about, but did not (1 Tim 1:6–7). See Johnson, *First and Second Letters to Timothy*, 312; Marshall and Towner, *Critical and Exegetical Commentary on the Pastoral Epistles*, 677.

41. See Towner, *Goal of Our Instruction*, which details the connection between right doctrine and right behavior. He states, "The *christliche Bürgerlichkeit* model argues that the goal of this existence (referring to Christian existence) as the Pastorals express it is to live respectably and peacefully in the world. And it claims to have discovered theological developments that underlie this understanding." Towner, *Goal of Our Instruction*, 17.

42. This statement does stand in contrast to what Paul argued in 1 Corinthians 7:8–9, "But I say to the unmarried and to widows that it is good for them if they remain even as I. But if they do not have self-control, let them marry; for it is better to marry than to burn." However, in the context of 1 Timothy and the church at Ephesus, Paul is interested in who is on the list and how the resources of the church there can be best utilized. There must have been a pledge ("first faith," whether formal or informal is hard to tell) once put on the list that some had afterward disregarded (1 Tim 5:12).

43. In this passage, the ones teaching the different doctrine were guilty of several things, including using "godliness as means of gain." This passage finds a relative parallel in Titus 1:10–11.

The Ephesian Opposition and the NPP

William Mounce conflates the opponents in all three letters, which makes the characterization of the opponents and understanding Paul's polemic harder to decipher in 1 Timothy.[44] The conflation of all opponents in the PE unnecessarily complicates identifying them. Though there are obvious semantic correlations between 1 Timothy and Titus, there are also important contrasts.[45] Johnson argues that the opponents are "an intellectual elite that demands performance measured by law and asceticism rather than by grace and conscience."[46] This characterization demands that the opponents be part of the church and the architects of problems within the church. Furthermore,

44. In fact, one of the difficulties in constructing a sketch of the various opponents in 1 Timothy is the lack of treatment found in commentaries. In most commentaries, the PE are treated as a group from start to finish. This study is not abject to their relative grouping based on their similarity, but they are distinct letters. Even Robert Karris deals with 2 Timothy, then 1 Timothy and Titus because 2 Timothy is a different type of letter. See Karris, *Pastoral Epistles*. Luke Timothy Johnson points out the problem of lumping all opponents together in his commentary. He states, "Each letter addresses a particular situation, has its own literary form, and uses its own mode of argumentation. Each letter must therefore be considered individually and in particular rather than in general and as a part of a larger group." Johnson, *First and Second Letters to Timothy*, 98. He points this out in reference to the false teachers as well, stating, "It is important to observe that the profile of the opponents in 1 Timothy is distinctive" (146).

45. Some of these similarities include the qualifications of elders (1 Tim 3:1–7; Titus 1:6–9) and similar semantic descriptions of opponents (1 Tim 1:3–6; cf. Titus 1:10–15). However, the letters are arranged differently, and have a different agenda from the start (1 Tim 1:3; Titus 1:5). They also share considerable vocabulary. For example, from 1 Timothy 1 only: "rebellious," 1 Tim 1:9; cf. Titus 1:6, 10; "true child" (γνωσίῳ τέκνῳ), a phrase only used in 1 Tim 1:2; Titus 1:4; "genealogies" (γενεαλογία), used only in 1 Tim 1:4; cf. Titus 3:9; "to speak confidently" (διαβεβαιόομαι), used only in 1 Tim 1:7; Titus 3:8. What is also important is the amount of material shared only by 1 and 2 Timothy. For example, also from 1 Tim 1: "miss the mark, depart" (ἀστοκέω), only used in 1 Tim 1:1:6; 6:21; cf. 2 Tim 2:18; "turn" (ἐκτρέπω), 1 Tim 1:6; 5:15; 6:20; cf. 2 Tim 4:4; "lawfully" (νομίμος), used only in 1 Tim 1:8; cf. 2 Tim 2:5; "unholy, wicked" (ἀνοσίος), 1 Tim 1:9; 2 Tim 3:2; "worldly, godless" (βέβηλος), 1 Tim 1:9; 4:7; 6:20; cf. 2 Tim 2:16 (even more specific is the phrase, βεβύλους κενοφωνίας, repeated in 1 Tim 6:20 and 2 Tim 2:16); "empowered, strengthened" (ἐνδυναμόω), 1 Tim 1:12; cf. 2 Tim 2:1; 4:17; "ministry, service" (διακονία), is used often in Paul, but it is not present in Titus, 1 Tim 1:12; cf. 2 Tim 4:5, 11; "blasphemer" (βλάσφημος), 1 Tim 1:13; cf. 2 Tim 3:2; "example" (ὑποτύπωσις), only used in 1 Tim 1:16; cf. 2 Tim 1:13; the name Hymenaeus, only mentioned in 1 Tim 1:20; cf. 2 Tim 2:17; "worldly and empty chatter" (1 Tim 6:20; cf. 2 Tim 2:16). All of these similarities were traced only in 1 Timothy 1, but the similarity in vocabulary alone demonstrates that, though 1 Timothy and Titus share common themes and discussions, 2 Timothy is still similar to 1 Timothy in its own way. What has been fascinating in this study as well, though not demonstrated here, is the level of semantic similarities the PE have with Hebrews.

46. Johnson, *First and Second Letters to Timothy*, 146.

these various problems may be dealing not with one group of people, but, like in 1 Corinthians, with a few distinct groups, individuals, and situations, all of which are contributing to the instability of the church.[47]

For the present task, what is important to see with regard to 1 Timothy is the depiction of the opponents and problems within the church in Ephesus. The occasion for writing, as witnessed in the different language used and matters discussed, is different than that of Romans or Galatians. Instead, 1 Timothy more closely resembles 1 Corinthians and some of the problems faced in that church, and Paul's reaction to those problems. The type of Jewish influence found in Galatians seems to be minimal, if at all present, in 1 Timothy. Rather than a move toward rabbinic Judaism, or more exactly, a more Jewish identity focused on "covenantal identifiers" or law-keeping, it seems that the anonymous opponents of 1 Timothy are engaged in controversies born from the conflation of Judaism and proto-gnosticism. James Dunn argues that the attraction of myths and genealogies (likely from the OT, which is why Paul mentions the proper use of the law) is what has led some astray.[48] He contends that it is not Judaizing covenantal works like circumcision, but using the Torah as a test of pedigree, attested in places like *1 Enoch*. Because of the different battle Paul is fighting, it is difficult to place Paul's thoughts here within the hermeneutical rubric of the NPP. The NPP is a new perspective on Judaism, first, and by that a Pauline perspective. The absence of the type of justification language used in Romans and Galatians, as well as "works" in a pejorative sense,[49] makes the comparison even more difficult. However, as will be discussed below, there are a few other parallels that require special attention and do not prohibit a NPP approach to 1 Timothy. Paramount to the present project, and study of the PE as a whole, is the unique nature of the recipient of this letter (Timothy)[50] as well as the unique opponents of Paul in the church in Ephesus. These men were likely *in* the church, affecting the church with their teaching, which is evidenced by the expulsion of Alexander and Hymenaeus. What can also be derived

47. For example, the "certain ones" who fancy themselves teachers of the law are likely not Hymenaeus and Alexander, who were "handed over to Satan," although they could be two named figures among a larger group.

48. Dunn, "First and Second Letters," 790–91.

49. This pejorative sense of "works" stands in contrast to the performance of "good works" found in 1 Tim 2:10; 3:1; 5:10, 25; 6:18.

50. The letters to Timothy (and Titus, for that matter) are not typical letters written from one individual to another. These letters, though written to an individual, may likely have been intended to be read by others as a teaching tool and apostolic backing for Timothy. See Johnson, *Letters to Paul's Delegates*, 29–33; and Mitchell, "New Testament Envoys in the Context of Greco-Roman Diplomatic and Epistolary Conventions," 641–62.

is the other problems within the church, not in direct connection to the supposed "teachers of the law," such as the care for widows (1 Tim 5:3–16), the adornment and role of women in regard to teaching (1 Tim 2:9–15),[51] the factiousness of men (1 Tim 2:8), and the danger of riches (1 Tim 6:9–10, 18–9) do not sufficiently coincide with the categories of chapter 1 to test within the hermeneutic of the NPP.

1 Timothy 1:6–16: Translation

(6) Some, having departed,[52] have turned[53] to fruitless talk,[54] (7) wanting to be teachers of the law, neither understanding what they say nor concerning the things they confidently assert.[55] (8) Now, we know that the law is good, if one uses it lawfully, (9) knowing this, that the law was not laid down for the righteous,[56] but for the lawless and rebellious,[57] the godless and sinners, unholy and irreligious, killers of father and mother, murderers, (10) fornicators, homosexuals, kidnappers, liars, perjurers, and whatever else is opposed to sound teaching (11) according to the gospel of glory of the great God, with which I have been entrusted.

51. An interesting element of this passage is Paul's use of the foundational story of the fall as proof of his argument, which is one of the few explicit connections to the OT in the PE. See Towner, "1–2 Timothy and Titus," 894–98. Paul has a similar, more subtle connection to Eve's being deceived in 1 Tim 5:15 in reference to young widows who have "turned aside to follow Satan." Paul alludes to the garden of Eden on several other occasions in "undisputed Paul" as well (Gal 3:28, "male and female"; 1 Cor 15:22, 45; Rom 5:14, references to Adam in contrast to Christ; 2 Cor 11:3, "as the serpent deceived Eve").

52. ἀστοχέω is used only in the PE (1 Tim 1:6; 6:21; 2 Tim 2:18) and carries the meaning to "miss the mark, depart." See BDAG, 146.

53. κτρέπω ("turn, turn away") is used four times in the PE (1 Tim 1:6; 5:15; 6:20; 2 Tim 4:14) and once in Heb 12:13. See "ἐκτρέπω," BDAG, 311.

54. ματαιολογία ("empty talk") is a NT *hapax legomenon*. See "ματαιολογία," BDAG, 621.

55. διαβεβαιόομαι is used again only in Titus 3:8. See "διαβεβαιόομαι," BDAG, 226.

56. δίκαιος is used only once in each of the PE (1 Tim 1:9; 2 Tim 4:8; Titus 1:8).

57. ἀνυπότακτος ("rebellious") is used in 1 Tim 1:9; Titus 1:6, 10 and once in Heb 2:8. The "lawful" use of the law was against such men, who undoubtedly were a problem in both Ephesus and Crete.

(12) I am grateful for the one who empowered[58] me, Christ Jesus our Lord, because he considered me faithful,[59] placing me into service, (13) being formerly a blasphemer and a persecutor and a violent man, but I was shown mercy, because I acted ignorantly in unbelief. (14) But, the grace of our Lord overflowed with the faith and love which are in Christ Jesus. (15) Faithful is the saying and worthy of all acceptance, that "Christ Jesus came into the world to save sinners," of whom I am first. (16) But, on account of this, I was shown mercy, so that in me, the first, Christ Jesus might demonstrate all patience, for an example for those about to believe in Him for eternal life.

This passage follows Paul's thesis statement for 1 Timothy, "But the goal of our instruction is love from a pure heart and a good conscience and a sincere faith" (1 Tim 1:5), made in opposition to the different/contrary teachings of some men in Ephesus. The passage is usually broken into 1 Timothy 1:3–7, 1:8–11, and 1:12–17. However, this study has chosen to break the passage up in this way (1 Tim 1:6–16) in order to highlight specific elements of the NPP: Paul's view of the law and Paul's conversion.

The Law

Paramount to the hermeneutic of the NPP—or any Pauline hermeneutic, for that matter—is the function of the law.[60] The law, in NPP thought, refers most often not to "law" generally speaking, or even to elements within the law (ceremonial or otherwise), but to the Torah.[61] Paul is able to speak both

---

58. ἐνδυναμόω ("empowered") is used in Paul (Rom 4:20; Eph 6:10; Phil 4:13; 1 Tim 1:12; 2 Tim 2:1; 4:17), and only once outside of Pauline literature, describing Paul after his persecution of the church and conversion (Saul; Acts 9:33).

59. Cf. 1 Cor 7:25, "I give an opinion as one who by the mercy of the Lord is trustworthy."

60. The work done on Paul and the law is vast. Richard Hays says of it, "Like the stone steps of an ancient university building, the topic of 'Paul and the Law' has been worn smooth by the passing of generations of scholars." Hays, "Three Dramatic Roles: The Law in Romans 3–4," 151. Though not an exhaustive list, other works that identify the problems with the complexity of the law in Pauline thought are: Cranfield, "St. Paul and the Law," 43–68; Das, *Paul, the Law, and the Covenant*; Hübner, *Das Gesetz bei Paulus*; Martin, *Christ and the Law in Paul*; Räisänen, *Paul and the Law*; Sanders, *Paul, the Law, and the Jewish People*; Schreiner, *Law and Its Fulfillment*; Thielman, *Paul and the Law*; Ware, "Law, Christ, and Covenant," 513–40; Westerholm, "Law and the 'Just Man' (1 Timothy 1, 3–11)," 79–95; Wright, *Climax of the Covenant*; Kruse, *Paul, the Law, and Justification*, 265–66.

61. James Dunn states that when Paul speaks of "law," context is the guide, in contrast to the presence or absence of an article. Dunn, *Theology of Paul the Apostle*,

of the usefulness of the law, as well as its goodness, but also the function of the law as being that which brings sin and death (Rom 5:13; 7:7–9), or, what Rosner calls, the "negative use" of the law.[62] Paul's use of, and thoughts concerning, the law is complex and variegated. However, most would maintain that it is consistent and coherent.[63] Here, in this passage, Paul speaks to the goodness of the law, in its "lawful" use, or, in other words, as long as the law is used within its proper boundaries. The word "lawful" (νομίμος) is used only one other time in the NT (2 Tim 2:5) and refers to the rules or boundaries of competition. What is evidently outside those rules is placing the restrictions of the law on the "righteous." Instead, the law is for the "lawless and rebellious." What follows this statement is a long list of characterizations and sins that seem to coincide with the Decalogue.[64] James Dunn

---

131–32. He also states, regarding some Second Temple literature and the connection between νόμος and *Torah*, "This does not provide any support for a further link, *nomos* = legalism. But it does mean that Paul's subsequent use of *nomos* to sum up Israel's covenant obligations, as set out by Moses (the Mosaic Law), is not in itself a distortion or misrepresentation of is Jewish heritage." Dunn, *Theology of Paul the Apostle*, 132. Similarly, Sanders states, "In all of these passages, the law is thought of as all of one piece." However, like Räisänen, and even citing his work, Sanders thinks that Paul's thought is not altogether consistent, stating, "All Paul's statements cannot be harmonized into a logical whole, but each one can be understood as coming from the application of different of his central convictions to diverse problems." Sanders, *Paul, the Law, and the Jewish People*, 86. Wright has a lengthy, complex discussion of the purpose of the law, what he calls, "Torah," in *Paul and the Faithfulness of God*. He explains, "It is increasingly apparent to many readers of Paul, whether or not they fully work the point through, that when Paul writes the word *nomos* he normally means, the Jewish law, the Torah." See Wright, *Paul and the Faithfulness of God*, 505, 1032–37. Even Wright in his *Paul for Everyone* commentary on the PE, has a section in the back defining certain terms. When defining "Torah, Jewish Law" he identifies the complexity of law by defining the law by the Pentateuch (along with the narrative sections), the entire OT, and "the developing Jewish legal tradition" which was codified in the Mishnah. Of primary significance is his last sentence in the paragraph, "Doing what Torah said was not seen as a means of earning God's favour, but rather of expressing gratitude, and as a key badge of Jewish identity." Wright, *Paul for Everyone*, 181.

62. Rosner, *Paul and the Law*, 45–109. Rosner's thesis is that Paul's use of the law is coherent, and he takes a mediating position between the Lutheran perspective and the NPP by asking the question, "How does the law relate to the issue of how to walk and please God?" In response to this question, he focuses on Paul's "movements" from repudiation, replacement, and appropriation of the law. Rosner, *Paul and the Law*, 43–44, 208–16.

63. See n61 wherein it is pointed out that both Räisänen and, to a lesser extent, Sanders see inconsistencies and contradictions in Paul's treatment of the law. It is in these cases that the NPP's assumptions about early Judaism takes precedent over Paul's own argumentation.

64. Several commentators point this out. For example, see Wright, *Pastoral Letters*, 9–10; Johnson, *First and Second Letters to Timothy*, 176; Dunn, "First and Second

suggests that the law does not seem to be being used by these opponents as what must be followed for morality's sake (e.g., legalism), but as a mine for myths, genealogical speculation, and fruitless talk.[65] Within the context of both Paul's definition of the law's proper usefulness and his indictment against the opponents regarding myths, genealogies, speculation, and fruitless talk, Dunn's suggestion makes sense. However, it is hard to connect the moralistic elements of Paul's listing to the other, more speculative elements, like "myths and genealogies." Paul's argument may be that the proper use of the law is to demonstrate sinfulness, which is rather straightforward (particularly in this list), in opposition to using the law as a means of mythological speculation, which serves to disrupt and obfuscate. Through Paul's strategy, the supposed teachers of the law are themselves unrighteous in their misuse of the law, in that he concludes the list with "whatever else is contrary to sound teaching" (1 Tim 1:10).

The idea of a "righteous one" (δικαίῳ) seems to contradict Paul and his string of quotations in Romans 3:10–19 which begins with a quotation of Psalm 53:3, "There is none righteous, not even one." However, if Paul has taught Timothy previously that righteousness only comes through Christ, then the "righteous" would, of course, mean a believer, not a do-gooder, or better, a "Law-keeper."[66] Both Dunn and Wright argue that righteousness is not given to a believer as a quality, instead, "to be righteous," is to receive God's own covenantal righteousness.[67] There are exceptions even in undisputed Paul, wherein "righteous" is a quality,[68] even though Paul does not use the term "righteous" often.[69] In fact, three of the uses are quotations of the OT (Rom 1:17; 3:10 [Ps 53:3]; Gal 3:11) and, two of those, are quoting the same text (Rom 1:17; Gal 3:11; cf. Hab 2:4). Though in his primary theology Paul argues that righteousness only comes through faith (Rom

---

Letters," 791; Mounce, *Pastoral Epistles*, 30–31; and Towner, *Letters to Timothy and Titus*, 127–29. Mounce ties the first couplets with "offenses against God" which coincides with the first four commandments. Then, the final, remaining vices/sins correspond to the last five commandments in the Decalogue.

65. Dunn, "First and Second Letters," 791.

66. Mounce, *Pastoral Epistles*, 18, explains, "Because the Ephesian heresy most likely lacked a well-defined theological core, because the letter is a repetition of what Paul and Timothy had earlier discussed, and because Timothy already knew Paul's teaching, there is no need for Paul to go into a theological discussion of why the opponents are wrong."

67. For example, see Dunn, *Theology of Paul the Apostle*, 341–46; Wright, *What Saint Paul Really Said*, 96–98.

68. Rom 2:13; 3:10; 5:7; 7:12; Gal 3:11; Eph 6:1; Phil 1:7; 4:8.

69. Rom 1:17; 2:13; 3:10, 26; 5:7, 19; 7:12; Gal 3:11; Eph 6:1; Phil 1:7; 4:8; 1 Tim 1:9; 2 Tim 4:8; Titus 1:8 (see also 2 Thess 1:5–6).

4:3–8), the nature of the word itself can also mean "righteous" as a moral quality (Rom 3:10; 5:7). The word used more often in 1 Timothy with regard to morality and ethics is "good": καλός[70] and ἀγαθός.[71] In 1 Timothy (as well as the PE, as a group), καλός is used more often than ἀγαθός,[72] and both are used more in 1 Timothy than either 2 Timothy or Titus.[73] This moral quality of "good," is illustrated elsewhere in undisputed Paul. For example, in Rom 5:7–8, Paul compares the "righteous," for whom one might die, with the "good" (ἀγαθός) and "sinners" (ἁμαρτωλῶν) for whom Christ died. Paul may be simply using this scenario as a hypothetical situation for argument's sake, but it does demonstrate one example of the word "righteous" being used as a moral quality and standing rather than a status or judicial pronouncement. In fact, in the previous verse (Rom 5:6), Paul states, "At the right time, Christ died for the *ungodly*" (ἀσηβῶν), which has as its correlative "sinners" (Rom 5:8). Thus, in Romans 5:6–8, Christ died for the "ungodly" and "sinners," with whom Paul identifies (Paul uses first-person plural pronouns in Rom 5:8). Perhaps not coincidentally, ἀσηβῶν is also designated as one of those against which the law is used in 1 Timothy 1:9, coupled with sinners ("ungodly and sinners").

Another important passage to consider is Romans 2:13. Paul argues, "It is not the hearers of the law who are righteous (δίκαιοι) before God, but the doers of the law shall be justified." This passage has been traditionally understood to represent the impossible standard against which all are measured, leading to reliance upon faith in contrast to doing the law (cf. Gal 3:12).[74] However, the NPP argues that what Paul is stating is axiomatic

---

70. 1 Tim 1:8, 18; 2:13; 3:1, 7, 13; 4:4, 6; 5:10, 25; 6:12–13, 18–19.

71. 1 Tim 1:5, 19; 2:10; 5:10.

72. καλός (2 Tim 1:14; 2:3; 4:7; Titus 2:7, 14; 3:8, 14); ἀγαθός (2 Tim 2:21; 3:17; Titus 1:16; 2:5, 10; 3:1)

73. See Marshall with Towner, *Pastoral Epistles*, 227–29. In "Excursus 6," Marshall discusses the meaning of "good" in relation to works as used in Paul and the PE. He opposes the idea that the high frequency of the qualifying adjective "good" in the PE is a reflection of bourgeois Christianity, or what J. Wanke calls "an altered view of Christianity." Ultimately, Marshall states, "It is undeniable that there is a greater stress on good works in the PE, but this is no basis for claiming an 'altered understanding of Christianity.' The difference from Paul is one of degree rather than of kind." Marshall with Towner, *Pastoral Epistles*, 229. See also Wanke, "κάλος," *EDNT*, 2:245.

74. For example, Cranfield writes, "In its context in Romans this sentence can hardly be intended to imply that there are some who are doers of the law in the sense that they fulfill it as to earn God's justification. Rather is Paul thinking of that beginning of grateful obedience to be found in those who believe in Christ, which though very weak and faltering and in no way deserving God's favour, is, as the expression of humble trust in God, well-pleasing in His sight." Cranfield, *Critical and Exegetical Commentary on the Epistle to the Romans*, 1:155. In contrast, Ulrich Wilckens believed the argument of

and fits within Paul's understanding of salvation and *final* justification with regard to the doing of the law.[75] So, with regard to use of the law, and it not being for the righteous, one wonders, then, how 1 Timothy 1:8 fits within the NPP rubric. Paul's use of the word, "righteous" is variegated. Paul can, at one and the same time, say that no one is "righteous" (Rom 3:10), but that a righteous status can be given (if even, hypothetically, for the sake of argument) to doers of the law (Rom 2:13) and to those who live by faith (Rom 3:10; Gal 3:11; cf. Hab 2:4).[76]

Towner argues that the "righteous" in view are Christians of "genuine conversion,"[77] but he also suggests that there is no need to make connections to Paul's justification theology via the "righteous" word group. He states, "He simply means authentic believers, for whom the law as a written moral code serves only a very limited purpose."[78] However, this explanation seems to miss the point of Paul's argument. Paul is arguing the law is *not* for the righteous. The limited purpose is for the "godless" and "sinner." Instead, what Paul seems to be doing is insinuating his opponents are not

---

Rom 2:13–14 to be a positive representative of Jewish thought. Westerholm sums up Wilckens's view: "for Wilckens's Paul the pursuit of the righteousness of the law was positively enjoined on the Jews, who, however, failed to attain their goal because they transgressed the law. . . . But the demand to fulfill the law, now seen as summed up in the love commandment, remains valid for believers." Westerholm, *Perspectives Old and New on Paul*, 159. See also Wilckens, *Der Brief on die Römer*, 145–51.

75. Dunn points out in his commentary on Romans that Paul is comparing the attentive hearing of the law done by Jews to *actual* doing. He does not understand the passage to be a complete theological unpacking, which comes later in Romans; "Rather, his concern is to put in question the prevailing Jewish understanding of who the 'righteous' are and of the grounds on which they can hope for final justification." Dunn, *Romans 1–8*, 98. He adds, "Like his fellow Jews and the whole prophetic tradition, Paul is ready to insist that a doing of the law is necessary for final acquittal before God; but that doing is neither synonymous with or dependent upon maintaining a loyal membership of the covenant people." Dunn, *Romans 1–8*, 98. Similarly, Wright maintains that this passage remains in some continuity with traditional Jewish eschatology (final justification). He states, "Romans 2:1–16 does indeed embody traditional Jewish eschatology, but it has been rethought around the Messiah and around the principle of 'no respect of persons' which, while itself rooted in the ancient scriptures, had attained a new focus through Paul's understanding of the gospel and the gentile mission." Wright, *Paul and the Faithfulness of God*, 1089.

76. For example, Paul uses the law (by way of a prophet; Hab 2:4) as proof that righteousness and faith are connected. So, a line is drawn from doing the law, to righteousness, to doing the law (living) by faith. Similarly, Wright goes so far as to say, "There is a hint, too, that Paul sees faith as the fulfilment of the law in (Rom) 3:27." Wright, *Paul and the Faithfulness of God*, 1089. Cf. also 1 Cor 7:16, which states, "Circumcision is nothing, and uncircumcision is nothing, but keeping the commandments of God."

77. Towner, *Letters to Timothy and Titus*, 124.

78. Towner, *Letters to Timothy and Titus*, 124.

"righteous" (if they were, they would not need the law), but that they are, in their teaching, "contrary to sound doctrine" and on equal plane with sinners, killers of parents, and the sexually immoral (cf. 1 Cor 6:9–10). If there be any doubt their teaching was contrary, and by that sinful, once coupled with these types of sins, Paul erases that doubt. Thus, more than anything, it seems Paul is pointing out that these "teachers of the law," by their unlawful use of the law, are ironically, themselves under the same umbrella with the sins that follow.

When Paul states, "The Law is good" (καλὸς ὁ νόμος), one cannot help but think of Romans 7:16.[79] In Romans 7:12, the term "righteous" is used to describe the law ("commandment," ἐντολή) as well.[80] The law, Paul says, is made for "the lawless and rebellious, for the ungodly and sinners, for the unholy and profane, for those who kill their fathers or mothers, for murderers and immoral men and homosexuals and kidnappers and liars and perjurers, and whatever else is contrary to sound teaching" (1 Tim 1:9–10). The first three couplets are relatively vague, but the charges become more precise. Within the bounds of 1 Timothy, it is not surprising that the law is also for "whatever is contrary to sound teaching."[81] Paul is exposing the weakness of these opponents, in that they misunderstand the law so badly, they have failed to recognize that even within the law, the "sound teaching" of Paul is found, the sound teaching which is according to the "glorious gospel" and that their own teaching is of a sinfulness on par with breaking the Ten Commandments on the most grandiose scale.

It is this shift from "whatever is contrary to sound doctrine" to "the glorious gospel" that helps define Paul's use of the law and the law's understood (οἴδμεν, "we know") function. The "glorious gospel" is not the law, but the gospel does incapsulate the sound teaching which is partially found in the law. In other words, the proper use of the law is not found in genealogies, myths, disputes, or even in "righteousness."[82] Instead, the proper

79. Even though a different word for "good" is used in each case (ἀγαθός in Rom 7:12; καλός in Rom 7:16). It is also worth pointing out that in both Rom 7:14 and 1 Tim 1:8 the opening phrase is οἴδαμεν δὲ (γαρ) ὅτι.

80. In this verse Paul says that "the law is holy, and the commandment (a possible synonym or subcategory of the law) is holy, righteous, and good." The word commandment (ἐντολή) is used six times in Romans 7 (7:8, 9, 10, 11, 12, 13) of the total of only fourteen in all Pauline literature (Rom 13:9; 1 Cor 7:19; 14:37; Eph 2:15; 6:2; Col 4:10; 1 Tim 6:14; Titus 1:14).

81. This exact phrase (ὑγιαινούσῃ διδασκαλίᾳ, "sound teaching") is only repeated in Titus 2:1. However, the term "sound" is used again in 1 Tim 6:3 as "sound" words in contrast to a different doctrine. So, in 1 Timothy, the word is used in contrast with error, or more specifically, "different teaching" (cf. 1 Tim 1:3).

82. Although secondary to the issues at hand, a word needs to be said about Rom

usefulness of the law is found in recognizing sin, sin here equated with heterodoxy. Some may understand Paul to be arguing that the law is meant to steer the sinner back onto course, and make him righteous through obedience.[83] Others suspect that the righteous are already on course, so they do not need the law, and that when Paul says "righteous," he is referring to both "gift and virtue."[84] However, both of these interpretations fail to account for Paul's statement, "Christ Jesus came into the world to save sinners, of whom I am the foremost" (1 Tim 1:15). Paul serves as the example

---

10:4, because it is such an important part of the discussion of Paul's view of the function of the law. Paul states, "For Christ is the end of the law for righteousness for all who believe." There are two basic understandings of this passage. The first understanding can be represented by C. E. B. Cranfield. He understands the word "goal" (τέλος) to mean both "fulfillment" and "goal" and that "law" (νόμος) refers to the OT. He states, "We conclude that the verse as a whole means: For Christ is the goal of the law, and it follows that a status of righteousness is available to everyone who believes." Cranfield, *Romans*, 519–20. In contrast, the second view expressed by Wright is that of "goal, fulfillment, *and* termination," in that Paul's theology of law and Christ incorporates all three of these options, including the law's cessation. Wright, *Pauline Perspectives*, 47–48. Sanders describes the end of the law as the already present eschaton. He explains further, "Christ is the end of the law in that he is the turning point from law to faith." Sanders, *Paul and Palestinian Judaism*, 535. James Dunn explains, "The word 'end' therefore is probably intended in the primary sense of 'termination, cessation.'" Dunn, *Romans*, 597. See also Wright, *Justification*, 73, 103, 244.

Regarding the "righteous" in 1 Tim 1:9, Philip Towner argues that Paul has in mind believers as the righteous, as well as his own theology of justification that Timothy would already know. However, the discussion seems more akin to Rom 5:1–5 wherein Paul mentions the "righteous" for whom someone may die in his hypothetical argument concerning the death of Christ for "sinners," and not the righteous.

83. For example, Benjamin Fiore explains, "Another apparently non-Pauline usage. The immediate context leans toward the secular Greek meaning of one who satisfies ordinary legal norms, and therefore implies the idea of becoming just by one's law-abiding actions." Fiore, *Pastoral Epistles*, 42. See also Gordon Clark, who in opposition to Donald Guthrie states, "That the Law does not apply to Christians is false because, first, Christians are not sinless; and second, the context is clear: the Law is good, if one uses it lawfully." He, instead, concurs with Calvin who suggests that Paul's arguments were against these "certain ones," and that the use of the term is "sarcastic," because he also insists, "Unfortunately there is none righteous, no, not one. Therefore we all need the Law." Clark, *Pastoral* Epistles, 15–17.

84. Mounce, *Pastoral Epistles*, 33–36. Mounce understands Paul to have in mind the forensic element of being made righteous, as well as the eschatological righteousness given at judgment. He states about righteousness, "It is forensic in that the righteous person is declared not guilty and eschatological in that the person will ultimately be declared righteous at the final judgment. It is not only a gift appropriated by faith but also a virtue to be sought." One wonders why this explanation would be necessary in the present passage. Paul is not defining "righteous," but explaining the proper use of the law. Mounce's description demonstrates the centrality of justification/righteousness language among scholarship, even when Paul seems to have something else in mind.

par excellence of God's mercy and Christ's patience. Thus, in part, Paul's definition of the law uses a hypothetical "righteous" person in opposition to the *sinful* use of law similar to the argument found in Romans 5:1–5. Ironically, then, it is Paul's acknowledgment of his ignorant sinfulness (not his "righteousness") that provides the background for the faithful saying, "Christ came to save sinners."

Paul's argument regarding the law follows his statement that the "the goal of our instruction is love from a pure heart and a good conscience and a sincere faith" (1 Tim 1:5). L. T. Johnson points out, "The norm of Christian righteousness is found, not in a law that stands outside the person, but in the commandment of love which is rooted in internal dispositions."[85] In other words, righteousness is not found in the law, or in obedience to it. This statement, in contrast to the "lawful use of the law" for sinners, is similar to Paul's statement in Galatians 5:22–23 concerning the fruit of the Spirit, two of which are found in 1 Timothy 1:5,[86] "against such things there is no law." Thus, although many point to Romans 7 because of the stark, almost identical similarities,[87] Galatians 5:19–23 also offers some parallels to the argument Paul is making in 1 Timothy 1:5–11.[88]

Paul's use of the law in this passage, and his delineation of its function, fits very well within the broader matrix of the NPP hermeneutic. The opponents were likely concerned more with the Pentateuch, because of their focus on myths and genealogies. Paul's specific focus is on the Decalogue, perhaps not only critiquing the way in which they used the law (its function), but also which parts of the law were still useful. Wright characterizes the law in this passage as "a map which only marks danger."[89] He even points to the similarity of the last vices in this list to the last of the commands in the Decalogue. Dunn has virtually no discussion of Paul's use of the law in this passage, except its similarity in wording to Romans 7:12, 16, and, he argues that the author (not Paul) "focuses exclusively on its function as law and implies that other use is unlawful."[90] Dunn does state, however, that "the

---

85. Johnson, *Letters to Paul's Delegates*, 116.

86. ἀγάπη and πίστις.

87. Some think the shared vocabulary between Rom 7:12, 16 and 1 Tim 1:9 are *too* similar, and thus see it as a quotation from Paul. For example, see Dibelius and Conzelmann, *Pastoral Epistles*, 22, wherein he states, "The author produces literally a phrase from Paul's reflections on the law (see Rom 7:16, 12), and introduces it with the phrase 'we know' (οἴδαμεν) as an acknowledged principle."

88. "πορνεία" (Gal 5:19) and "πόρνος" (1 Tim 1:9).

89. Wright, *Pastoral Letters*, 8.

90. Dunn, "First and Second Letters," 791. These two passages, although mentioning similar sins, do not mention the law. Romans 1:32 comes closer in its mention of

teaching is consistent with Paul's views expressed earlier in Rom 1:26–27; 1 Cor 6:9–10."[91] What is missing in these two commentaries (to be expected, considering the type of commentaries they are) is a comparison of this view of the law with that of undisputed Paul. One supposes that in this case, this comparison is absent because there is significant continuity between 1 Timothy and Romans. However, the neglect of properly comparing this text with the rest of Paul is troubling in that this the only time the word νόμος is used in the PE. A proper understanding of the law plays such a major role in Paul's theology, and in the articulation of the NPP, one would expect to see further explanation.

Brian Rosner does engage 1 Timothy 1:8–10 with Paul's theology of law. He sees Paul's theology of the law as a three-step process. He focuses on the "big moves" Paul makes with regard to the law as repudiation, replacement, and appropriation. He compares this process to a waitress who was fired, then rehired as a maître d' and sommelier. He clarifies this solution and hermeneutical approach, saying, "Rather than asking which bits of the law Paul retains and which he rejects, a hermeneutical approach starts by acknowledging the unity of the law and asks instead, when Paul speaks positively or negatively about the law, in which capacity the law is functioning."[92] He classifies the use in 1 Timothy 1:8–9 as a *repudiation* which is subsequently replaced with the gospel (1 Tim 1:11) and *appropriated* by arguing for the payment (double honor) due to elders who rule well (1 Tim 5:18; cf. Deut 25:4). Although, as he claims, this is a broad characterization, one can see a slight problem with terminology and oversimplification in this case. This use of the law is a repudiation of the law, on the one hand, ("if one uses it lawfully"), and a re-appropriation on the other ("it is not for the righteous, *but* for the . . . "). Paul's explanation is not altogether negative, but it is a nuanced critique of his opponents' use of the law, as well as a positive, agreed-upon appropriation ("we know").

One must be careful not to bring in Paul's polemic elsewhere in a systematization of Paul's thought, even though the language and phraseology are similar. There is no need to apologize for Paul, or to help him make his point. For example, in Galatians, Paul uses a "pedagogue" as an analogy of the law. He does not use this specific analogy anywhere else. So, here in

---

the "ordinances of God." A better comparison may be Rom 2:12–23 in which Paul compares being righteous to doing the law, which some gentiles had done without actually having the law themselves. In this passage, he calls the Jew who knows the law and so teaches others as liable to obey the law themselves. He uses three of the Ten Commandments as examples (adultery, idol worship, and stealing).

91. Dunn, "First and Second Letters," 791.

92. Rosner, *Paul and the Law*, 208.

1 Timothy, Paul is not providing an all-encompassing treatise on the law, but he is highlighting one aspect of the law to combat these self-appointed teachers. In this case, it would be difficult to argue Paul has in mind "law," generally speaking. What he envisions is the Torah, and more specifically, the Decalogue.

It should also be noted that this depiction of the law does not necessitate a legalistic understanding of the law in that following the law is not "legalistic," but necessary, if the law was one's standard. Paul's argument is that the law is a standard of only what *not* to do in this case. More likely, Paul uses this function of the law, not in contrast to legalistic tendencies, but in high-minded, speculative reading and fruitless talk of men who do not know what they are talking about. The polemic against the law being used for the righteous, is that these "teachers of the Law," are themselves equated with the list of sins against which the law speaks, because they themselves are teaching "whatever is contrary to sound doctrine." In so many words, Paul's argument here is reminiscent of his thoughts on the law (and its teachers) in Romans 2:1–23 where he argues (in essence), "if you teach the law, then you claim to know it, and you ought, in that way, to do it." Similarly, Paul claims in Romans 13:8–10, that the law can be fulfilled (not abolished) in the love commandment (cf. 1 Tim 1:5). Also, in connection with this passage in 1 Timothy, is the list of laws in Romans 13:8–10 that are taken from the Decalogue as well.

In sum, the law here likely refers to the Pentateuch (or possibly even the entire OT). However, the lawful use of the law is to demarcate sin, not to *make* one righteous. And, a more subtle, but important corollary is that the law is meant to combat "whatever is contrary to sound doctrine," a major aspect of the purpose of 1 Timothy. For Paul, the law, and even the moralistic sections of the Decalogue, are compatible with his own teaching.

Paul's Conversion: Salvation For "The Chief of Sinners"

One of the major issues with regard to the NPP is Paul's "conversion." Based on his definition of covenantal nomism, E. P. Sanders maintains that Paul was not responding to a plagued conscience when turning to Christ. Instead, Paul was moving from "solution to plight."[93] Christ provided an answer to a problem Paul did not know he had. When referring to his previous life, Paul comments, "as to the righteousness that was in the law, found blameless" (Phil 3:6). In other words, Paul saw himself perfectly

---

93. Sanders, *Paul and Palestinian Judaism*, 442–43.

fitted within the boundaries of Judaism before Christ's call. In fact, he adds that he did not have "a righteousness of my own from the Law" (Phil 3:9), insinuating that his own righteousness is not how one is found in Christ, a righteousness he believed he had while in Judaism. The question at hand for this project is whether or not this same conclusion can be drawn from Paul in 1 Timothy 1:12–16. The glorious gospel with which Paul had been entrusted is evidenced in and through his own conversion and call. This section seeks to establish what Paul converted from, what he was called to do, and particularly how his call and conversion in 1 Timothy 1:12–16 compares with the hermeneutic of the NPP.

Considered Faithful

Paul begins the recollection of his conversion by offering thanks to Jesus who "considered me faithful" (ὅτι πιστόν με ἡγήσατο). Πίστος can mean "faithful," "trustworthy" or "dependable."[94] Paul does not use the term "righteous" here, as he did in 1 Timothy 1:9, but he does speak to Christ's faith in him ("I thank Jesus Christ, who strengthened me, because he considered me faithful"), even prior to his conversion. Paul was not bothered by a "plagued conscience" in the sense that he was unsatisfied with his life in Judaism. Knowing what he knows now, he certainly would have felt guilty, and his guilt can be sensed in the aftermath of this conversion. However, Paul's call was not a guilty conscience searching for, then finding solace in, Christ. Instead, Paul's call is about a guilty man, ignorant of his own guilt, who was somehow considered trustworthy then put into service.

Paul argues that his call and conversion serve as the ultimate example of Christ's patience in saving sinners, not a relentless search that finally comes to a conclusion in Christ. In fact, this same faithfulness may be seen in Timothy's mother and grandmother, who may or may not have been believers.[95] Paul uses this word (πίστος) often—most often in 1 Timothy.[96] However,

---

94. See Bultmann, "πιστεύω," *TDNT*, 6:174–228; BDAG, 816–18. A more nuanced definition may also include "obedience," though that is not likely the meaning here, considering Paul speaks of his former life only to highlight his sinfulness. He probably thought he was being obedient and served with a good conscience, but he was proven otherwise by Christ.

95. Acts 16:1; 2 Tim 1:5. In Acts 16:1, Timothy's mother is called "a faithful Jewish woman" (γυναικὸς Ἰουδαίας πιστῆς). In 2 Tim 1:5, similarly, the sincere faith (ἀνυποκρίτου πίστεως) of Lois (his mother) and Eunice (his grandmother), Paul also hopes to find in Timothy.

96. 1 Cor 1:9; 4:2, 17; 7:25; 10:13; 2 Cor 1:18; 6:15; Gal 3:9; Eph 1:1; 6:21; Col 1:2, 7; 4:2, 9; 1 Thess 5:24; 2 Thess 3:3; 1 Tim 1:12, 15; 3:1, 11; 4:3, 9–10, 12; 5:16; 6:2; 2 Tim

πίστος is not used at all in Romans or Philippians, and only once in Galatians (Gal 3:9), which once again demonstrates the similarity of 1 Timothy and 1 Corinthians. Twice in 1 Corinthians Paul states that God is faithful (1 Cor 1:9; 10:13), and even states, "I give an opinion as one who by the mercy of the Lord is trustworthy," which is similar to his statement in 1 Timothy 1:12–13, wherein he looks to his faithfulness and the Lord's mercy. In the case of 1 Timothy 1:12–13, "faithful" is likely not "faithful" in an obedient, works-based sense, but more likely, "trustworthy." If Paul was "faithful" with regard to works, it may give one the impression Paul thought he had earned the right to his ministry through faithfulness of action, when he outright states the opposite. Instead, even before his conversion he possessed trustworthiness as a trait. In fact, Paul's active verbs in this case have "Christ Jesus our Lord" as their actor. Christ "strengthened" (ἐνδυναμώσαντω) Paul, "considered" (ἡγήσατο) him faithful, and "put" (θέμενος)[97] him into service.

One must consider to what Paul was faithful. Paul was certainly faithful, at least if in his own mind, to Judaism, and by that to God and his covenant with Israel. However, in light of Paul's theology elsewhere, there is little reason to think that Paul thought his actions somehow justified his call to ministry. Instead, it was an act of mercy and graciousness, which is Paul's point in this passage. As a matter of fact, Paul changes the rules when boasting of his right to apostleship in 2 Corinthians 11:22–23, wherein his Jewishness plays a secondary role to his suffering. His early life with all its accomplishments was considered "refuse" (Phil 3:8; σκύβαλα), and his boasting was now found in his willingness to suffer (2 Cor 11:22–30), which, in a way, is a reversal—the persecutor becomes the persecuted. In both cases, whether in his pre-conversion Jewish perspective, or by his perspective as the apostle to the gentiles, Paul had been "faithful."

Overemphasizing this point, Krister Stendahl, a NPP representative, states, "We look in vain for a statement in which Paul would speak about himself as an actual sinner."[98] One does look in vain if 1 Timothy 1:15 is not considered a Pauline recollection of his conversion. However, to be fair, Stendahl may well be correct, if he is speaking of Paul's pre-conversion notion of himself and his life within Judaism. Paul likely knew he was a "sinner" as recognition of his humanity and imperfection, but he saw himself as a sinner within the boundaries of Judaism, and thus not the

---

2:2, 11, 13; Titus 1:6, 9; 3:8.

97. Cf. 2 Tim 1:11

98. Stendahl, "Apostle Paul and the Introspective Conscience of the West," 210. See also Stendahl's similar statement, "We look in vain for any evidence that *Paul the Christian* has suffered under the burden of conscience concerning personal shortcomings which he would label 'sins'" (202, italics original).

same as a sinner outside Judaism and outside the people of God (cf. Gal 2:15; "We are Jews by nature and not Gentile sinners"), or even a Jewish "sinner." However, the question becomes, in this case, did Paul see himself as a sinner in need of a savior other than God and obedience to Torah before his conversion? It seems relatively straightforward that he did not. What *is* important is how Paul's conversion as related in 1 Timothy segues into his gospel and ministry to the gentiles. Paul's conversion (1) led him to understand his sin more fully, which would find resonance with the gentiles who also needed their sinfulness pointed out, (2) demonstrated that righteousness came from faith, not in being Jewish (or in obeying the law), (3) demonstrated God's mercy, (4) and demonstrated how ignorant sinfulness can be transformed into salvation.

For Paul, his sins of blasphemy, violence, and persecution are seen as sins, only in retrospect. There is no indication that Paul, before his conversion, thought these specific things were sinful. In fact, in his former life, he likely saw these things as a service to God in keeping with Judaism. What he calls "zeal" is given in his list of his impressive Jewish pedigree (Phil 3:5–6) and as a favorable quality of the Jews, if it were accompanied by knowledge (Rom 10:2). N. T. Wright describes Paul's former life as a sinner, "Not that it had seemed like it at the time, of course; he had thought he was doing God's will. . . . He was doing to God's true people what the wicked pagans had done to Israel in times past. The fact that he thought he was defending Israel against heresy only made it worse."[99] One can sense Wright's underlying assumption in this short passage—Christians were God's "true people," in opposition to Jews like Paul.[100] But, Paul's actions were not due to his moral corruption, but rather to his ignorant zeal. Wall writes in regard to this passage, "God gives second chances to those whose prior rejection of God's Messiah is a matter of their ignorance of Scripture's messianic way of salvation rather than a matter of bad character."[101] Nonetheless, as will be noted below, Paul's conversion provides an example for others, who may themselves be morally corrupt (not "righteous"). Paul moves from the foremost sinner who acted in ignorance, to "sinners," generally speaking (cf.

99. Wright, *Pastoral Letters*, 12–13.

100. Worth noting is James Dunn's and N. T. Wright's view of God's people, specifically the passage wherein one finds "all Israel will be saved" (Rom 11:26). The gentiles had now become part of Israel (Rom 11:25). Paul does not use the term "Jew" in this passage. Instead, "all Israel" refers to all true Israel, once the fullness of the gentiles had come in. Dunn, *Theology of Paul the Apostle*, 526–30. Similarly, Wright maintains, "Paul's meaning is not a temporal sequence—first the Gentiles, *then* the Jews. Rather, it is the interpreter of a particular process *as* the salvation of 'all Israel.' And in this context 'all Israel' cannot possibly mean 'all Jews.'" Wright, *Climax of the Covenant*, 249–50.

101. Wall and Steele, *1 & 2 Timothy and Titus*, 72.

Rom 5:14). Just as God's mercy and Christ's patience is witnessed in Paul's call, other "sinners" may also be saved. This is an important segue that represents Paul's flexible theology of salvation to be further demonstrated in 2 Timothy 1:8–12 and Titus 3:3–7.

Mercy and Ignorance: "And yet I was shown mercy because
I acted ignorantly in unbelief."

The word ἀγνοέω ("to be ignorant") is used only here in 1 Timothy 1:13 in all of the PE. In fact, every other instance of this word in Paul is found within undisputed Paul.[102] Of these many instances, Romans 10:2–4 stands out as particularly similar because the Jews themselves, though zealous, were ignorant about God's righteousness. Instead, they were busy with a righteousness of their own, a righteousness not derived from God. Paul writes, "For I bear them witness that they have a zeal for God, but not in accordance with knowledge. For not knowing about God's righteousness, and seeking to establish their own, they did not subject themselves to the righteousness of God" (Rom 10:2–3). This description by Paul is likely not in an individual sense of "works-righteousness," but it represents Jewish attempts to exalt themselves as Jews, rather than the "righteousness of God" which is found also in the faith of the gentiles (Rom 10:3–12). So, Paul is able to say "Christ is the end of law for righteousness of all who believe" (Rom 10:4).[103] In both 1 Timothy 1:13 and Romans 10:2–4, the law is juxtaposed with belief (or, in the case of 1 Timothy 1:13, "unbelief"). Paul's ignorance can even be characterized in 1 Timothy as a righteousness of his own doing, of being "zealous," trying to be the best Jew possible, maintaining the traditions of Judaism and persecuting the church. He was both "faithful" in a sense, as well as ignorant. Another parallel with 1 Timothy 1:13 is Romans 2:4, wherein his audience "is ignorant" that God's kindness, and patience, leads to repentance. In 1 Timothy 1:16, Paul states that it was the "patience" of Christ Jesus that was demonstrated in him.[104] Although the word "super-abounding," (ὑπερεπλεόνασαν δὲ ἡ

---

102. Rom 1:13; 2:4; 6:3; 7:1; 10:3; 11:25; 1 Cor 10:1; 12:1; 14:38; 2 Cor 1:8; 2:11; 6:9; Gal 1:22; 1 Thess 1:13.

103. See note 82 of this chapter.

104. See also Rom 9:22–24, wherein Paul, looking to both Jews and Greeks, asks, "What if God, although willing to demonstrate His wrath and to make His power known, endured with much patience vessels of wrath prepared for destruction?" He responds, "This he did in order that he might make known the riches of his glory upon vessels of mercy." Also note that Rom 2:4 and 9:22 are the only places outside of 1 Tim 1:16 in Pauline literature that the word "patience" is used outside a listing of qualities

χάρις)[105] is used only here (1 Tim 1:14), there is a slight parallel in Romans 5:20 (ὑπερεπερίσσευσεν ἡ χάρις, "grace abounded more").

As noted above, in Romans 5:8 Paul explains that one does not die for the good, or the righteous, but Christ died for "sinners."[106]Although not calling himself a "sinner" *per se*, Paul does use the first-person plural with regard to saving us from "our" sins (Rom 5:8; Gal 1:4). Paul is not using the first-person plural simply for the sake of argument, but to demonstrate that as Christ died for the sake of "sinners," Christ also died for him. He calls himself "the foremost sinner" here in 1 Timothy 1:15 (cf. 1 Cor 4:9; 15:9). Although not claiming to be the "first" or "foremost" sinner elsewhere, Paul does consider himself the "least" of the apostles in 1 Corinthians 15:9 (cf. also Eph 3:8). In either case, Paul considers his position superlative as the "first" (πρῶτος) sinner and the "least" (ἐλάχιστος) apostle. In fact, in both cases, the reason Paul is "least" or "foremost" is due to his persecution of the church.[107]

Paul's Conversion in the NPP

The relevance of this passage when testing the NPP is Paul's consideration of his conversion and from what he was converted. Within the NPP, there is no completely unified consensus about how to describe Paul's conversion. As stated above, E. P. Sanders refers to Paul's conversion as moving from "solution to plight," and it is within that matrix Paul creates his own thoughts regarding salvation, and in Romans and Galatians, justification.[108] James Dunn, on the other hand, questions the validity of using the term "conversion," in that, like Frank Thielman, and in some ways N. T. Wright, Paul did not convert from one religion to another, since "Christianity" did not yet exist.[109] Wright contends that Christ fulfilled the Scriptures and

---

(the other Pauline uses are 2 Cor 6:6; Gal 5:22; Col 1:11; 3:12; 2 Tim 3:10; 4:2). Col 1:11 is the closest parallel to Rom 2:4; 9:22; 1 Tim 1:16.

105. "ὑπερπλεονάζω," BDAG, 1034.

106. 1 Cor 15:3; 2 Cor 5:21; Gal 1:4.

107. See also Gal 1:13–14; Phil 3:4–6; 2 Cor 12:11.

108. Sanders explains, "There is no reason to think that Paul felt the need of a universal savior prior to his conviction that Jesus was such." Sanders, *Paul and Palestinian Judaism*, 443. This statement is what is taken up by Wright in that he thought Paul did think Israel needed a Savior because of their continued exile.

109. Though Dunn sees the term as appropriate as a "general description," he notes two major issues in calling Paul's (and, in this case, mostly others') call a "conversion." The first is the lack of Paul's use of the term "to turn around" (Gal 4:9; 2 Cor 3:16; 1 Thess 1:9). Second, Paul also does not frequently use similar terms, "repentance" or

God's promise to Abraham, and in that way, did not oppose "Judaism," Israel, or even the Torah. Wright sees two plights for which Christ was the solution: the plight of Israel who was "not free" and the plight of the sinner.[110] Although varied in these precise details, the basic NPP position is that Paul's conversion was not a step from one religion to the next, but that his theology was in both continuity and discontinuity with the Judaisms of his day, and that his conversion was not a move from a primarily works-based "pattern of religion" to a grace-centered one.

Since this is the only time in the PE Paul recounts his conversion, as well as his former life, a word needs to be said about what it was from which Paul turned, what is usually designated as "Judaism." Paul only uses the term "Judaism" twice, both in a single passage (Gal 1:13–14), and that, in reference to his former life.[111] What has been sufficiently demonstrated in modern scholarship is that Judaism was itself variegated.[112] The Qumran community represents a different form of Judaism than rabbinic Judaism, even though both groups may share certain beliefs and practices in common. Paul helps us characterize from what type of Judaism he comes when he references his prior life. However, in the case of 1 Timothy 1:12–13, Paul does not say much about that life in Judaism and how he excelled in that life. Instead, in keeping with his motif of salvation offered to all through Christ's mercy, grace, and patience, Paul accentuates his sinfulness, *a result of what his prior life produced*. The Judaism from which Paul was called, was one of zeal (Gal 1:13; Phil 3:6; see also Acts 22:3–4), promotion/

"forgiveness." Dunn, *Theology of Paul the Apostle*, 326–28. For a further discussion of Paul's own "conversion," see Dunn, *New Perspective on Paul*, 341–59, wherein he maintains that Paul's conversion was characterized by his move from a nationalistic "Judaism," and from those laws that separated the Jew from gentile, to one based on faith. See also Thielman, *Paul and the Law*, 242–43, wherein Thielman marks great continuity with the law in Paul. Though, he also states, "Continuity and discontinuity, then, are a hallmark of Paul's view of the Law." Thielman, *Paul and the Law*, 242.

110. Wright, *Pauline Perspectives*, 295–97. He writes, "What is more—and this lies close to the heart of his freshly reworked theology of the cross, the main subject of this paper—he may have already glimpsed, as Jesus and the other prophets before him had done, the dangerous truth that Israel's problem was related to the world's problem, in the sense not just that Israel was the innocent victim and the world was the guilty aggressor, but that Israel herself was composed of human beings who, despite being given Torah and Temple, were themselves still sinners. Whether he has already thought of it like that or not, this is the point he now offers as the most profound analysis: *Israel too is in Adam*." Wright, *Pauline Perspectives*, 296, italics original.

111. The reference in Gal 1:13 (ἐδίωκον) and 1 Tim 1:13 (διώκτην) both use a form of the word "persecute" to describe Paul's former life. In fact, a participial form of the word is also used in Phil 3:6 (διώκων) as well.

112. For example, see the two-volume series edited by Carson et al., *Justification and Variegated Nomism*; See also, Thielman, *Paul and the Law*, 48–68.

advancement (Gal 1:14), tribalism (both within Israel apart from gentiles, as well as distinction from fellow Jews),[113] and law-keeping (Phil 3:6; "as to righteousness found in the law, blameless"). These features help define both Paul's former life and conversion. They also provide the backdrop for the gospel, wherein Paul comes to realize that there are sinners of all types, even those who are ignorant, like himself. In this regard, then, the standard view among the NPP is that Paul emerged from rabbinic Judaism, even though the comparison is not perfectly tidy.[114]

As for Sanders's contention that Paul moves from "solution to plight," 1 Timothy does not necessarily prove or disprove that thesis. Paul, in retrospect, saw himself as a "sinner," and likely saw himself as a "sinner" even beforehand, though his concept of "sinner" and "salvation" was altered after his encounter with Christ. However, there is no indication in 1 Timothy 1:12–16 that Paul was searching for salvation apart from Judaism before his conversion. He certainly would not have considered himself the "foremost" sinner in his life in Judaism. When coupled with passages like Philippians 3:2–7 and 1 Corinthians 15:9, one sees remarkable continuity in the way Paul characterizes his conversion—from a zealous Jew to a "sinner," the "least" of the apostles, saved and set aside for God's ministry to the gentiles. In reality, Paul, in the words of Stendahl, had a rather "robust"[115] conscience. Paul's theology of salvation, under which justification functions, is itself robust enough to have Christ save sinners, even the ones who, before they knew Christ, did not know the full measure of their sinfulness. In other words, although Paul likely knew he was a sinner of sorts in Judaism, his encounter with Christ demonstrated sinfulness of which he was unaware. Also, it could be argued, though his sinfulness was observed in his violence, persecution, and blasphemy, it was more deeply rooted in "ignorance" and "unbelief," a characterization he may have used purposefully in the polemic against the supposed teachers of the law, who themselves were ignorant (1 Tim 1:7; "not knowing," μὴ νοοῦντες).

113. Paul's zeal, notion of advancement, and tribalism is a more subtle point in that by the nature of being a Jew he was separate from "Gentile sinners" (Gal 2:16), but, the way in which he characterizes himself, and his pedigree as "Hebrew of Hebrews," and "of the tribe of Benjamin," he also saw himself as distinct from his fellow Jews. This mentality spills over, but by way of suffering, into Paul's mission as apostle to the gentiles (2 Cor 12:22–28). He sees himself as more of a servant of Christ than the other apostles (with whom he shares ethnicity), because of the sufferings he had undergone.

114. Sanders is unsure concerning Paul's background. He does not see Paul fitting neatly into either Palestinian, rabbinic, or Hellenistic Judaism. Sanders, *Paul and Palestinian Judaism*, 549–56. Wright finds that Saul closely resembles Shammaite Pharisaism. Wright, *What Saint Paul Really Said*, 30.

115. Stendahl, "Apostle Paul and the Introspective Conscience of the West," 200.

Salvation, Mercy, and Ignorance

In Paul's depiction of his conversion in 1 Tim 1:12–16, it is fully initiated by God. Paul purposefully draws Timothy's attention to his ignorance. Paul thought he was doing what was right. However, Jesus was patient, God was merciful,[116] his grace was overabundant, and Paul now serves as an example of salvation for the ignorant sinner, whether it be parent killers, or those ignorantly teaching what is contrary to sound doctrine. This "gospel of glory," and its inclusive nature, is what these supposed teachers had missed, and in missing it, they had created dissention and strife. The purpose of the law was to demonstrate sin, but it was instead being used for their high-minded controversies.

πιστὸς ὁ λόγος: Faithful Is the Word

This phrase (πιστὸς ὁ λόγος) is only found in the PE. There are five of these "faithful sayings" in the PE (1 Tim 1:15; 3:1; 4:9; 2 Tim 2:11; Titus 3:8).[117] In some of the sayings, it is difficult to distinguish whether or not the saying precedes the phrase πιστὸς ὁ λόγος or follows it. However, in 1 Tim 1:15, it seems clear enough Paul is referring to *what follows* as the faithful saying. George Knight argues that the saying entails "Christ Jesus came into the world to save sinners." The phrase, "among whom I am foremost," is an addition to the saying to complete his thoughts concerning his conversion and the example it set for those who come to believe.[118] This "faithful saying" sums up this section of Paul's thought. The law had been misunderstood and appropriated wrongly by these teachers, when instead, the law's purpose was to demonstrate the need for salvation. Paul's ministry and mission were based on this need for salvation, for both Jew and Greek. Paul himself had misunderstood the law and his role within the purpose/plan of God. The "gospel of glory" now makes Paul, not only a teacher, but an example, of God's salvation.

---

116. Paul twice repeats that he was shown mercy (1 Tim 1:13, 16).

117. Frances Young posits that though there could be some difficulty in deciphering whether or not what follows or precedes is the faithful saying, "The formula is invariably attached to a statement about salvation. This would suggest that the phrase does not simply signal a reliable Pauline tradition, or a secure doctrine, but rather heralds an assurance of the gospel." Young, *Theology of the Pastoral Letters*, 56.

118. Knight, *Faithful Sayings in the Pastoral Letters*, 32. See also Marshall with Towner, *Pastoral Epistles*, 399–400.

1 Timothy 2:3–7: Translation

(3) This is good and acceptable[119] before our savior, God,[120] (4) who wants all men to be saved and to come to the knowledge of the truth.[121] (5) For God is one, and there is one mediator of God and man, the man, Jesus Christ, (6) the one who has given himself as a ransom[122] for all, the testimony at the proper time, (7) for whom, I was made a herald and apostle (I am speaking truth and not lying),[123] a teacher[124] of the Gentiles[125] in faith and truth.

Salvation for All

This passage has been included because of Paul's description of his apostleship. One of the major tenets of the NPP is the assumption that Paul's doctrine of justification is a teaching born from his mission to the gentiles, and by that, serves a specific polemical function.[126] In 1 Timothy 1:11–12, Paul mentions his ministry (διακονία), but he does not define the parameters of that ministry, only that he had been put into "service." However, in 1 Timothy 2:3–7, Paul explains his mission further with regard to the

---

119. ἀπόδεκτος ("pleasing, acceptable") is found only in 1 Timothy (1 Tim 2:3; 5:4). See "ἀπόδεκτος," BDAG, 109.

120. The attribution of God as Savior is typical of 1 Timothy and Titus, but not so elsewhere in Paul (1 Tim 1:1; 2:3; 4:10; Titus 1:3, 4; 2:10, 13; 3:4, 6). In fact, Paul only uses the term three times outside 1 Timothy and Titus as a designation for Christ (2 Tim 1:10; Eph 5:23; Phil 3:20).

121. Cf. 1 Cor 10:32–33.

122. ἀντίλυτρον ("ransom") is a *hapax legomenon*. However, a similar term, and possible synonym (λύτρον), is used in Matt 20:28 and Mark 10:45. See "ἀντίλυτρον," BDAG, 89.

123. Cf. Rom 9:1; 2 Cor 11:31; Gal 1:20.

124. The entire phrase (εἰς ὃ ἐτέθην ἐγὼ κῆρυξ καὶ ἀπόστολος καὶ διδάσκαλος) is repeated in 2 Tim 1:11, in which the term, κῆρυξ, is only used in these two passages (1 Tim 2:7; 2 Tim 1:11). These two passages are also the only times Paul explicitly calls himself "teacher." Although Paul taught (1 Cor 4:17, "as I teach in every church."), he preferred to designate himself as "apostle."

125. The word "Gentile" (ἔθνος) is used three times in 1 and 2 Timothy (1 Tim 2:7; 3:16; 2 Tim 4:17), each referring, in some way, to the gospel (1 Tim 3:16) or to Paul's mission to the gentiles (1 Tim 2:7; 2 Tim 4:17). It is not used at all in Titus.

126. This assumption of the NPP regarding the polemical function of justification by faith was demonstrated in chapter 2, beginning in the work of William Wrede and Albert Schweitzer and brought into the discussion of the NPP by E. P. Sanders. Sanders argues that two major convictions "governed Paul's Christian life." The first was Jesus Christ as Lord who brought salvation to all, and the second was that Paul was "called to be the apostle to the Gentles." Sanders, *Paul and Palestinian Judaism*, 441–42.

salvation of "all humankind" (ὃς πάντας ἀνθρώπους θέλει σωθῆναι; cf. 1 Tim 2:1; 4:10). The salvation of all mankind is linked to the prayers offered on behalf of kings and rulers (1 Tim 2:1–2). Just as the relationship between Jew and gentile, slave and free, male and female (Gal 3:27–28) is paramount elsewhere in Paul's articulation of the gospel, so too, here, "all men" includes those in authority. He points to the *Shema* and the oneness of God as evidence, which he does elsewhere with regard to unity.[127] Thus, for Paul, his ministry to the gentiles is part and parcel of salvation for all mankind. In other of his letters, particularly Romans and Galatians (but also found in Philippians, Philemon, and Ephesians), Paul insists that salvation is available to all on the basis of faith. This concept is not isolated to 1 Timothy 2:3. In the case of Galatians and Romans, the terminological focus is on justification[128] and the erasure of the distinction between Jew and gentile and the search for righteousness in the gospel rather than "salvation."[129] So, though the language is different, Paul's foundational conviction is the same: There is one God who desires salvation for all. The point need not be limited to only the Jew-gentile dilemma of Galatians and Romans. Salvation is here extended to kings and rulers (just as elsewhere it is extended to Jew and gentile alike).

God, Our Savior

The term Savior (σωτήρ) is only used twice by Paul outside the PE (Eph 5:23; Phil 3:20), each referring to Christ. However, the term is used ten times in the PE,[130] only four of which refer to Christ.[131] God being called "Savior" as a Pauline phenomenon is only found in 1 Timothy and Titus, another example of which will be seen in the passage under consideration in chapter 5 (Titus 3:3–7).[132] Within the context of 1 Timothy 2:3–7, God as Savior

127. Rom 3:29–30; 1 Cor 8:6.

128. For example, the word σῴζω ("to save") is used in Rom 5:9–10; 8:24; 9:27; 10:9, 13; 11:14, 26, and not at all in Galatians. In contrast, it is used seven times in the PE (1 Tim 1:15; 2:4, 15; 4:16; 2 Tim 1:9; 4:18; Titus 3:5).

129. Paul also mentions slave/free, male/female, barbarian, Scythian, circumcised/ uncircumcised, but "Christ is all, and in all." See Rom 10:12; 1 Cor 7:19–22; Gal 3:28; 5:6; 6:15; Col 3:11.

130. 1 Tim 1:1; 2:3; 4:10; 2 Tim 1:10; Titus 1:3–4; 2:10, 13; 3:4, 6.

131. 2 Tim 1:10; Titus 1:4; 2:13; 3:6.

132. 1 Tim 1:1; 2:3; 4:10; Titus 1:3; 2:10, 13; 3:4. Cf. also Jude 25 and 2 Pet 1:1. Titus 2:13 (τῆς δόξης τοῦ μεγάλου θεοῦ καὶ σωτῆρος ἡμῶν Ἰησοῦ Χριστοῦ) could be rendered as "the glory of *our* great God and our Savior, Jesus Christ," although Mounce argues that it should be rendered "the glory of our great God and Savior, Jesus Christ."

makes perfect sense in that he, as Savior, is the one who desires all men to be saved. God's desire is matched by his initiative. He desires men to be saved, so he saves them.

Wright connects these prayers for rulers to the continuing Babylonian exile.[133] Certainly, the idea of God as Savior, although carrying Jewish, eschatological overtones, stands in contrast to these rulers, who may themselves have been considered "saviors."[134] So, for these rulers, in the gospel the "savior" becomes the "saved." However, if Paul is addressing rulers as "savior," his point is subtle. He is overtly backing his claim that these rulers should be prayed for, even though, historically, they often stood in opposition to Christians. Dunn states that this passage asserts "Christian universalism," by which he means not that all *will* be saved necessarily, but that God desires that all be saved.[135] Dunn makes a proper observation about acceptance of those on the outside, "The uncomfortable fact is that such universalism inevitably involves a fair degree of openness to the other and acceptance of the other in terms broader than one's own perspective."[136] Rather than universalism understood as the actual salvation of all, Paul has in mind God's will for the salvation of all which is demonstrated in Paul's ministry to the gentiles through the gospel of faith, and the prayers offered for "all mankind (men)."

These "kings and ones in authority" are representative of gentiles and God's mission and will to save all men. Even so, neither Dunn nor Wright discuss the implications of this passage for Paul's mission to the gentiles, which is Paul's major focus in Romans and Galatians. In fact, the term ἔθνος is only used two other times in the PE (1 Tim 3:16; 2 Tim 4:17[137]),

---

For the lengthy discussion of this verse, see Mounce, *Pastoral Epistles*, 425–31. The main argument from grammar is the Granville Sharp Rule (TSKS; article-substantive-καί-substantive) which basically states, "The second noun refers to the *same* person mentioned with the first noun when: (1) neither is *im*personal; (2) neither is *plural*; (3) neither is a *proper* name." See Wallace, *Greek Grammar Beyond the Basics*, 270–90.

133. Wright, *Pastoral Letters*, 19.

134. Dibelius and Conzelmann, *Pastoral Epistles*, 100–3, points out the varied nature of the designation "savior" in the early Jewish and Greco-Roman period. In Jewish literature it is always God who saves, but as noted above, often in Paul the term is used of Jesus as well, even though Jews did not make this attribution to the Messiah, which conveys a rather obvious message concerning Jesus's status in Paul's mind. Dibelius also connects "savior" to the Hellenistic "saving" deities (e.g., Asclepius) and to mystery religions, and also to "the cult of the ruler."

135. Dunn, "First and Second Letters," 798.

136. Dunn, "First and Second Letters," 799.

137. In 2 Tim 4:17, Paul is again recounting his mission to the gentiles, and he also uses the term "strengthened" (ἐνδυναμόω) in recounting his conversion in 1 Tim 1:12.

but prolifically in Romans and Galatians.[138] With such a small sampling to pull from in the PE, one would think there should be a natural draw to its novelty within the PE (or, more precisely, 1 and 2 Timothy) compared to the ubiquity of the term in Romans and Galatians. Furthermore, the term is not used at all in Philippians and only once in Colossians (Col 1:27), which, as in 2 Timothy 3:16, is used in a quasi-creedal description of the gospel. Thus, the mere presence of the term ought to draw one's attention. Paul describes his mission using ἔθνος because, as teacher of the gentiles (coupled with an appeal to the oneness of God), these rulers are not excluded from God's salvation. However, the reason Paul uses the term here is to highlight not the "gentile-ness" of the leaders, though the authorities he has in mind were likely gentiles. Instead, Paul uses the term to illustrate the continuity between his gospel to the gentiles and the salvation of everyone, which included these rulers as a subset of "all humankind."[139] This inclusion of rulers into the universality of the gospel is an important distinction to make. For example, the term "all" is also used in the saying of 1 Timothy 2:6 ("ransom for all"). While Wright, for example, focuses on the rulers and authorities, they themselves are an unpopular group of "all men." One can see the transition Paul is making as apostle to the gentiles—a gospel that includes gentiles, slaves, and women, and also includes rulers and authorities.[140]

One God and One Mediator

Paul, for the sake of praying for the authorities, which is both praying for gentiles as well as for enemies (cf. Rom 12:18–13:5), appeals to the oneness of God for support. Because God is one,[141] and there is only one Mediator

138. Rom 1:5, 13; 2:14, 24; 3:29; 4:17–18; 9:24, 30; 10:19; 11:11–13, 25; 15:9–12, 16, 18, 27; 16:4, 26; Gal 1:16; 2:2, 8–9, 12, 14–15; 3:8, 14.

139. Cf. Phil 4:22 where Paul sends greetings from the saints that included those of Caesar's household.

140. The word used for "those in authority" (ὑπεροχή) is used only one other time in Paul (and the NT) referring to his coming not in "superiority of speech" (1 Cor 2:1). One wonders if the term could refer not only to those in positions of authority in government, but those in authority within the church. The word is not used of elders or deacons, or even of Paul. However, there seems to have been problems within the eldership, which would have made a quiet, peaceful life in the church difficult. Certainly, government officials and authorities would have been included, but the phrase is periphrastic, which may have included other types of authorities as well.

141. N. T. Wright understands Jewish monotheism (the oneness of God) to lie at the foundation of Judaism and Pauline theology. He argues that though this Jewish monotheism is "redefined" by Paul in light of the coming of Christ Jesus, the *Shema* (Deut 6:4) is one element that continues to find expression in the NT highlighting the NT

(μεσίτης), then "all men" are unified in their need to be ransomed. The only occurrence of "mediator" in the LXX is Job 9:33 which states, "There is no mediator (μεσίτης) between us, who may lay his hand upon us both." A. T. Hanson argues that the author of 1 Timothy is alluding to this passage in Job, but he also insists that the meaning behind the passage in Job attributed to Christ is "very un-Pauline,"[142] because, Paul would not have considered Jesus an arbitrator between God and man.[143]

The use of this term is not especially significant for the current project, except that it is used by Paul elsewhere (Gal 3:19–20) in a negative way.[144] The two seemingly opposing uses of the word, and the concept that underlies the usage, speaks to Paul's fluidity of argument from one situation to the next. In the context of Galatians, Paul is answering the question, "Why the Law?" The law was not the meditator, but presumably Moses is, though Paul does not say so explicitly.[145] The troublesome part is Paul's almost direct contradiction. In one case, Christ is the *one* mediator between man and the *one* God (1 Tim 2:5). In the other case, the oneness of God is why there is not a need for a mediator (Gal 3:19–20). Of course, most scholars, if given the option of which is Pauline and which is not, will side with Galatians and argue the writer of 1 Timothy has misrepresented Paul. However, when approaching the text from the canonical perspective, an answer must be found as to why the two seem to disagree.

The answer is found in Paul's polemic and argumentation. Towner argues, "In any case, unlike the rather negative use of the concept elsewhere in Paul that associates the reception of the law with a certain distance

---

continuity with, and climax to, the OT Scripture. See Wright, *Paul: In Fresh Perspective*, 83–107. Although not alluding to 1 Tim 2:3–7, Wright argues that "monotheism, election, and eschatology are thus closely interrelated." These three provide the foundation for much of Wright's understanding of Pauline theology, and they are expressed in 1 Tim 2:3–7. See Wright, *Paul: In Fresh Perspective*, 84. For Wright's most thorough treatment of Jewish monotheism, see Wright, *Paul and the Faithfulness of God*, 619–773. The use of the *Shema* for the sake of unity and the inclusive nature of the gospel is used by Paul in 1 Cor 8:4–6; Eph 4:1–6; and Col 1:15–20.

142. Hanson, *Pastoral Letters*, 34–35. Also see Quinn and Wacker, *First and Second Letters to Timothy*, 183–86.

143. μεσίτη is also used in Heb 8:6; 9:16; 12:24.

144. "Why the Law then? It was added because of transgressions, having been ordained through angels by the agency of a mediator, until the seed should come to whom the promise had been made. Now a mediator is not one, but God is one."

145. Both Quinn and Wacker's commentary and Philip Towner make reference to the *Testament of Dan* 6:2, which states, "Draw near to God and to the angel who intercedes for you, because he is the meditator between God and men for the peace of Israel. He shall stand in opposition to the kingdom of the enemy." See Quinn and Wacker, *First and Second Letters to Timothy*, 183–84; and Towner, *Letters to Timothy and Titus*, 180.

from God (Gal 3:19–20), the present use is clearly a positive description of Jesus."[146] In the case of Galatians, the mediator is *not one*, representing separation, in contrast to God, who is one. The oneness of God in Galatians is highlighted as a oneness of continuity, the "mediator" implying some level of disjunction. In 1 Timothy, however, one is not dealing with the giving of the law, but with the salvation of all mankind. That salvation is brought about between the one God and the one mediator between God and man, "the man Christ Jesus."[147] There is also the possibility that the mediator in Galatians is not Moses, but the law itself as something to stand in the meantime between Abraham (Gal 3:18) and the promised seed (Gal 3:19). Like Wright, Raymond Collins sees the humanness of the mediator in direct opposition to the various gods, and emperor gods, of the Roman Empire.[148] Andreas Köstenberger rightly explains, "Since there are other monotheistic religions besides Christianity, Paul goes on to emphasize that there is only one mediator between God and humanity, 'the man Jesus Christ, who gave himself as a ransom for all.'"[149]

Herald, Apostle, and Teacher

The term "herald" (κῆρυξ) is found nowhere else in the NT outside these two occurrences (1 Tim 2:7; 2 Tim 1:11). Paul more often calls himself an "apostle."[150] In Romans 11:13, he uses a similar phrase as here in 1 Tim 2:7, designating himself as the "apostle of the Gentiles" (ἐθνῶν ἀπόστολος) rather than "teacher of the Gentiles" (διδάσκαλος ἐθνῶν). Paul also calls his apostleship, his διακονία ("ministry," cf. Rom 11:13), which is the same word used above in 1 Timothy 1:12 when Paul speaks of his conversion. However, nowhere else outside of 2 Timothy 1:11 does Paul call himself a διδάσκαλος,[151] though he uses the term three times in lists of gifts within the church (1 Cor 12:28–9; Eph 4:11).[152] Paul does say he "taught" in 1 Cor 4:17, and he refers

146. Towner, *Letters to Timothy and Titus*, 181.

147. For a full discussion of this passage, see Stout, *"Man Christ Jesus,"* 13–63.

148. See Wright, *Pastoral Letters*, 19; Collins, *I & II Timothy and Titus*, 61. See also Gloer, *1 & 2 Timothy-Titus*, 139. Wright also makes this point in Wright, *Paul and the Faithfulness of God*, 279–347.

149. Köstenberger, *1-2 Timothy and Titus*, 101.

150. E.g., Rom 1:1; 1 Cor 1:1; 9:1–2; 2 Cor 1:1; Gal 1:1; Eph 1:1; Col 1:1; 1 Tim 1:1; 2 Tim 1:1; Titus 1:1.

151. Other than the omission of ἐθνῶν ("of the Gentiles") and the aside, "I am telling the truth, I am not lying," the phrases in 1 Tim 1:12 and 2 Tim 1:11 are identical.

152. "Teacher" is used two other times, once in regard to the supposed "teacher of the immature" (Rom 2:20) and the other regarding teachers amassed to tickle ears

to his own "teaching"[153] (2 Tim 3:10). So, the fact that he does not call himself teacher elsewhere is not altogether significant. Regarding the phrase "I am not lying," there are other similar Pauline occurrences (Rom 9:1; 2 Cor 11:31; Gal 1:20). In all three cases, Paul uses the phrase as proof of something personal, something for which his recipients would have to take his word. The closest parallel of this passage is Galatians 1:20, wherein Paul recounts his conversion, and more specifically, his call to "preach Him among the Gentiles" (Gal 1:14–15). This parallel is significant in that it demonstrates Paul's difficulty in proving his apostleship to outsiders. One may wonder why he would need to say such a thing to Timothy, unless, as it seems, Paul intended this letter to be read by others as well. It also may have been added for the sake of highlighting his identification as "teacher of the Gentiles" in response to the supposed teachers of the law mentioned earlier.

Conclusions for 1 Timothy: To Save Sinners

The opponents of 1 Timothy set the tone of the letter. It is obvious that Paul is not combatting the same sort of heresy found in Galatians, even though the core of the gospel and his mission remains the same. Paul is also likely not combatting Gnosticism—at least, not later Gnosticism of the second century. Instead, what seems to be the issue is actually twofold. Like the Corinthians, there is more than one set of problems, even though these problems may have a similar genesis. The major, most dangerous problem within the church in Ephesus is the self-appointed teachers of the law, among whom may have been some elders. Paul saw their teaching, not only as a distraction from the gospel (or, "sound teaching"), but as contrary to it, on par with other, base sins. The second set of problems were problems within the church itself, possibly born from these other teachers. There were young widows who were taking advantage of church aid (1 Tim 5:9–16), men who, instead of praying, lifted hands in anger (1 Tim 2:8), issues with modesty and women's roles (1 Tim 2:9–15), problems within the eldership (1 Tim 3:1–7; 5:19–22), and problems with social distinction and riches (1 Tim 6:1–10, 17–19).

For a proper comparison with the NPP, many of the internal struggles specific to the Ephesian church are relatively insignificant. However, the teachers of the law provide enough commonality to recognize that even

---

(2 Tim 4:3).

153. This word, διδασκαλία, is found only four times outside the PE in Paul (Rom 12:7; 15:4; Eph 4:14; Col 2:22), but it is used heavily within the PE (1 Tim 1:10; 4:1, 6, 13, 16; 5:17; 6:1, 3; 2 Tim 3:10, 16; 4:3; Titus 1:9; 2:1, 7, 10).

though they are not exhibiting the same error as that of Galatians or Romans, Paul's foundational considerations of the law are consistent (cf. Rom 7:12, 16; 1 Tim 1:7–9). As in Romans 7 and Romans 13:8–10, Paul in 1 Timothy 1:8–11 acknowledges the purpose of the law in exposing sin (Rom 7:7–11), and in that purpose, focuses on the Decalogue.[154] What is absent in 1 Timothy is the more nuanced subtlety concerning the law found in Galatians and Romans, as well as the outright dismissal of some elements of the law (Rom 8:3–4; 1 Cor 15:56; 2 Cor 3:6; Gal 2:19–21; 3:19–21). Paul would have no need to express to Timothy the totality of his theology of the law, in that likely Timothy was already aware of it. The nature of Paul's description of the law demonstrates the significant differences between the problems of Romans, Galatians, and 1 Timothy.

Paul recounts his conversion in response to the misunderstanding of the law by the supposed teachers—the gospel stands in opposition to their contrary teaching. In the recollection of his conversion, Paul is able to have both a "robust conscience," as characterized by his achievements in Judaism, as well as his achievements as an apostle, and a retrospective awareness of his sinfulness in persecuting the church. So, on the one hand, in Philippians 3:1–7, Paul is able to speak of his zeal that led to persecution of the church and blamelessness with regard to the law. On the other hand, he is keenly aware of his position as the least of the apostles because of that same zeal (1 Cor 15:9). First Timothy offers a similar portrait of Paul's self-understanding. Paul was thankful to God for his ministry and empowerment, even though he had formerly been a persecutor. Paul tells Timothy that Jesus came into the world to save sinners, "among whom I am chief." Though not an exact parallel to 1 Corinthians 15:9, there is remarkable similarity in that Paul denigrates himself over his actions against the church in his former life. His statement in 1 Timothy 1:15 is also quite similar to Romans 5:8, wherein Paul includes himself among those for whom Christ died and "sinners." There is no indication, in either passage, that Paul would have considered himself the "chief of sinners," or the "least" of his apostolic contemporaries prior to his conversion. So, in this, the NPP can certainly find resonance. In fact, Paul expresses in 1 Timothy 1:13 that in his blasphemy, persecution, and aggression he was acting "ignorantly in unbelief."

There is also continuity in semantics and language (grace, saved, faith) between undisputed Paul and 1 Timothy. However, like any of Paul's letters, there is also distinct vocabulary (e.g., "blasphemer" and "man of violence").

---

154. In Rom 7:7, Paul uses covetousness as an example and in Rom 13:9 Paul uses the commandments of adultery, murder, stealing, and covetousness as being fulfilled in loving one's neighbor (Lev 19:18).

In 1 Timothy 1:6–16, the verb δικαιόω is not present,[155] which reinforces the NPP concept of justification—that it is primarily a doctrine of a particular polemic against Jewish exclusion of gentiles based on "works of law." Paul was not a gentile coming into Christianity. Instead, he was an "ignorant" sinner, a word he also uses of Jews in their zeal (Rom 10:3). Paul's articulation of his sinfulness and conversion in 1 Timothy 1:12–16 is different than his usual description of his conversion. It seems in Paul's articulation of the gospel, his conversion served as a demonstration to himself that he was a sinner, that the Jewish mindset of moral and ethnic superiority comes to an end in Christ and faith (Rom 10:4), and that his sins of persecution and violence were born from this ethnic superiority. His empowerment from the foremost sinner to an apostle to the gentiles demonstrates to Jew and gentile alike the perfect patience of Christ. One must keep in mind, that for the gentiles to come to faith, God sent to them a Jew who had to learn that ethnicity and Torah-keeping were not the way of salvation. Timothy himself was a type and demonstration of both of these worlds. The lack of justification (δικ-) language (except for the term "righteous" in 1 Tim 1:9) demonstrates Paul's gospel as one that need not use that language for explanation. Instead, "saved" serves as more encompassing term, a term that is slightly more ubiquitous in Paul.[156] Paul's point can even be seen in the description of his conversion in 1 Timothy 1:12–16. He states that he was considered "faithful" by God, not "righteous," which was the catalyst for God's placing him into service. In other words, he was not made "righteous," pronounced "righteous," nor was he "righteous" in the context of 1 Timothy 1:12–16. Though Paul's sins were not moral failings *per se* and were born of zeal, the foundation of the gospel remains that "Christ Jesus came into the world *to save* sinners." Paul serves as an example, even for all who would come to believe, not just those coming from a form of Judaism into the gospel. As demonstrated from the second passage, 1 Timothy 2:3–7, the gospel is given for all, Jew as well as gentile.

Although the Jew/gentile relationships and the involved discussion of such things is not as obvious and central in 1 Timothy, these aspects of the gospel are nonetheless there. In fact, though other readings are possible, the NPP hermeneutic easily fits within the context of 1 Timothy 1:6–16 and 2:3–7. Although there is no full discussion of the law, what Paul does say about the law in 1 Timothy 1:8–11 is substantiated elsewhere (Rom 7:7–16).

155. δικαιόω is also not present in 2 Corinthians, Ephesians, Philippians, Colossians, 1 and 2 Thessalonians, and 2 Timothy. It is used only twice in 1 Corinthians (1 Cor 4:4; 6:11), once in 1 Timothy (1 Tim 3:7), and once in Titus (Titus 3:7).

156. The verb σῴζω is found in every Pauline letter except Galatians, Philippians (σωτηρία is used three times, 1:19, 28; 2:12), and Colossians.

Though Paul speaks of his own conversion, he does so, not alluding to his Jewish pedigree, but by characterizing his conversion by his "ignorance." As he articulates his sinfulness in his former life, nothing is said of his inability to keep the law or his search for salvation. Instead, his sinfulness was found in his treatment of the church and his unbelief. One could even argue that Paul's conscience was plagued by his sin *after* his conversion more so than before. In fact, one could also argue that prior to his conversion, Paul felt completely justified in his persecution of "the way" (Acts 9:2).

Everyone seems to agree that Paul was the "apostle to the Gentiles." However, the point of contention rests in what that meant for Paul's articulation of the gospel and his theology. Obviously, in Romans and Galatians, that meant discussing and defining justification through faith. However, when writing to gentiles uninfluenced by the same type of Jewish interference as the Romans and Galatians, the moniker "apostle" or "teacher" of the gentiles has new significance. As elsewhere, Paul weaves the *Shema* and the oneness of God, a reconfigured Jewish element of his theology, into the fabric of God's desire to save all men, which is a not-so-different claim than "there is neither Jew nor Greek, slave nor free, male and female: You are all one in Christ Jesus" (Gal 3:28). However, rather than the argument revolving around the Jew/gentile debate, it instead revolves around salvation for all, including kings and authorities. So, there continues to be relative continuity between 1 Timothy, the rest of the Pauline corpus, and the NPP.

Although there are other tertiary conclusions to be drawn, for the purpose of the present work, when comparing Paul's use and articulation of the purpose of the law, his conversion and his apostleship to the gentiles, there is significant correlation with the NPP. The NPP argues that Paul's positive use of the law is varied, but that the primary purpose of the law is to expose sin, which is corroborated by 1 Timothy 1:8–11. The NPP also maintains that Paul's conversion was not one based on an existential search for salvation, but that Paul lived with a good conscience until his encounter with Christ, also corroborated in 1 Timothy 1:12–16. Finally, the NPP understands Paul's mission, polemic, and argumentation in undisputed Paul to revolve around his apostleship to the gentiles, again corroborated in 1 Timothy 2:3–7, even though the exact problem is not the same. The Ephesian church could have easily dismissed praying for kings and authorities, just as the Jews had intended to exclude gentiles, or make them follow some Jewish customs to gain their justification.

While 1 Timothy 1:6–16; 2:3–7 found relative resonance with the NPP, the next chapter will focus on 2 Timothy 1:3, 8–12. These two short passages offer different challenges to the NPP hermeneutic. In 2 Timothy 1:3, Paul explains that he worships God with a clean conscience just as his forebears did. In 2 Timothy 1:8–12, Paul contrasts "our works" with salvation and calling without mentioning justification or righteousness. So, the major tenets of the NPP as outlined in chapter 1 that will be examined are Paul's relationship to his former life in Judaism, justification/salvation terminology, and "works."

4

"Not According to Works"

2 Timothy 1:3, 8–12

Introduction

THIS CHAPTER WILL EXAMINE 2 Timothy 1:3, 8–12 in conversation with the NPP. The last chapter concluded that 1 Timothy 1:6–16 and 2:3–7 hold relative consistency within the rubric of the NPP hermeneutic. Special attention was given to Paul's discussion of the purpose of the law, his conversion, and his apostleship to the gentiles. Like chapter 3, this chapter will identify the opponents of 2 Timothy, followed by a translation of 2 Timothy 1:3, 8–12 and comparative exegesis engaging the NPP. The primary focus of this passage is Paul's view of Judaism (2 Tim 1:3), salvation, and the definition and function of "works" within the context of salvation. These passages will be compared and contrasted with the NPP and undisputed Paul in an attempt to test the NPP's validity within 2 Timothy.

Although the PE, as a whole, have not enjoyed a place in Pauline theology, 2 Timothy has come under less scrutiny, and has experienced a greater reception as Pauline in content.[1] There are various compositional hypotheses of 2 Timothy, ranging from Pauline authorship to the use of a

---

1. For example, see Wright, *Paul and the Faithfulness of God*, 61; Prior, *Paul the Letter Writer and the Second Letter to Timothy*; Murphy-O'Connor, "2 Timothy Contrasted with 1 Timothy and Titus," 403–18; Murphy-O'Connor, *Paul: A Critical Life*, 357–59; Towner, "Portrait of Paul and the Theology of 2 Timothy," 151–70. Wright says of 2 Timothy, "If this were the only 'Pastoral' we had, I suspect it would never have incurred the same questioning that it has endured through its obvious association with 1 Timothy and Titus." Wright, *Paul*, 394. Because of 2 Timothy's better reception, Wright advocates a second Roman imprisonment, stating, "If 2 Timothy is genuine, then, it reflects a complex journey—and a return to Rome—of which we know nothing else." Wright, *Paul*, 396.

secretary and even Lukan authorship.[2] Although these two selections are from the same passage, this study has chosen to bracket the first selection off (2 Tim 1:3) from the rest (2 Tim 1:8–12) because of how the passage relates to Paul's pre-conversion faith and his continuing concern for Israel. Also, as stated in chapter 1, this study will remain focused on the stated thesis, which is to test the validity of the NPP in the PE. The short introduction to 2 Timothy will help gain a proper understanding of the letter as a whole. Though this chapter focuses on only two short passages, one must see these passages within the larger rubric of the context of the letter, and as pointed out in the Methodology, within the larger corpus of canonical Pauline literature, and in comparison with the NPP.

Opponents and Occasion for the Letter

Since many commentaries deal with the opponents of the PE by grouping them together, deciphering the occasion of the letter proves difficult.[3] Although 1 Timothy seemed to have been written in response to some specific instances within the Ephesian church, 2 Timothy seems to have a different agenda. This letter does not seem to have "opponents" in mind in a specific sense, although there are some specific names mentioned of people to whom Paul was opposed (Hymenaeus, Philetus, and Alexander[4]; 2 Timothy 2:17; 4:14).[5] However, the problems Paul mentions are not what instigated

2. James Miller argues that 2 Timothy was a composite document made up of authentic Pauline fragments (or "notes"). Miller, *Pastoral Letters as Composite Documents.* Both H. C. G. Moule and C. F. D. Moule opt for Lukan authorship at the dictation of Paul. See Moule, *Second Epistle to Timothy*, 9–10; Moule, "Problem of the Pastoral Epistles," 117. For Lukan authorship, see also Wilson, *Luke and the Pastoral Epistles.* For a more thorough treatment of these issues, see sections "From Paul to Pseudonymity" and "The PE Reconsidered: 2 Timothy" in chapter 2 of this work.

3. For example, though espousing Pauline authorship, William Mounce deals with the opponents of all three letters as a group. Mounce, *Pastoral Letters*, lxix–lxxxiii. Even those who argue for pseudepigraphical authorship understand the PE to be dealing with the same issues, by the same author, using Timothy and Titus as false recipients to engage their contemporary, second-century problems. See Houlden, *Pastoral Epistles*, 18–44. Houlden admits the relative distinctiveness of 2 Timothy as opposed to the stark similarities of 1 Timothy and Titus. However, he maintains that 2 Timothy is nevertheless written to a fictitious Timothy from the "Pastor." Similarly, see Collins, *I & II Timothy and Titus*, 3–14.

4. Philetus and Hymenaeus (2 Tim 2:17–18) are those who said the resurrection had already taken place.

5. Paul lists many names in 2 Timothy: Timothy (1:1), Lois and Eunice (1:5), Phygelus and Hermogenes (1:15), Onesiphorus (1:16; 4:19), Philetus and Hymenaeus (2:17), Demas (4:10), Crescens (4:10), Titus (4:10), Luke (4:11), Mark (4:11), Tychicus

the writing of the letter. Unlike 1 Timothy and Titus (and other of Paul's letters), there is no specific place indicated to where this letter is sent. The letter is sent to Timothy, who could have been in a variety of places, although most think he may have still been in Ephesus.[6] Paul is encouraging Timothy in his ministry and warning him about the dangers that accompany the type of ministry in which Paul, and now Timothy, are engaged. Paul sees his own life and ministry coming to an end, so he writes to inspire Timothy to lay aside shame and timidity, and to "rekindle the gift of God which is in you through the laying on of my hands" (2 Tim 1:6). Timothy's faith is to emulate the faith found in his mother and grandmother (2 Tim 1:5), Paul (2 Tim 1:13; 3:10–12), and the Scriptures (2 Tim 3:14–6). His faith and ministry are also defined in contrast to other opposing teachings, attitudes, and actions (2 Tim 2:14–18, 23–26; 3:1–9, 13; 4:3–5).

As 1 Timothy resembles 1 Corinthians, 2 Timothy significantly resembles Philippians.[7] However, in contrast to the joyful tone of Philippians,[8] the tone of 2 Timothy is somber.[9] As L. T. Johnson points out, there is also the dark reality of the letter of Paul's having "fought the good fight" (2 Tim 4:7), now approaching the end of his ministry. Johnson writes concerning 2 Timothy's differences with Philippians, "In 2 Timothy, the mood is much grimmer. Paul does not express any hope of this-life deliverance, but sees his death as imminent (4:6)."[10] Andreas Köstenberger classifies 2

(4:12), Alexander (4:14), Prisca and Aquila (4:19), Erastus (4:20), Trophimus (4:20), Eubulus (4:21), Pudens (4:21), Linus (4:21), and Claudia (4:21).

6. For example, see Fee, *1 and 2 Timothy, Titus*, 13. However, Paul refers to the help of Onesiphorus in Ephesus, which may indicate Timothy was no longer there (2 Tim 1:18). Also, Paul tells Timothy Tychicus was sent to Ephesus (2 Tim 4:12). However, Paul also tells Timothy to greet the household of Onesiphorus (4:19) who had helped him in Ephesus, which may indicate Timothy was in Ephesus, or going to Ephesus.

7. For example, Timothy is one of the co-sponsors of Paul's letter to the Philippians (Phil 1:1) and, in both 2 Timothy and Philippians, Paul describes his relationship to Epaphroditus and Timothy as that of a soldier (Phil 2:25; 2 Tim 2:3–4; cf. also 1 Cor 9:7). See Johnson, *First and Second Letters to Timothy*, 319–20, 368–69.

8. Phil 1:18; 2:17–18; 3:1; 4:4.

9. In Philippians, as Paul is in chains, he focuses on joy and contentment (Phil 4:4, 9–18). He knows his death looms and welcomes his departure (Phil 1:19–24). On the other hand, in 2 Timothy, there is a darker element to his discourse. Though he is confident in his race and fight (2 Tim 4:7), he no longer speaks of his continued service.

10. Johnson, *First and Second Letters to Timothy*, 319.

Timothy as Paul's "last testament"[11] and as a "personal paraenetic letter."[12] In relation to this genre identification, Johnson writes, "The letter, then, is personal not only in its tone, but also in its focus."[13] This personal tone affects the way in which the letter is read, and the reason for its composition. Paul is not writing to combat specific people or problems. Instead, with similar vocabulary to that found in 1 Timothy,[14] he rehearses both present and possible threats to Timothy's ministry.

Sometimes in 2 Timothy, Timothy is warned of the opposition that is coming and the opposition that already exists (2 Tim 3:1, 5; 4:3). Myths played a significant role in helping identify the opponents of 1 Timothy because of their coupling with other facets of the Ephesian heterodoxy, like genealogical disputes and asceticism (1 Tim 1:4; 4:3).[15] However, 2 Timothy, although sharing vocabulary and style, is a different type of letter than 1 Timothy and Titus. Like Köstenberger, Johnson identifies 2 Timothy as a parenetic/protreptic letter.[16] He states, "The false teachers become the

11. The "last testament" described by Köstenberger is not the same testament of antiquity such as the *Testament of Abraham*, *Testament of the Twelve Patriarchs*, or *the Testament of Job*. Johnson argues that though Paul's death is looming and that Acts 20:17–35 fits the mold of the testament/farewell discourse genre, 2 Timothy better fits the paraenetic/protreptic letter genre. Johnson, *First and Second Letters of Timothy*, 321. Köstenberger states, "Since it (2 Timothy) is Paul's last recorded letter—written from a second and much more severe Roman imprisonment with Paul's martyrdom apparently imminent—it seems to some to take on the character of a last testament in certain respects, similar to 2 Peter, though in light of some important differences, it may be best to classify 2 Timothy as a personal paraenetic letter." Köstenberger, *Commentary on 1–2 Timothy and Titus*, 46.

12. Köstenberger, *Commentary on 1–2 Timothy and Titus*, 45–46.

13. Johnson, *First and Second Letters to Timothy*, 320.

14. As noted in the last chapter, there are significant verbal parallels between 1 and 2 Timothy and there are similar "problems" discussed in each. However, 2 Timothy portrays a different agenda and setting. For example, Paul mentions those "coming to the knowledge of the truth" (identical phrases) in 1 Tim 2:4 and 2 Tim 3:7. In 1 Tim 2:4 (εἰς ἐπίγνωσιν ἀληθείας ἐλθεῖν), Paul uses the terminology in a positive sense ("who desires all men to be saved and come to the knowledge of truth"). On the other hand, in 2 Tim 3:7 (εἰς ἐπίγνωσιν ἀληθείας ἐλθεῖν), Paul is warning Timothy of a certain type of man (or the women they teach) he is to avoid "who are always learning, but never able to come to the knowledge of truth." Cf. also Titus 1:1.

15. In other words, "myths" by themselves would have proven harder to identify without the connection with genealogies and asceticism.

16. Paraenesis and protrepsis are similar genres. Abraham Malherbe states, "Paraenesis is the moral exhortation in which someone is advised to pursue or to abstain from something." Malherbe, *Moral Exhortation*, 124. See also Johnson, who defines the parenetic letter as "advice in the form of exhortation that encourages certain actions and discourages others." Johnson, *First and Second Letters to Timothy*, 322. Similarly, the protreptic letter is common among philosophical schools, "which encourage

negative model that Timothy is to avoid."[17] In other words, the polemic of the letter is not the "reason" for having written the letter, but it is used "as a negative foil to the ideal image presented by Paul himself."[18] Paul is the model that Timothy is to imitate.[19] Johnson compares 2 Timothy to *To Demonicus* as the "best example of paraenesis in antiquity."[20] In this comparison, Johnson points out that 2 Timothy contains certain elements in an alliterative list: memory, model, mimesis, and maxims.[21] Paul draws Timothy's mind to the memory of his (Paul's) ancestral faith (2 Tim 1:3), Timothy's mother and grandmother's faith (1 Tim 1:5), Paul as a model to be imitated (2 Tim 1:13; 2:1–4; 3:10–11), and certain "maxims" that accompany the mimesis (2 Tim 2:22–26; 3:1–9, 12; 4:1–5). Johnson also points out that 2 Timothy is similar to Hellenistic moral philosophy, in that it is not only about knowing, but about practice. He states, "character is best learned by imitation."[22] The letter is sharply focused, not on community shaping (as in 1 Timothy), but on the shaping of Timothy's personal character, which shapes the character of community because of his vocation as teacher. Johnson concludes, "2 Timothy, then, has the overall form of a paraenetic letter. Since Paul is concerned, however, not simply with his delegate's personal virtue, but, above all, with his character as a delegate—that is, as a teacher of churches—he uses polemic in a way it is used in protreptic discourses, as a negative foil to the ideal image presented by Paul himself."[23]

The genre of the letter plays a significant role in its interpretation, even with regard to 2 Timothy 1:3, 8–12. As a paraenetic letter, Paul uses himself and his ancestors as examples of faithfulness to follow (2 Tim 1:3). The salvation (and calling) of Paul and Timothy is articulated as an axiomatic statement (or, maxim), rather than in response to a specific polemic,

---

young men to pursue the life of philosophy or, for those already professing the philosophical life, to live up to the ideals of their profession" (323). The major thrust of the protreptic letter as defined by Johnson is that the teacher provides the proper example for imitation, and that the imitation is accompanied by "maxims ('do this, avoid that') in antithetical fashion, using the polemic against false teachers in order to portray in vivid colors that which should be avoided" (324). For example, see 2 Tim 2:14–18, 23–26; 3:1–9, 13; 4:3–5.

17. Johnson, *First and Second Letters to Timothy*, 323.

18. Johnson, *First and Second Letters to Timothy*, 324.

19. Cf. 1 Cor 4:15–17; 11:1; Phil 3:17 where Paul instructs the churches to be imitators of him. 1 Cor 4:15–17 has special significance in that Paul urges the Corinthians to imitate him like children imitate a father, using Timothy as an example and teacher.

20. Johnson, *First and Second Letters to Timothy*, 322.

21. Johnson, *First and Second Letters to Timothy*, 322–23.

22. Johnson, *First and Second Letters to Timothy*, 325.

23. Johnson, *First and Second Letters to Timothy*, 324.

like that found in Galatians. He is not teaching Timothy anything new *per se*, instead he is relying on the agreed upon axiomatic rendering of the gospel in order to dispel any shame Timothy may feel toward the gospel, or of Paul, a prisoner of the gospel.

Translation: 2 Timothy 1:3

I give thanks to God who I worship from my forefathers[24] with a clean conscience[25] as I have constant[26] mention of you in my prayers night and day,

Paul's Clean Conscience ἀπό προγόνων

This passage has been selected because of Paul's reference to his προγόνοι, a word meaning "parents" or "forefathers."[27] One can be certain that Paul's forefathers were Jewish and, by that, worshiped the same God Paul did even after his conversion to Christianity.[28] However, much discussion of Pauline theology, if not stated, assumes Paul's disjunction from Judaism, or at least some forms of Judaism. There is no doubt that Paul has broken away from his former life that was characterized by zeal, professional advancement, and persecution of the church (Gal 1:14; Phil 3:4–9). However, there are also ways in which Paul maintains his Jewish heritage in its grounding in Scripture (2 Tim 3:16), the promise and purpose of God

24. The word used is πρόγονος ("parents") used only here (2 Tim 1:3) and 1 Tim 5:4 in the NT.

25. Although the term "conscience" (συνείδησις) is used regularly in Paul, this is the only time the word is used in 2 Timothy. Paul refers to "conscience" twice in Acts. Once, he refers to an "all good conscience" (Acts 23:1) and a "blameless conscience" (Acts 24:16).

26. This word, ἀδιάλειπτος ("constant"), is a NT *hapax legomenon*. See "ἀδιάλειπτος," BDAG, 19–20.

27. Johnson translates the term as "forebears." See Johnson, *First and Second Letters to Timothy*, 337.

28. When Paul defends his right to apostleship, he begins with his Jewish pedigree. He describes his lineage in several ways: as a Hebrew (2 Cor 11:22; Phil 3:5), "of the tribe of Benjamin" (Rom 11:1; Phil 3:5), an Israelite (Rom 11:1; 2 Cor 11:22; Phil 3:5), of the seed of Abraham (Rom 11:1; 2 Cor 11:22), "circumcised on the eight day" (Phil 3:5; "circumcision" is a ubiquitous way for Paul to refer to the Jews; e.g., Rom 2:29; 4:12; 15:8; 1 Cor 7:19; Gal 2:12; Eph 2:11; Phil 3:2–3; Col 2:11; 4:11; Titus 1:10), and a Pharisee (Phil 3:5; this is the only occurrence in all Pauline literature). He also describes his former life as one lived within "Judaism" (Gal 1:13–14; this is the only passage in which this term is used in the NT).

(Rom 15:8), monotheism (1 Cor 8:6), election (Rom 11:7), and morality (Rom 13:8–10).[29] One of the major characteristics of the NPP is emphasis on Paul's continuity with Judaism, so this passage is considerably important for the present work.

To begin, one must consider the precise identity of these "parents/forefathers." In context, Paul is likely speaking of his Jewish heritage that extended beyond his immediate ancestors.[30] Although the term πρόγονος is used only twice in the NT, both of which in the PE (1 Tim 5:4; 2 Tim 1:3), it is also used in ancient Greek literature, as well as in the LXX.[31] Originally the term referred to an older child, or sibling, but came also to mean either "parents," directly, or as L. T. Johnson translates it, "forebears."[32] It is clear that in 1 Timothy 5:4, the meaning is "parents" or "grandparents," or close lineage. Paul states that the children whose mother has been widowed should "make a return to their parents," echoing the command to honor father and mother (Exod 20:12; Deut 5:16; cf. 2 Tim 5:3). So, Paul could be referring to his actual mother and father (cf. 2 Tim 1:5) or simply his ancestors, generally speaking (2 Cor 11:22; Phil 3:5).[33] There is also the slight chance that this

29. Much of the discussion of continuity and discontinuity stands at the center of the debate surrounding the NPP. Often, the issue is not whether Paul maintained some Jewish elements, but to what extent he maintained these Jewish elements. For example, on Paul's continuity with the Scriptures, see Wright, *Pauline Perspectives*, 547–53. See also Dunn, *New Perspective on Paul*, 241–58. In this essay, "How New Was Paul's Gospel? The Problem of Continuity and Discontinuity," Dunn focuses on the continuity and discontinuity of the Pauline gospel. N. T. Wright focuses on Paul's continuous, but reconfigured, notions of monotheism, election, and eschatology. See Wright, *Paul and the Faithfulness of God*, 609–18 for his most robust discussion. He also discusses these three elements of Paul's gospel in Wright, *Pauline Perspectives*, 407–21.

Paul's use of Scripture is complex and variegated. He both dismisses the efficacy of the law, and yet often quotes, alludes, and "echoes" the OT Scriptures as evidence for the truth of the gospel or theology. Although beyond the scope of this project, there are several works that have proven invaluable in the discussion of Paul's use of the OT. See Moyise, *Old Testament in the New*, 117–48; Hays, *Echoes of Scripture in the Letters of Paul*; Hays, *Conversion of Imagination*; Watson, *Paul and the Hermeneutics of Faith*; Ellis, *Paul's Use of the Old Testament*; Dodd, *According to the Scriptures*. See also Dodd, *Old Testament in the New*. Dodd deals more in the use of the OT in the Gospels than with Paul, yet his is still an important work in biblical theology.

30. Jerome Quinn and William Wacker demonstrate that the term (πρόγονος) as used outside the NT is "most of the time" referring to "the forefathers of the Jews and in fact to rather more distant ancestors than grandparents." Quinn and Wacker, *First and Second Letters to Timothy*, 573.

31. Quinn and Wacker, *First and Second Letters to Timothy*, 573. Philip Towner also notes the ambiguous construction (ἀπὸ προγόνων) is attested in inscriptions even though it is rare in the NT. See Towner, *Letters to Timothy and Titus*, 449.

32. Johnson, *First and Second Letters to Timothy*, 337.

33. Quinn and Wacker point out that the term as used in the LXX most often refers

usage of the word may refer to his "parents" in the Christian faith, though there is no precedent for the word's usage in that way. Paul prefers the term "child"[34] and "father"[35] when speaking of the family of faith. Instead, Paul is more likely celebrating the clean conscience he shares with those in his family (or, ancestors in a more general sense) who came before him. Further evidence is Paul's reference to Timothy's "parents" (2 Tim 1:5; 2 Tim 3:14–5). William Mounce states that this reference points to the commonality of "spiritual heritage,"[36] which for Paul, was his Jewish heritage and belief in the one God of Israel, his promises, and the Scriptures. Though the phrase ἀπὸ προγόνων is ambiguous,[37] James Dunn concludes, "Either way, the phrase underlines the conviction that the religion of his ancestors (not just the Judaism that he had previously practiced; see Gal 1:13–4) had sought to serve God in good faith and that Paul's apostolic ministry was in direct continuity with it."[38] Dunn sees continuity in this passage with Paul's former faith. He writes, "The emphasis is in marked contrast with a considerable portion of Christian history wherein Christianity has found it necessary to establish its own identity by denigrating the Judaism that preceded it—Christianity as 'gospel' to Judaism's 'law.'"[39] Dunn takes the opportunity to demonstrate a foundational pillar of the NPP: that there was considerable continuity between Paul's Jewish faith and his faith in Christ, something (he argues, at least) has been missed by much of "Christian history."

Similarly, Paul instructs Timothy to "continue in what you have learned and become convinced of, knowing from whom you have learned it, and how from childhood you have known the sacred writings that are able to instruct you for salvation through faith in Christ Jesus" (2 Tim 3:15). Paul teaches the continuity of the ancient faith found and attested in the "sacred writings." So, just as Paul often quoted the Scripture as evidence

---

to "ancestors." See Quinn and Wacker, *First and Second Letters to Timothy*, 573. See also 3 Macc 6:38 for the use of πό with προγόνων.

34. τέκνον: 1 Cor 4:14, 17; 2 Cor 6:13; 12:14; Gal 4:19; Phil 2:22; 1 Thess 2:7, 11; 1 Tim 1:2; 2:18; 2 Tim 1:2; 2:1; Titus 1:4.

35. πατήρ: Rom 9:5; 11:28; 1 Cor 4:15; 1 Thess 2:11; 1 Tim 5:1–2.

36. Mounce, *Pastoral Epistles*, 467.

37. This ambiguous construction is attested in 3 Macc 6:28. George Knight offers "as my ancestors did" as the best translation. Knight, *Pastoral Epistles*, 367.

38. Dunn, "First and Second Letters," 833.

39. Dunn, "First and Second Letters," 834. He continues, "Denigration of predecessors is an unlovely way to advance one's own claims at any time" (834). In danger of making the same mistake, but worth pointing out, is that the NPP could be accused of such denigration of the traditional Reformed perspective, at least in its first articulations by Stendahl and Sanders.

of his own theological positions,[40] so here Timothy is to remember the Scripture so that he may be "equipped for every good work" (2 Tim 3:16).[41] In no way in 2 Timothy can one get the impression that Paul was opposed to "Judaism" as a whole. Instead, the faith of his "forebears," as well as the faith of Timothy's mother and grandmother, coupled with an appeal to the OT Scripture, provided the proper foundation for "salvation through faith in Christ Jesus" (2 Tim 3:15).

Paul's continuity with his ancestors is also witnessed elsewhere in his writings.[42] For example, in Romans 9:3–5 Paul acknowledges Israel's right to receive adoption as sons, stating,

> For I could wish that I myself were accursed, *separated* from Christ for the sake of my brethren, my kinsmen according to the flesh, who are Israelites, to whom belongs the adoption as sons, and the glory and the covenants and the giving of the Law and the *temple* service and the promises, whose are the fathers, and from whom is the Christ according to the flesh, who is over all, God blessed forever (NASB, italics original).

Paul also refers to the Israelites in the wilderness as "our fathers" to the Corinthians, who (one can assume) were primarily gentile (1 Cor 10:1). Thus, for Paul, faith in Christ meant somehow connecting with, and learning from, the forebears of Judaism, even if one was not ethnically Jewish (cf. Rom 2:28–29; Gal 6:15–16).[43] Also, in Romans 9:7–8, Paul redefines the "seed" or "descendants" (σπέρμα) of Abraham from a purely fleshly descent to the "children of promise." He states, "It is not the children of flesh who are the children of God, but the children of the promise are regarded as descendants" (τὰ τέκνα τῆς ἐπαγγελίας λογίζεται εἰς σπέρμα; Rom 9:8). He looks backward to the faith of Abraham as a proper continuous expression of faith to be emulated.

In Philippians 3:4–9, Paul mentions the things in his former life he gave up (ἡγοῦμαι σκύβαλα, "considered rubbish") for the sake of the gospel.

40. Paul quotes from the OT often. A few examples include: Rom 3:10–18; 4:7–9; 1 Cor 10:1–11; 2 Cor 9:9; Gal 3:8–10; Eph 5:31–32; Phil 2:10.

41. See Kruse, *Paul, the Law, and Justification*, 269.

42. It may be worth noting here that Paul, as he pointed to his own pedigree and circumcision as evidence of his equality with other apostles (2 Cor 11:22; Phil 3:5, "circumcised on the eight day"), he also had Timothy circumcised "because of the Jews in that place, for they all knew that his father was a Greek" (Acts 16:3). In other words, he had Timothy maintain his Jewish heritage, not for the sake of salvation, but in order to appease the Jews of the area.

43. Romans 2:28–29 is especially significant because Paul uses the term Jew, but explains it is a matter of the heart, not the flesh, that makes one "a Jew inwardly."

In contrast, in 2 Timothy 1:3, Paul acknowledges the positive aspect of the worship of his "forebears." Paul had not forsaken his God, which is exhibited in his use of the *Shema* (1 Cor 8:6; 1 Tim 2:5). In fact, Paul continues to find ways in which the promises of the OT find expression and fulfillment in Christ.[44] He had not outright rejected the faith and worship of his parents. Instead, what he had received from them was reimagined in Christ. Often, many assume that when Paul speaks of Timothy's "sincere faith," which was also found in his mother and grandmother, that this faith is that of faith in Christ.[45] Paul does use "faith" (πίστις) in this way most of the time. However, "faith" is also used to speak of Abraham's faith (Rom 4:9), the faith of the righteous (Heb 2:4), and the disputed statement, "from faith to faith" (Rom 1:17). Paul even asks, "Do we nullify the law through faith?" answering, "Let it not be! We establish the law" (Rom 3:31). So, for Paul, faith is both the foil for and establishment of the law. In Romans 4:16, Abraham is called the "father of us all" through his faith. Paul assumes continuity between Abraham's faith, God's promise, and faith in Christ Jesus. Johnson states regarding Eunice, "It is her character as a believer in God that is significant and exemplary."[46] In other words, "faith" is not restricted to only faith in Christ, though here, this is likely the case.[47]

One final aspect to consider is to what extent, and to which "forebears" is Paul referring? Paul highlights various aspects of his ethnicity and pedigree in response to critics and as an example of the futility of such things as ethnicity in the gospel. He uses his pedigree to characterize his apostleship positively in 2 Corinthians 11:22, using several different aspects of that pedigree: Hebrew (Ἑβραῖος), Israelite (Ἰσραηλίτης), and seed of Abraham (σπέρμα Ἀβραάμ). On the other hand, he uses several of these same terms in Phil 3:5 (ἐκ γένους Ἰσραήλ),[48] Galatians 1:13–14, Romans 9:3–5, and 11:1 in contrast to his life in Christ. Interestingly, though, Paul never uses προγόνος

---

44. E.g., Rom 4:17; 8:3–4; 9:32–33; 11:25–27; 15:8–9; 2 Cor 9:8–9; Gal 3:16.

45. E.g., see Guthrie, *Pastoral Epistles*, 124–25 who argues that Eunice was likely a Christian because of her marriage to a Greek. See also Fee, *1 and 2 Timothy, Titus*, 223; Knight, *Pastoral Epistles*, 369; Clark, *Pastoral Epistles*, 128; and, Marshall and Towner, *Critical and Exegetical Commentary on the Pastoral Epistles*, 694–95.

46. Johnson, *First and Second Letters to Timothy*, 339.

47. Cf. Acts 16:1. Acts calls Timothy's mother (though not named) a "Jewish woman of faith," or a "faithful Jewish woman" (γυναικὸς Ἰουδαίος πιστῆς). This may be in reference to her being a "believer" or to her faithfulness as a Jew. The fact that Timothy himself was already a believer seems to indicate his mother was also a believer. See Wright, *Paul for Everyone*, 86.

48. He adds here φυλῆς Βενιαμίν ("tribe of Benjamin") and κατὰ νόμον Φαρισαῖος ("as to the Law, a Pharisee"). He also includes his circumcision on the eighth day as part of his Jewish heritage as proof that he was born a Jew.

anywhere outside of 2 Timothy 1:3 to refer to his ancestors or his ancestral tradition. The inclusion here emphasizes Paul's attempt to resonate with Timothy, who himself shares the faith of his "parents." Within the framework of "memory, model, and mimesis,"[49] Paul looks to the clear conscience of his fathers as another level of continuity in his teaching.

2 Timothy 1:3: Resonance with the NPP

Paul's continuing concern for Israel and the inclusion of the gentiles is central to the articulation of his gospel. N. T. Wright is known for pointing to Romans 9–11 as the climax of Paul's theology in Romans.[50] Just because Paul is the apostle to the gentiles does not mean he has abandoned the Jews (Acts 9:15; 18:6; 22:21). In fact, even in Acts, Paul's ministry to the gentiles came about because of the Jewish refusal to listen, not Paul's reluctance to bring the gospel to them (Acts 18:5–6). This can also be witnessed in Paul's own writing. He states, "For I could wish that I myself were accursed, separated from Christ, for the sake of my brothers, my kinsmen according to the flesh" (Rom 9:1–5). Then again, in Romans 11:13–14, he states, "Inasmuch then as I am an apostle of Gentiles, I magnify my ministry, if somehow I might move to jealousy my fellow countrymen and save some of them." So, although only a passing reference in 2 Timothy, with regard to the memory and mimesis mentioned by Johnson, Paul is accentuating his un-ashamedness even in the midst of imprisonment. He emphasizes his resonance with his forebears, rather than demonstrating how he (or, they) has detracted from faith. As they worshiped in good conscience, so does he. The idea of a "clean conscience" is significant in its connection not to the forefathers alone, but in contrast to his being in chains. Even in imprisonment for the gospel, Paul's conscience is clean. For Paul, the gospel means suffering, which is attested, even in Galatians, as proof of the legitimacy of Paul's ministry (Gal 5:11). This segues into the next passage to be discussed where Paul asks Timothy not to be "ashamed" of the testimony of our Lord or of Paul himself, "his prisoner" (2 Tim 1:8).

Whereas in 1 Timothy the law is seen in a positive sense by way of exposing sin, now the "forebears" (of the ancient Jewish faith) are also seen positively. However, one must consider in what sense Paul's conscience finds resonance with his ancestors. It is in this distinction one finds Paul's thoughts concerning Judaism, and in some ways, the roots of his own

49. Johnson, *First and Second Letters to Timothy*, 322.

50. Wright, *Climax of the Covenant*, 231–56; Wright, *Pauline Perspectives*, 115–20, 392–406; Wright, *Paul and the Faithfulness of God*, 1156–1257.

faith and calling. Traditionally, discussions of Paul have revolved around the sharp dichotomy between "law" and "grace," and within that, between Judaism and faith in Christ. However, a seemingly innocuous statement like this one in 2 Timothy 1:3 demonstrates a relative level of continuity and mimicry on Paul's part to the ancient faith of his ancestors.[51] In fact, when Paul needed to do so, he used his Jewish pedigree, not as "rubbish" (Phil 3:8), but as evidence of his equality with some of the other apostles (2 Cor 11:22).[52] The very idea of righteousness being reckoned according to faith is taken from Abraham's faith prior to his circumcision (Gen 12:6) and demonstrates Paul's commitment to the permanence of the promise of God found in both Jews and gentiles.

After this short section on Paul's inherited faith, what is clearly shown is that although Paul may have been preoccupied with advancement in his prior life, the Jewish faith is not altogether characterized as one opposed to Christ. Rather, when properly approached, it is one that finds continuity with faith in Christ, or better, as one that understands Christ as its fulfillment. Both Paul and Timothy, in some fashion, learned faith from their "parents." Johnson explains,

> The first (of three dimensions of Paul's emphasis on faith) is how Paul makes no distinction between the faith of his Jewish ancestors (and Timothy's) and that shared by Timothy and himself (as "Christians"). This sense of continuity is deeply consonant with Paul's own emphasis on faith, especially in Romans, which argues that the fundamental human response is always toward or away from the living god, so that the faith of Abraham, the faith of Jesus, and the faith of Christians is much more continuous than it is discontinuous (Rom 3–4).

51. J. L. Houlden argues that the positive view of Paul's ancestors in 2 Tim 1:3 is pseudo-Pauline. He states, "The tension involved in Paul's movement from Judaism to Christ has been eliminated. For pseudo-Paul, that issue is dead, at least as far as it concerned the life of Paul." Houlden, *Pastoral Epistles*, 109.

52. In this passage, Paul refers, first, back to his Jewish heritage, then to his sufferings in Christ. In fact, for the only time, Paul refers to himself as a "Hebrew," an "Israelite," and a "descendant of Abraham," all in one place. He does refer to himself with these terms in other places (Rom 11:1; Phil 3:5), but not all together. This ordering is not arbitrary, but Paul's appeal to the origins of the gospel. He refers, not only to his tribal heritage (Israel), but to his heritage as the "seed" of Abraham, which he articulates more fully in Gal 3:16 and Rom 4:16–17. The point for Paul, in this passage, is that he is not an outlier coming into the flow of the main river, but that he had always been part of the flow, and now, more so, because of his willingness to suffer. In other words, his concern was not his ethnicity so much as his path to apostleship. Because, in this case, he is not referring to what he accomplished in his prior life and how he gave it up for the sake of the gospel.

In light of the crypto-Marcionism that afflicts so much Christian theology that bases itself on Paul, 2 Timothy highlights an important aspect of Paul's understanding in the undisputed letters that often is overlooked.[53]

Marshall also comments on the continuity with Paul and his ancestors. He explains, "The statement implies that Paul's ancestors also served God with a clear conscience, and thus a line of continuity is drawn between the faithful service of Israel and the service of Christians."[54] Also observe Acts 23:1, where a similar statement is used. His statement, "I have lived with a perfectly good conscience to this day," likely refers both to his prior life in Judaism and his continued "good conscience" even though he was being tried as a criminal. In both cases (Acts 23:1 and 2 Timothy 1:3), Paul's conscience is clean despite accusations and imprisonment.[55]

2 Timothy 1:8–12: Translation

(8) Therefore, do not be ashamed[56] of the testimony[57] of our Lord nor me his prisoner[58] but suffer with me[59] for the gospel according to the power of God (9) who saved us and called with a holy calling, not according to our works but according to his

---

53. Johnson, *First and Second Letters to Timothy*, 342. It is worth noting that Johnson in making this statement does not even discuss the NPP. His thoughts concerning Paul's continuity with the faith of his ancestors is founded upon this passage and passages within other Pauline epistles, and not from the hermeneutic of the NPP.

54. Marshall with Towner, *Pastoral Epistles*, 691.

55. J. N. D. Kelly writes, "As in the whole of this letter, he is painfully conscious of his position as a prisoner on a criminal charge, and is by implication protesting his innocence." Paul's imprisonment and suffering for the sake of Christ are central to his encouragement to Timothy to not be ashamed. Kelly, *Pastoral Epistles*, 155.

56. Rom 1:16; 6:21.

57. Raymond Collins contends that this "testimony" (μαρτύριον) is not synonymous with the gospel, but a reference to Christ's trial and crucifixion, which Paul is comparing to his own trial as a prisoner. Though this may be a viable option for interpretation in this passage, the use of the word elsewhere in Paul does not bear this meaning (1 Cor 1:6; 2 Cor 1:12; 2 Thess 1:10; 1 Tim 2:6). The only places the meaning of "testimony" as Christ's trial and crucifixion may be attested is Matt 10:18 and Mark 13:9. See Collins, *I & II Timothy and Titus*, 198–99.

58. Acts 23:18; 25:14 (Paul is called "prisoner"); Eph 3:1; 4:1; Phlm 1:1, 9.

59. This word ("to suffer with") is used only in 2 Tim 1:8; 2:3. I. Howard Marshall points out that the "simplex" form is used in 2 Tim 2:9 and 4:5, but that "the compound appears to be a new creation by the author for the occasion." Marshall with Towner, *Pastoral Epistles*, 703. Also, see "συγκακοπαθέω," BDAG, 951.

own purpose[60] and the grace which was given to us in Christ Jesus from all eternity, (10) but now having been revealed by the appearing[61] of our Savior Christ Jesus, who has abolished[62] death and brought to light[63] life and incorruptibility[64] through the gospel, (11) into which I was placed a preacher and apostle and teacher. (12) For this reason,[65] I also suffer[66] these things. For I know whom I have believed and I am convinced[67] that he is able to keep my deposit[68] until that day.

Suffering and Shame

Paul prepares Timothy for the inevitable suffering that comes with their calling.[69] He encourages Timothy, "do not be ashamed" (2 Tim 1:8) of the "testimony of our Lord" or of "me his prisoner." Paul uses himself as the proper example for suffering without shame. Even through his suffering, he exclaims, "but I am not ashamed" (2 Tim 1:12). Being a prisoner carried

60. The word, πρόθεσις ("plan, will, purpose"), is used in Rom 8:28; 9:11; Eph 1:11; 3:11; 2 Tim 1:9; 3:10. See "πρόθεσις," BDAG, 869.

61. ἐπιφάνεια ("appearing") is used only in the PE (1 Tim 6:14; 2 Tim 1:10; 4:1, 8; Titus 2:13) and once in 2 Thess 2:8. This is the only instance that refers to Christ's first coming. All other times refer to his second coming. The word ἐπιφαίνω is used in Titus 2:11 and 3:4, but the meaning is not as explicit with regard to Christ's coming in the flesh, but more about the appearance of God's grace, kindness, and love for humanity. See Lau, *Manifest in the Flesh*, 114–29, 160–76, 236–42, 250–56.

62. Although used quite often in Paul outside the PE (Rom 3:3, 31; 4:14; 6:6; 7:2, 6; 1 Cor 1:28; 2:6; 6:13; 13:8, 10, 11; 15:24, 26; 2 Cor 3:7, 11, 13, 14; Gal 3:17; 5:4, 11; Eph 2:15; 2 Thess 2:8), this is the only time καταργέω is used in the PE (2 Tim 1:10).

63. Used only three other times in Paul (φωτίζω, "to give light, enlighten"; 1 Cor 4:5; Eph 1:18; 3:9). See "φωτίζω," BDAG, 1074.

64. This word (ἀφθαρσία) is only a Pauline word used primarily in reference to the resurrection (Rom 2:7; 1 Cor 15:42, 50, 53, 54; Eph 6:24; 2 Tim 1:10).

65. The word used here (αἰτία) is used only by Paul in the PE (2 Tim 1:6, 12; Titus 1:13). However, it is used often in Acts (Acts 10:21; 13:28; 22:24; 23:28; 25:18, 27; 28:15, 20).

66. This is the only time this word (πάσκω) is used in the PE (2 Tim 1:12), although Paul uses the word elsewhere (1 Cor 12:26; 2 Cor 1:6; Gal 3:4; Phil 1:29; 1 Thess 2:14; 2 Thess 1:5).

67. This verb (πείθω) is used often in Paul (Rom 2:8, 19; 8:38; 14:14; 15:14; 2 Cor 1:9; 2:3; 5:11; 10:7; Gal 1:10; 5:7, 10; Phil 1:6, 14, 25; 2:24; 3:3, 4; 2 Thess 3:4; 2 Tim 1:5; 1:12; Phlm 1:21), but the similarity of 2 Tim 1:12 and Rom 14:14 ("I know and I am convinced") is worth pointing out.

68. παραθήκη ("deposit") is used only in the PE (1 Tim 6:20; 2 Tim 1:12, 14). See "παραθήκη," BDAG, 764.

69. Cf. Rom 8:16–23; 2 Cor 4:7–18.

shame, even for those who would associate with Paul. Paul uses the verb ἐπαισχύνομαι only in Romans and 2 Timothy.[70] Second Timothy 1:12 ("I am not ashamed") holds remarkable resemblance to Paul's statement in Rom 1:16, "For I am not ashamed of the gospel . . . ." In Romans 1:16, Paul describes the gospel as "the power (δύναμις) of God for salvation." Similarly, in 2 Timothy 1:12 Paul also finds his strength in God, "who is able (δυνατός) to guard what I have entrusted to him for that day." Paul also explains that God does not grant a spirit of timidity, but one of power (2 Tim 1:7; δύναμις). Paul knows that suffering and a society opposed to you and your teaching can easily produce shame about the message being proclaimed. It is shame and suffering that stand at the center of this passage and help provide a proper context for 2 Timothy 1:9–10 and Paul's contrast between salvation/calling and "our works." The verb ἐπαισχύνομαι serves as book ends to this passage: Timothy is not to be ashamed, just as Paul himself is not ashamed (2 Tim 1:8, 12).[71]

In this regard, Johnson discusses a culture of honor and shame in the Greco-Roman world and how Paul is appealing to a "higher court of opinion."[72] Obviously, through his imprisonment and the rejection of the Christians by the Jews and Romans alike, Paul's message was dishonorable to the world around him. However, Paul is convincing Timothy that the "court of opinion" that mattered was that of his ancestors/parents (2 Tim 1:3, 5), Paul himself (2 Tim 1:8, 11–12), the testimony of Jesus (2 Tim 1:8, 12), and the power of the gospel (2 Tim 1:8–10). These witnesses to the higher court of opinion help one understand Paul's statement of the gospel in 2 Timothy 1:9–10. Paul is not defining his theology of "law" and "works," as he does in Romans, Galatians, or even 2 Corinthians (2 Cor 3:1–8). Instead, he is explaining to Timothy that "our works" (which include imprisonment) are not the reason for God's salvation and call. It is instead God's purpose and grace. Shame need not accompany suffering and imprisonment if one is an instrument of God's purpose—"a herald and apostle and teacher" (2 Tim 1:11).

70. Rom 1:16; 6:21; 2 Tim 1:8, 12, 16.

71. There are striking parallels between 2 Tim 1:8–12 and Rom 6:21–23, except in the case of Rom 6:21–23, "shame" is used to denote the things done in a former life "of which you are now ashamed."

72. See Johnson, *First and Second Letters to Timothy*, 357–59.

The Gospel and Suffering[73]

Paul was in prison, not for being a criminal, but for the sake of the gospel and the opposition it caused.[74] Mounce writes, "Paul is αὐτοῦ, 'his,' i.e., Christ's, prisoner."[75] Paul's gospel, like Jesus's ministry and death, is founded upon suffering. As noted in the previous chapter, Paul appeals not to his accolades and accomplishments for his apostleship, but to his suffering and weaknesses (2 Cor 11:23—12:10). Paul tells Timothy later in this same letter, "Indeed, all who want to live a godly life in Christ Jesus will be persecuted" (2 Tim 3:12). A similar assumption can be seen in Galatians 5:11. Paul states, "But, brothers, why am I still being persecuted if I am still preaching circumcision? In that case the offense of the cross has been removed." Paul's assumption is that if he is preaching the "cross," in contrast to "circumcision," then he expects persecution to follow. In fact, Paul refers to the cross (or Christ) as a scandal, or offense.[76]

Paul's focus on suffering is an indispensable aspect of his salvation and calling. Paul encourages Timothy to "suffer with me for the gospel" (συγκακοπαθέω). Rather than a cause for shame, suffering is a testament to God's power. God's power is highlighted in weakness (2 Cor 12:9; 2 Tim 1:7–8), which is a thoroughly Pauline theological motif and the way in which Paul characterizes his apostleship. The interconnectedness of Paul's apostleship and suffering is recognized by both the NPP and traditional Pauline perspectives alike.

Saved

Shame is abated and suffering is endured "according to the power of God who saved us (κατὰ δύναμιν θεοῦ τοῦ σωσαντος ἡμᾶς)."[77] The verb σώζω is

73. This passage (and much of 2 Timothy, for that matter) demonstrates that Paul's message to Timothy contrasts with what some scholars like Philip Towner argue, that the PE accentuate a Bourgeoise Christianity, or what he calls *christliche Bürgerlichkeit*. See Towner, *Goal of Our Instruction*, 17. Those pursuing a "middle-class" life need not be encouraged to not be ashamed or be warned about suffering.

74. Robert Wall points out that Paul's suffering comes at the hands of the Romans, though he had not purposely sought to combat the empire. He states, "Rather, it is because the embrace of the gospel forges a vision of daily life and practices that threaten the empire's way of doing business." Wall and Steele, *1 & 2 Timothy and Titus*, 230.

75. Mounce, *Pastoral Epistles*, 480. The point is that Paul did not consider himself a prisoner of the state, and certainly not a criminal, but as a prisoner for the sake of Christ.

76. The word used is σκάνδαλον. See Rom 11:7–12; 9:32–33; 1 Cor 1:23.

77. Johnson claims that Paul's statement, "the God who saved us," is "intensely

used only twice in 2 Timothy (1:9; 4:18). The use in 2 Timothy 4:18 refers to Paul's (future) salvation "into his (the Lord's) heavenly kingdom." As noted in the explanation of one of the major tenets of the NPP, salvation plays a major role in Pauline theology, with justification as part of that process.[78] However, justification language is nearly absent in 2 Timothy.[79] In this specific passage, it is altogether absent. Thus, one can conclude that justification is not the specific aspect of the gospel necessary for Paul to encourage Timothy with regard to their calling.[80] In fact, Paul's discussion of salvation (and calling) is not the primary reason for his writing this letter.[81] Instead, Paul is stating what seems to be axiomatic. Even though he and Timothy had been saved,[82] it was not of their own doing (οὐ κατὰ ἔργα ἡμῶν, "not according to our works").

---

personal and experiential," comparing it to 1 Tim 1:15. Johnson, *First and Second Letters to Timothy*, 348.

78. Cf. Rom 5:9 and Titus 3:5–7. "Called" (καλέω, thirty-three times) is used roughly as often as "saved" (σώζω, twenty-nine times). In fact, in the following examples of the use of the word "called," only here in 2 Tim 1:9 is "saved" and "called" used in close proximity. One should note that the count is only for the word καλέω. If any cognates such as ἐπικαλέω or παρακαλέω are added, the frequency is higher.

79. Cf. 2 Tim 2:22; 3:16; 4:8.

80. Although the term justified (δικαιόω) is not used, Mounce states, "the thought and vocabulary of verses 9–10 are so fully Pauline that they may be viewed as Paul's own discussion of the gospel." Mounce, *Pastoral Epistles*, 481.

81. Even Robert Cara calls 2 Tim 1:8–10 a "wonderful digression." See Cara, *Cracking the Foundation*, 166.

82. The word σώζω is often found in the future in the undisputed Pauline epistles (Romans 5:9–10; 9:27; 10:9, 13; 11:14 [could be an aorist subjunctive], 26; 1 Cor 3:15; 7:16; the word σώζω is not used at all in Galatians). However, σώζω is also found in the aorist subjunctive (1 Cor 5:5; 9:22; 10:33; 1 Thess 2:16), and the aorist infinitive (cf. 1 Cor 1:21), which do not indicate a temporal element. Garwood Anderson points out that salvation is usually future-referring, while justified is always (with one exception; Rom 2:13) past-referring. See Anderson, *Paul's New Perspective*, 301–2. However, in Titus 3:5 "saved" is in the aorist indicative (ἔσωσεν) and refers to a past event. Cf. Rom 5:9–10 where "saved" is in the future tense (σωθησόμεθα), but the participial use of "justified" is the same as that found in Titus 3:7 (δικαιωθέντες). In this regard, Dunn states, "The consistent aorist tenses (describing what has already been accomplished) need not imply a changed perspective from the earlier Paulines (where salvation is essentially a future good, the goal of the saving process; see e.g., Rom 5:9–10; 1 Cor 1:18); note, after all, 2:10." Dunn, "First and Second Letters," 835–36. See also Gordon Clark's response to C. K. Barrett who argues that the PE are not authentic based (in part) on the PE's use of salvation language. See Clark, *Pastoral Epistles*, 132–33. He explains, "We do not deny that Paul often used the word σώζειν with a future reference. We simply reject Barrett's statement that 'In Paul salvation refers *almost exclusively* to a final eschatological act.'" Similarly, see Johnson, *First and Second Letters to Timothy*, 355.

Paul's statement of salvation and calling corresponds in some ways to Eph 2:8–10 and combats any idea of self-achieved salvation. The issue at hand is why Paul would articulate the gospel in this way ("saved and called") compared to the way in which he does in Romans or Galatians. The gospel is articulated in a similar way in undisputed Paul, but usually in a general statement, not in response to specific problems (1 Cor 1:21–29; Gal 1:14).[83] So, even here, one does not get the impression that Timothy was advocating "works-righteousness," or that even those with whom Timothy was engaged did. However, Paul is careful to let Timothy know that suffering with him for the sake of the gospel is at the initiative of God ("purpose and grace") just as were their salvation and calling. This truth is self-evident and fully Pauline. However, Robert Cara states, "All of this emphasis on what God did for us in salvation shows that 'works' as a *contrast* must be considered works-righteousness theology."[84] And, by that, he means as a contrast to "covenantal nomism." If anything has been demonstrated up to this point, it is that Paul is appealing first to his continuative faith with his ancestors. He is not combating their works-righteousness (though, they may have been "legalistic"), or better, he is not combatting them at all. Cara's emphasis demonstrates a reading of Paul within the boundaries and categories of Pauline scholarship. In this passage, Paul does not seem to have these same categories in mind.

More informative than the coupling of salvation apart from "our works" is the absence of justification (δικ-) language. This absence reiterates the NPP's argument that justification is not Paul's primary category of salvation, but often serves as a response to a certain polemic, or is used as a specific metaphor, not as a response to legalism. This statement by Paul, without doubt, disproves the veracity of "legalism." That much is clear. However, Paul does so in order to help Timothy stay away from such a mindset—a mindset not necessarily picked up from a legalistic form of Judaism (though it could have been), but a mindset Paul anticipates could be drawn from his salvation and call in the gospel, or as an axiomatic statement of the gospel as a means to encourage Timothy in the face of shame and suffering. Paul is demonstrating that suffering or not, imprisonment or not, "works" are not what save. It is as if, for the sake of strengthening his argument, that Paul is reiterating a well-known, understood fact of the gospel in contrast to the ubiquitous nature of mankind's struggle for accomplishment.

---

83. When Paul uses the term "called," it is sometimes accompanied by "justified" (cf. Rom 8:28–30). Besides 2 Tim 1:9, "saved" and "called" are not used together by Paul.

84. Cara, *Cracking the Foundation*, 168, italics original.

Called

The verb "called" (καλέω) is used only twice in the PE (1 Tim 6:12; 2 Tim 1:9).[85] The word "calling" (κλῆσις) is used only here in the PE (1 Tim 1:9). The idea of one's calling is not only reserved for apostles or those in leadership positions like Timothy and Paul. Paul speaks to the Corinthians in reference to their calling, as well as specifically to slaves (1 Cor 7:20). In fact, it seems in every instance, except for this one, that Paul speaks of "calling" as that which is common to all Christians (Rom 11:29; 1 Cor 1:26; Eph 1:18; 4:1, 4; 2 Thess 1:11). In this case, one gets the impression that when Paul is speaking to Timothy, he is referring to the special calling they share, but that is not necessarily the case.[86] When referring to the calling of others, Paul also mentions their special, specific gifts (1 Cor 7:17-21). In the context of 2 Timothy 1:9, what Paul and Timothy share is salvation, calling, suffering, and grace (1 Tim 1:8).[87]

The phrase "holy calling" (κλήσει ἁγίᾳ) could be understood in two ways. First, "holy" may be modifying calling, indicating that the call itself is what is holy (i.e., it comes from God).[88] However, secondly, "holy" may be a call to a holy life.[89] Mounce argues that it could mean both. He states, "In other words, God's call is ethical: God does not just call believers; he calls them toward himself, toward holiness."[90] In Romans 1:7, Paul uses the phrase κλητοῖς ἁγίοις, referring to Christians as "called saints." Similarly, I. Howard Marshall highlights Ephesians 4:1, wherein the holiness of the calling is what leads to a holy life, "Live in a way which is worthy of the

85. Although only used twice in the PE, as noted above, "called" (καλέω) is used just as often in Paul as "saved." Although simply word frequency and not taking into account other aspects of "calling" and "salvation," the frequency of usage of the term "called" by Paul demonstrates the importance for Paul's theology.

86. In fact, what is likely the case is that, although Paul is speaking of their specific calling, the truth of the nature of every Christian's calling is assumed. In other words, Paul is moving from the overall truth to its specific manifestation in himself and Timothy. Johnson notes the problems one faces in interpreting this section on "calling." He concludes, "Given the following contrast between human effort and God's gift, it is probable that the wider sense of 'calling to God's people' is intended." See Johnson, *First and Second Letters to Timothy*, 348.

87. Garwood Anderson identifies this use of "call" as a soteriological use. See Anderson, *Paul's New Perspective*, 18n10.

88. See Köstenberger, *1-2 Timothy and Titus*, 218, who seems to prefer this meaning opting for the translation, "holy calling," stating, "The holy God has set us apart for ministry."

89. For example, see Kelly, *Pastoral Epistles*, 162.

90. Mounce, *Pastoral Epistles*, 482.

calling by which you were called."[91] For Paul, salvation and calling are interconnected (Rom 9:24–27). However, "calling" has not been a primary
category used in discussions of Paul, law, and grace, even though God's call
is listed in the actions of God for those for whom things work together for
good (Rom 8:28–30).[92] The significance of the call in 2 Timothy 1:9 is to
highlight the holiness of the call, which is not characterized by "our works,"
but by the holiness and initiative of God.

"Not According to Our Works"

One of the tenets of the NPP outlined in chapter 1 is that of the law and
"works of law." The specific terminology, "works of law (ἔργα νόμου)," is restricted only to Romans and Galatians in contrast to justification by works.[93]
The idea of "works," generally, is usually regarded positively by Paul in the
PE.[94] One could argue that even in 2 Timothy 1:9, the idea is not negative
per se, but just that "works" are not the catalyst for salvation and calling.
Both Paul and Timothy will have participated in good works before their
salvation and calling, and they may also have been "accomplished" as far
as their contemporaries were concerned.[95] These works are not dismissed
outright, though they are dismissed with regard to salvation and calling. In
contrast to the underlying assumption that bad works and sinfulness earn
death (Rom 3:23), and that good works earn life (Rom 2:6–8), in this case,
no works (whether bad or good) remove one from God's purpose or earn
his favor (cf. Rom 8:28–30; 9:10–11).

91. See Marshall with Towner, *Pastoral Epistles*, 705. Marshall decides "holy calling" as that which comes from God is the best option for the meaning of the phrase.
Raymond Collins states that there is a threefold meaning within this "holy" call. He
continues, "The call is holy not only because it proceeds from God; it is also holy insofar
as it is a call to live a holy life, a call to participate in the life of God's holy people." Collins, *I & II Timothy and Titus*, 199–200.

92. The term "justified" (δικαιόω) also appears in this list while "saved" does not.
It should be noted that following this list is Paul's discussion of calling in Romans 9,
where there is a clustering of καλέω being used (Rom 9:7, 12, 24–26). There is another
clustering of καλέω in 1 Corinthians 7 (1 Cor 7:15, 17, 18, 20, 21, 22, 24).

93. Rom 3:20, 27–28; Gal 2:16; 3:2, 5, 10.

94. 1 Tim 2:10; 3:1; 5:10, 25; 6:18; 2 Tim 2:21; 3:17; 4:5; Titus 1:16; 2:7. For a positive
sense of "works" outside the PE see Rom 2:6–7; 13:3; 1 Cor 3:13–14; 9:1; 15:58; 16:10;
2 Cor 9:8; Gal 6:4; Eph 2:10; Phil 1:6, 22; Col 1:10; 3:17; 1 Thess 1:3; 5:13; 2 Thess 2:17.

95. Timothy was a special delegate with a unique ministry, which may be seen as
an accomplishment. It is quite clear Paul was "accomplished" in Judaism before his
conversion to Christ (Gal 1:13–14; Phil 3:4–7).

Paul's teaching to Timothy is not the same as the argument being made in Romans 3:20–28 and Galatians 3:1–11 regarding justification by faith.[96] James Dunn, who has done the most work with the idea of "works of law" among NPP adherents, defines "works of law" as "'covenantal nomism,' where both words are important—law as functioning within and in relation to the covenant, law as expression of and safeguard for the covenant, law as indicating Israel's part of the agreement graciously initiated by God.'"[97] It is "covenantal nomism" that had created the problem of gentile exclusion exhibited in Romans and Galatians. One can even see this mentality in Paul's former life as expressed in Philippians 3:6–9, which was a life of exclusion and accomplishment. N. T. Wright concurs with Dunn's basic definition.[98] In contrast to some who might argue the NPP should include 2 Timothy 1:8–9 (as well as Titus 3:5–8) into its understanding of "works," Dunn discusses 2 Timothy 1:9 and Titus 3:5 in his essay, "Whatever Happened to 'Works of the Law?'"[99] Dunn's treatment of these passages is by no means extensive in that he deals with the passages together based on the assumption that "they share common features and seem to be making the same point."[100] According to Dunn, the point they make, in contrast to the specific polemic of Romans 3 and Galatians 2 and 3, is "all human acceptability before God is dependent not on human activity but on divine grace from start to finish."[101] He also explains, "The gospel is formulated not despite Israel or to contradict Judaism, but by appeal to Israel's most fundamental insight into divine grace."[102] Dunn concludes, "In a word, the Pastorals add little or nothing to

96. Roberts Karris discusses the omission of the phrase "works of law" by stating, "That question, reflected in Rom 3:28, is in the past. But our author is true to the Pauline gospel by retaining Paul's faith insight that humans do not save themselves." Karris, *Pastoral Epistles*, 16.

97. Dunn, *Theology of Paul the Apostle*, 355. As for his work on "works of law" see also Dunn, *New Perspective on Paul*, 111–30, 207–20, 333–40, 375–88, 407–22; and Dunn, *Epistle to the Galatians*, 135–38.

98. See Wright, *Pauline Perspectives*, 334–38. See also Wright, *Climax of the Covenant*, 142, wherein Wright translates the phrase as "works of Torah."

99. He explains, "The simplest solution of our small conundrum would seem to be, then, that when Paul speaks of 'works of the law' he meant 'works we have done,' and that the later writings, despite omitting 'of the law,' were in effect repeating just what Paul had said in Romans and Galatians. And this, indeed, is the solution which most hold—or to be precise, which most take for granted." Dunn, *New Perspective on Paul*, 376.

100. Dunn, *New Perspective on Paul*, 385.

101. Dunn, *New Perspective on Paul*, 386.

102. Dunn, *New Perspective on Paul*, 386. Raymond Collins similarly states, "The notion that God's salvific will is accomplished independently of human acts is biblical and Jewish." He cites Philo as evidence (*Leg.* 3.77, 83). See Collins, *I & II Timothy and Titus*, 200.

our quest for clarification of Paul's affirmation that 'by works of the law shall no flesh be justified before God' (Rom 3:20)."[103] So, though one may expect and assume that "works" are the same as "works of law," the position of the NPP is clear that "works of law" are specific covenantal works discussed in only Romans and Galatians and that they are not understood to be legalistic works. Dunn even states outright regarding 2 Tim 1:9,

> "Not according to our works" is an equally strong echo of a cen-
> tral Pauline statement of the gospel (Rom 3:20, 28; Gal 2:16),
> but there is a significant shift of emphasis. The concept of works
> seems to have broadened out from a more specific 'works of
> law' (Paul was usually thinking of the things the law required
> and that distinguished Israel from other nations) to "our works,"
> "anything we have done" (NIV, meaning any attempt to secure
> our own righteousness; cf. Eph 2:8; Titus 3:5).[104]

This "shift of emphasis" will be discussed further in some concluding remarks in chapter 6. For now, what is important to glean from the above statement of Dunn, is the realization, even by Dunn, that 2 Timothy 1:9–10 is a broad, generalized understanding of works, which is very much in line with the tra-ditional perspective, but also does not negate the position of the NPP.

The exact phrase "works of law" and $\delta\iota\alpha$- language are absent from 2 Timothy 1:8–12, both of which are usually found together in Romans and Galatians (Rom 3:20, 28; Gal 2:16; cf. also Gal 3:11).[105] As already pointed out, Paul does not discuss justification at all in 2 Timothy 1:8–12. Instead, Paul is reminding Timothy that their respective salvation and calling did not come by works, but the more fundamental truth that they came at the initiative of God. So, "works" in 2 Timothy 1:9 is likely broader than "works of law."[106] The natural understanding of recompense is that one is rewarded

---

103. Dunn, New Perspective on Paul, 53–54. This is an overstatement by Dunn. The PE do help in clarifying the more foundational relationship between works and salva-tion (and, in Titus 3:3–7, justification) outside the specific polemic of gentile inclusion and Jewish superiority. Even he, above, notices the "significant shift of emphasis," not an altogether different theology.

104. Dunn, "First and Second Letters," 836.

105. In Gal 3:11, the entire phrase "works of law" is not used, but only "works."

106. In defining "works of law" both Dunn and Wright point to a manuscript from the DSS, 4QMMT. Within this text is the phrase, "works of law," the only attested use of the phrase outside Pauline literature. They claim that the use in 4QMMT is compa-rable to the NPP's definition of Paul's use in Romans and Galatians. Because this study is not critiquing the NPP directly, there will be no extended treatment of 4QMMT and its parallels with "works of law" in Paul. For further study, and a more thorough explanation see Wright, Pauline Perspectives, 332–55; Dunn, New Perspective on Paul, 333–40; De Roo, "Works of the Law" at Qumran and in Paul; Abegg, "Paul, 'Works of

for doing good and punished for doing bad. Paul himself says so (Rom 2:5–8). In this immediate context, imprisonment does not mean Paul does not deserve God's call, or that if Paul had not been in prison, he would deserve his salvation and calling all the more. Like all Pauline theology, salvation and calling are rooted in God. This is the only place that Paul qualifies works with "our" (ἔργα ἡμῶν).[107] In the context of such a personal letter, this *our* likely refers to himself and Timothy (and not the inclusive first-person plural of all Christians, though the statement could be true for everyone else as well).[108] Even in Eph 2:8–10, Paul does not use the first person, but the third person (οὐκ ἐξ ὑμῶν) as well as "not from works" (οὐκ ἐξ ἔργων) which would exclude boasting. However, in Titus 3:3–7, Paul does use the first-person plural, and likely he does so in a more inclusive way incorporating himself, Titus, and the rest of the Cretan Christians.

This passage is similar to Romans 9:10–11. Paul writes, "For though they (Jacob and Esau) were not yet born, and had not done anything good or bad, in order that God's purpose according to his choice might stand, not because of works, but because of Him who calls." In the context of Romans 9, what is being emphasized is God's choice, even though it may seem unjust. Similarly, in 2 Timothy 1:9, Paul is confronting Timothy with the same truth—their calling and salvation have nothing to do with their works. The difference is the context of the argument.

Johnson translates ἔργα as "accomplishments."[109] I. Howard Marshall writes, "We need not doubt that the Jewish stress on the works of the law lies at the bottom of the phrase, but here it is generalized to cover any kind of deeds."[110] He adds, "It must be insisted that this is not a *difference* from Paul's teaching or a 'new soteriological conception.'"[111] One can see both Dunn and Marshall's point clearly. Neither argue that 2 Timothy 1:9 is un-Pauline, but that the problems faced in Romans and Galatians are not exhibited in 2 Timothy. Instead, Paul is stating a fact more foundational

the Law' and MMT," 53–55.

107. Compare with 1 Tim 1:8–16.

108. In fact, many commentators assume this refers to everyone without making an explicit statement saying so. For example, see Johnson, *First and Second Letters to Timothy*, 348. There are some who argue that 1 Tim 1:9–10 is an early Christian creed or hymn. For example, see Hultgren, *1–2 Timothy, Titus*, 112–13; Towner, *Letters to Timothy and Titus*, 466–67; Fiore, *Pastoral Epistles*, 141.

109. He states he translated ἔργα in this way "to avoid the more technical sense of 'works' that Paul sometimes employs (Gal 2:16) in favor of the broader sense of 'human deeds' that he uses more frequently (e.g., Rom 2:6–7; 15:18; 1 Cor 3:13–15; 9:1; 2 Cor 11:15; Gal 5:19; 6:4; Phil 1:22)." Johnson, *First and Second Letters to Timothy*, 348.

110. Marshall with Towner, *Pastoral Epistles*, 705.

111. Marshall with Towner, *Pastoral Epistles*, 705, italics original.

to his gospel— salvation and calling are according to the purpose of God, not to "our" works.

This declaration even finds expression in Romans 4:1–8. Paul states the fundamental truth that "work" involves wages and repayment (Rom 4:4). However, Abraham was reckoned righteous by his faith in God before his work, thus he was receiving, not what was due him, but what was "reckoned."[112] Even David writes that blessedness is reckoned by God because of forgiveness, not works (Rom 4:6–8).[113] It is this fundamental truth that leads Paul then to focus on circumcision (a "work of law") in Rom 4:9. His question is, "Is this blessing then upon the circumcised, or upon the uncircumcised also?" Paul works from the fundamental truth (that works earn, but favor is a gift) to the more specific example of circumcision. Paul does not have to make that move with Timothy. He simply states a foundational declaration of his gospel. Both he and Timothy agreed that nothing had been earned, but given.

The basic, underlying controversy with the NPP lies not in what Paul is arguing in 2 Timothy 1:8–12, or how his argument compares with Romans, Galatians, and even Ephesians 2:8–10. The controversy is the understanding of Judaism as either "legalistic"[114] or "covenantal nomistic" and Paul's response to it. In 2 Timothy 1:8–12, a specific controversy with Judaism cannot be traced. Whatever elements of Judaism are present, they are seen in a positive light (2 Tim 1:3; 3:16). So, the lines of contention as they have been drawn between the traditional perspective and the NPP do not prevent either from accepting Paul's axiomatic statement that God saves and calls "not according to our works," nor does 2 Timothy 1:9 necessitate a traditional reading of Galatians and Romans in those passages that contain the phrase "works of law." This is not to say that the NPP is "correct," but that in the context of 2 Timothy and "works," the hermeneutic of the NPP is not such that it cannot accommodate Paul's theology in 2 Timothy.[115]

---

112. The term used in Rom 4:3–11 is λογίζομαι ("to reckon, consider"). Thus, Abraham was considered righteous apart from works.

113. The term λογίζομαι is also used in Rom 4:6, 8, the latter being a quotation from Ps 32:2.

114. It should be noted that although this work often uses the term "legalistic" or "legalism," there is no semantic correlation in the early Jewish literature to "legalism." See Bird, *Anomalous Jew*, 32–35.

115. Similarly, even though not discussing the PE, Michael Bird issues a warning to either/or approaches to the NPP and Lutheran perspective. See Bird, *Saving Righteousness of God*, 88–112, specifically his discussion and nuance of "merit theology" (89–94).

Purpose and Grace

Although some understand the phrase "purpose and grace" to be a hendiadys, Mounce sees "his own" (ἰδίαν) as modifying only purpose because "which he gave" (τὴν δοθεῖσαν) modifies grace.[116] "Purpose" (πρόθησιν) is used only one other time in the PE and refers to Paul's purpose to be followed by Timothy (2 Tim 3:10). However, Paul does use the term in Romans and Ephesians (Rom 8:28; 9:11; Eph 1:11; 3:11). In these cases, he is referring to God's purpose. "Grace" (χάρις) is used often by Paul, but only once in connection with "purpose."[117]

As noted above, this passage (2 Tim 1:9–10) is remarkably similar to Romans 9:11 wherein Paul uses much of the same language referring to "calling," "works," and "purpose." Paul writes, "For though they (the twins, Jacob and Esau) were not yet born and not done anything good or bad, so that God's purpose (πρόθεσις) according to his choice (ἐκλογήν) would stand, not because of works (οὐκ ἐξ ἔργων) but because of Him who calls (τοῦ καλοῦντος)." One significant difference is that the term saved is not used.[118] Romans 8:28 also combines purpose and calling. "And we know that God causes all things to work together for good for those called according to his purpose (τοῖς κατὰ πρόθεσιν κλητοῖς)." Salvation by grace has its Pauline correlative in Eph 2:5, 10 (χάριτί ἐστιν σεσῳσμένοι),[119] whereas "justified by his (ἐκείνου) grace" in Titus 3:7 is also found in Rom 3:24 ("being justified as a gift by his [αὐτοῦ] grace;" cf. also Gal 5:4).[120]

116. Mounce, *Pastoral Epistles*, 483. The entire phrase is κατὰ ἰδίαν πρόθεσιν καὶ χάριν τὴν δοθεῖσαν ἡμῖν. See also Towner, *Letters to Timothy and Titus*, 469, who states, "But the two concepts 'purpose' and 'grace,' are distinct and should not be merged together."

117. It is used multiple times in every Pauline letter. Notable parallels to this passage include: Rom 11:6, "But if it is by grace, it is no longer from works, otherwise grace is no longer grace"; 1 Cor 15:10, grace is used three times in reference to Paul's own vocation and work; Gal 1:15, "he called me through his grace."

118. For further resemblance with the entire passage (2 Tim 1:3–12) and Paul's reference to his and Timothy's "forebears," see Rom 9:3–12.

119. Ephesians 2:5 and 8 are the only times σώζω is used in the perfect.

120. Although the purpose of this study is not to argue for or against Pauline authorship, the sophistication of the similarity of language between undisputed Paul and 1–2 Timothy is remarkable. It leads one to doubt a pseudepigrapher is capable of manufacturing such sophisticated use of Pauline vocabulary while maintaining a relative degree of originality.

Death and Life

Paul's suffering is endured because of his hope granted through Jesus: the abolition of death and the illumination (φωτίσαντος) of life and immortality. This is where Paul departs from his Jewish roots. The faith granted by his forebears bore witness to Christ, but Christ's death and resurrection are what provide hope and his appointment as "preacher and apostle and teacher" (2 Tim 1:11).[121] Although not directly relevant to the present study, Paul's suffering as preacher, apostle, and teacher is nonetheless an important aspect of Paul's life and theology. His suffering, what could be understood as "works" in this general sense, is not what instigated God's calling and salvation. Instead, his vocation and ministry are the reason for his suffering. He "works" because of his trust in the one to whom he has entrusted himself (cf. Eph 2:8–10).

Conclusions: Paul's Heritage of Faith, Works, and the NPP

In sum, these two passages (2 Tim 1:3, 8–12) find some resonance with the NPP. In 2 Timothy 1:3, Paul looks positively to his forebears (as well as Timothy's; 2 Tim 1:5) explaining, "I thank God, whom I serve with a clear conscience the way my forefathers did." Although no one could argue Paul was perfectly content with Judaism as it was after his conversion (based on other letters), Paul does find resonance with the worship and conscience of his forebears, rather than using Judaism, or the Torah, as an opponent of his gospel.[122] Pedigree and spiritual heritage are not "works," even though one does get the impression Paul may have considered his descent a resumé of sorts, particularly in regard to his equality with the other apostles and his desire for his kinsmen—through whom Christ came—to be saved (cf. Phil 4:7,

121. Cf. 1 Tim 2:7 where the identical phrase is used with the addition of "to the Gentiles." The phrases are so similar, a textual variant evidences the addition of "to the Gentiles" in 2 Tim 1:11. Regarding this phrase, Quinn and Wacker write concerning this phrase in contrast to the same one in 1 Tim 2:7, "It is also much more cunningly fitted into the total structure of this sentence where each part has telescoped out of the other into the order: God–Grace–Christ–Gospel–Apostle." Quinn and Wacker, *First and Second Letters to Timothy*, 602.

122. Although, as noted, 2 Tim 1:3 is not often discussed by scholars with regard to Paul's relationship with his past in Judaism, Dietrich Bonhoeffer in a letter to a friend does mention this passage using Paul as an example of the gift of the past. He states, "Continuity with our past is a wonderful gift! St. Paul wrote 2 Tim 1:3a as well as 1 Tim 1:11." See Bonhoeffer, *Letters and Papers from Prison*, 89. Bonhoeffer points out the complexity of Paul's relationship with the Judaism of his past.

"If anyone has a mind to put confidence in the flesh, I far more"; 2 Cor 11:22; Rom 9:3–4). Paul recognizes the difference between fleshly descent and spiritual descent (cf. Phil 3:2–3). Whereas his former life revolved around his fleshly descent and advancement within his own ethnic group, his new life continued to recognize the heritage of his spiritual descent. Sometimes, these two (spiritual and fleshly descent) overlap. For example, in Romans 9:6–7 Paul explains, "For they are not all Israel who are from Israel nor are they all children because they are Abraham's seed." For Paul, fleshly descent did not guarantee spiritual descent. Robert Wall clarifies, "This expression of continuity with his ancestors, then, lays claim to something more important than what appears at first reading: Paul's Gentile mission is in continuity with the biblical promises God made to Israel."[123] Paul states as much later in 2 Timothy, "But the Lord stood with me and strengthened me, so that through me the proclamation might be fully accomplished, and that all the Gentiles might hear" (2 Tim 4:17). So, for Paul, his gentile mission was predicated upon the faith of Israel and Israel's God (Rom 3:1–2).

The next passage, 2 Timothy 1:8–12, also finds relative resonance with the NPP, although a proper comparison is not altogether possible. This difficulty of a proper comparison demonstrates the need for a fuller articulation of Paul's theology, which must include the PE. The NPP has focused on terms like "works of law" and "justification," neither of which are present in this passage. However, one does find enough commonality with undisputed Paul (especially Romans) that 2 Timothy 1:8–12 does not necessarily disprove the NPP's hermeneutic regarding covenantal nomism, or the NPP's characterization of Paul's opponents in Romans and Galatians, or even his characterization of his former life in places like Philippians 3:4–7. However, in order to demonstrate the fundamental character of Paul's statement here, which can be missed if Paul's theology is bound to Romans, Galatians, and Philippians, Colin Kruse states, "Thus, even in a context which does not demand it, Paul's conviction that salvation is independent of human works, and dependent instead upon the grace of God manifested in Jesus Christ, is emphasized."[124]

To illustrate the problem of comparing this passage with the hermeneutic of the NPP, note that Robert Cara claims with regard to 2 Timothy 1:8–10, "In context, the past tense of these two aspects of God's work relates to justification and current sanctification."[125] Cara is straining the meaning of this passage. There is nothing said of justification in this

---

123. Wall and Steele, *1 & 2 Timothy and Titus*, 219.

124. Kruse, *Paul, the Law, and Justification*, 269.

125. Cara, *Cracking the Foundation*, 167.

passage, and for that matter, 2 Timothy as a whole. In fact, "righteousness" in 2 Timothy is something to be pursued (2 Tim 2:22) and learned (2 Tim 3:16), not a status that is received. He also states, "All of this emphasis on what God did for us in salvation shows that 'works' as a *contrast* must be considered works righteousness soteriology."[126] Again, there is no mention of "righteousness" in this passage. Cara assumes that the *us* here is referring to all Christians. Although the statement Paul makes is true of everyone who is saved and called, in this specific instance, he is speaking of himself and Timothy, with regard to shame and suffering.[127] As is often the case, preconceived questions and categories are brought into the core of a discussion, sometimes distorting the original meaning of the text which is clear in its original context. It seems Cara wants to compare this passage with Paul's theology of justification,[128] when this passage is better compared to Romans 9:10–12 and Ephesians 2:5, 8–10, the former of which focuses on calling and the latter to salvation.[129]

Cara's book, *Cracking the Foundation of the New Perspective on Paul*, was written to combat the notion of "covenantal nomism" as the subtitle indicates (*Covenantal Nomism Versus Reformed Covenantal Theology*). In this book, he deals specifically with 2 Timothy 1:8–10. Within his treatment of 1 Timothy 1:9, he states, "In context, the past tense of these two aspects of God's work relates to justification and current sanctification." Neither justification nor sanctification are overtly (or discreetly, for that matter) discussed in 1 Timothy 1:9. Cara makes the common mistake of conflating the two categories of salvation and justification. Although, as Dunn, Wright, and Marshall agree, the passage is indeed stating the foundational truth that salvation and calling are at the initiative of God in contrast to "works,"[130] covenantal nomism is not Paul's opponent evidenced by the absence of δικ- language and the absence of the word "faith."[131] This

126. Cara, *Cracking the Foundation*, 168, italics original. He states something similar earlier in the same paragraph (italics also his), "In sum, for our topic, Paul comments on God the Father's saving us by *contrasting* our 'works' (v. 9b) with God's 'purpose and grace' (v. 9c)." Cara, *Cracking the Foundation*, 168.

127. "Shame" is used three times from 2 Tim 1:8–16, and twice in 2 Tim 1:8–12. Paul urges Timothy, "Do not be ashamed" (2 Tim 1:8), and, then, he uses himself as an example, "For this reason, I suffer these things, but I am not ashamed" (2 Tim 1:12).

128. Or better, the Systematic, Reformed way of reading Paul.

129. Both are concerned with works, and Eph 2:8–10, like 2 Tim 1:9, is concerned with soteriology. Neither discuss justification, righteousness, or "current sanctification."

130. See Wright, *Pastoral Epistles*, 90–91; Dunn, "First and Second Letters," 836; Marshall with Towner, *Pastoral Epistles*, 705–6.

131. Paul does speak of the faith of Timothy's mother and grandmother (1 Tim 1:5) and the "faith and love" which are in Christ Jesus (1 Tim 1:13).

is not to say there is total disagreement with Cara, but like the NPP, Cara is working from a particular rubric, and one that does not, from the start, find common ground with the NPP. By no means is the NPP vindicated by 2 Timothy 1:3 or 2 Timothy 1:8–12, but after reviewing the passages and reading them from the NPP hermeneutic, there is no need to dismiss the NPP either. Paul's soteriological statement in 2 Timothy 1:8–12 demonstrates the fundamental aspects of Paul's theology in contrast to the polemically charged aspects highlighted in Romans and Galatians.

The next chapter will focus on Titus 3:3–7. The central point of that passage will be the relation of δικαιόω to salvation. The term "works" is also present, modified by "we have done in righteousness," which seems to combat the idea of "works-righteousness." Like the previous two chapters, this final chapter of exegesis will read this passage from the hermeneutic of the NPP with special emphasis on "works," "salvation," and "justification."

5

Justified by Grace

Titus 3:3–7

Introduction

IN CHAPTER 4, 2 Timothy 1:3, 8–12 was studied, demonstrating Paul's continuity with Judaism along with the specific challenges brought about by the gospel for which he was appointed "herald, apostle, and teacher" (2 Tim 1:11). Like 1 Timothy 1:6–16 and 2:3–7, justification (δικ-) language was missing from Paul's articulation of the gospel and his former life. In both cases, the major tenets of the NPP found expression through Paul's definition of the use of the law (1 Tim 1:9), his pre-conversion self (1 Tim 1:12–16; 2 Tim 1:3), his vocation (1 Tim 2:7; 2 Tim 1:11), and his articulation of the gospel/salvation (1 Tim 1:6–16; 2:3–7; 2 Tim 1:8–12). In 2 Timothy 1:8–12, Paul contrasted "our works" with salvation and calling that come from God. However, this statement does not necessarily dictate that Paul was reacting against "works-righteousness," but represented a more foundational expression of salvation than the "works of law"/faith dilemma of Galatians and, to some degree, Romans. Instead, Paul is warning Timothy of the danger that persecution and suffering can create. The calling they share did not consist of a list of good works or accomplishments by which they earn their salvation or special vocation.

The present chapter will focus on Titus 3:3–7 with a special emphasis on Paul's opponents and the themes of salvation, justification, and works. These categories were detailed as major tenets of the NPP in the first chapter. Of the four passages studied, this passage poses the biggest threat to the hermeneutic of the NPP because Paul uses the verb "justified" (δικαιόω), which the NPP maintains is a primarily polemical doctrine (metaphor) of Paul when discussing gentile inclusion into the people of God in contrast to the traditional view that argues "justification" is the imputed righteousness of Christ (or God; cf. 2 Cor 5:21). What follows is an interpretation of this passage with special attention given to the similarities and contrasts of Titus 3:3–7 with the NPP in an attempt to test the validity of the NPP hermeneutic.

Titus, Crete, and Paul's Opponents

As in the previous chapters, the opponents and Paul's reason for writing this letter play an important role in how Paul articulates his theology. Outside of this epistle, and even within it, little is known of Titus. Titus is mentioned eight times in 2 Corinthians, twice in Galatians, and once in 2 Timothy, but he is not mentioned at all in Acts.[1] Titus comforted Paul by his arrival (2 Cor 7:6, 13) and must have known, and been known by, the Corinthians relatively well (2 Cor 7:13–14; 8:6, 16, 23; 12:18). Paul writes that Titus went to Dalmatia, so he may have spent some time working there (2 Tim 4:10). Paul calls Titus his partner and fellow-worker (2 Cor 8:23). With these titles, as well as the similarity of the letter to Titus with 1 Timothy, one can assume that Titus held a position similar, if not identical to, that of Timothy. In fact, Paul calls both Timothy and Titus his "true child" in the introduction to the letters (γνωσίῳ τέκνῳ).[2] However, unlike Timothy who was both Jewish and Greek, Titus was Greek (Gal 2:3). Internal evidence relays the work of Titus and Paul's expectations of him and his ministry. He was left behind in Crete "to put in order what remained to be done" (Titus 1:5), which included the appointment of elders, a job Timothy was left in Ephesus to do as well (1 Tim 3:1–7). He was to teach "what is consistent with sound doctrine" in contrast to some rebellious men from the "circumcision" (Titus 1:10; 2:1). Among these duties were the reminders to the old, young, slaves, and masters regarding acceptable behavior, also similar to that found in 1 Timothy.[3]

---

1. 2 Cor 2:13; 7:6, 13, 14; 8:6, 16, 23; 12:18; Gal 2:1, 3; 2 Tim 4:10. See Barrett, "Titus," 2–3; Köstenberger, *Commentary on 1–2 Timothy and Titus*, 291.

2. The greetings of 1 Timothy and Titus are quite similar. However, in 2 Timothy, Paul calls Timothy his "beloved" (ἀγαπητός) child. The greeting of Titus is longer and includes a precursive statement of the gospel (Titus 1:1–4). However, 1 and 2 Timothy both contain the tripartite greeting ("grace, mercy and peace"; 1 Tim 1:2; 2 Tim 1:2), whereas Titus has only two ("grace and peace"; Titus 1:4). Some later texts added "mercy" to the introduction of Titus (e.g., A K L 81, and *the Textus Receptus*). Both 1 Timothy and Titus also use the term "faith" (ἐν πιστεί, "in faith"; κατὰ κοινὴν πιστίν, "according to a common faith") to qualify their relationship (1 Tim 1:2 and Titus 1:4, respectively).

3. A few examples of the similarities between 1 Timothy and Titus are: "true child" (1 Tim 1:2; Titus 1:4); both commissioned for a specific purpose (Ephesus, 1 Tim 1:3; Crete, Titus 1:5); directives for leadership (1 Tim 3:1–13; Titus 1:5–9); directives for the household of faith (1 Tim 5:1–2; 6:1–2; cf. Titus 2:1–10); subjection to rulers and

The island of Crete was home to the Minoans, one of the earliest civilizations (ca. 1700–1420 BC).[4] Crete did not have a good reputation, as Paul's quotation of a sixth century (BC) poet demonstrates (Titus 1:12).[5] Though coming near to Crete on Paul's journey to Rome recorded in Acts 27:6–21, Luke does not indicate that Paul actually visited the island at that time, and at any rate, he likely would not have had time to establish churches in the area. However, as L. T. Johnson points out, Acts does not include an exhaustive list of Paul's travels. Paul himself mentions a trip to Illyricum (Rom 15:19) of which Acts does not speak. Neither does Acts record Paul establishing churches in Galatia or Colossae, which he undoubtedly did.[6] However, Cretans are mentioned as having been at attendance on the Day of Pentecost (Acts 2:11) and could have taken their faith back to the island with them.[7]

---

authorities (1 Tim 2:1–2; Titus 3:1). For more parallels see, n45 in chapter 3. See also Mounce, *Pastoral Epistles*, lx–lxi.

4. Most commentaries do not say much about historical Crete. The omission may be due to the rejection of Pauline authorship, casting doubt on the Cretan situation which the letter addresses. However, even those like Luke Timothy Johnson who advocate Pauline authorship do not mention much about historical Crete. Johnson simply points to Paul's few-day visit there (Acts 27:1) and the likelihood that Crete was a new area of Paul's mission. See Johnson, *Letters to Paul's Delegates*, 211. However, see Köstenberger, *1–2 Timothy and Titus*, 296–99, for a more thorough treatment of historical Crete that outlines its many cities (cf. Titus 1:5) and the many Roman cults and religions represented in those cities. Köstenberger argues based on substantial evidence that Titus was likely based in Gortyn, which was near where Paul passed on his way to Rome (Acts 27:7–21), and may have been established alongside the Jewish population already there. For more information on ancient Crete and Titus, see Wieland, "Roman Crete and the Letter to Titus," 338–54; Zimmermann, "Wiederentstehung und Erneuerung," 284; van der Horst, "Jews of Ancient Crete," 183–200; and Johnson, *Letters to Paul's Delegates*, 213. For further discussion of the church and Jewish population of Crete, see Yarbrough, *Letters to Timothy and Titus*, 49–51; and Schnabel, *Paul and the Early Church*, 1284–86.

5. L. T. Johnson states that the "incivility" of the Cretan populace (and church) is, in part, what prompted the writing of the letter. He writes, "Not only is the native population described as mendacious and rough (1:12), but the same qualities may adhere to converts as well. The evidence in Titus suggests that in Crete the gospel is struggling to establish roots in a context of severe incivility." Johnson, *Letters to Paul's Delegates*, 213.

6. See Johnson, *1 Timothy, 2 Timothy, Titus*, 112. Johnson also suggests that Paul's statement, "I left you behind in Crete" (ἀπέλιπόν σε ἐν Κρήτῃ; Titus 1:5), does not necessitate Paul having been there, but that he left Titus "in that position" (112). Although it may be true that Paul was not there to leave Titus behind, the other two times the verb is used in Paul (2 Tim 4:13, 20) use the word in that way.

7. It is hard to place the writing of this letter within the Pauline timeline with any certainty. However, most place the writing near the time 1 Timothy was written. In fact, some think Titus may have been the first of the PE written. Paul does not speak of being in prison, which likely means he wrote this letter between his first and second imprisonment (AD 63–65). Johnson, *Letters to Paul's Delegates*, 211. For a thorough

Regardless of how the church there began, it seems from evidence within the epistle itself that the church was relatively young.[8]

As for the opponents of Titus, many commentators simply conflate these opponents with those of 1 Timothy.[9] However, there is a more easily detectable Jewish element in the opposition of Titus. For example, in Titus the myths of which Paul speaks are called "Jewish" myths (Titus 1:14) and Paul specifies that "those of the circumcision"[10] (οἱ ἐκ τῆς περιτομῆς; Titus 1:10) are exceptionally rebellious. Also, among the things Titus is to avoid are "genealogies" (γενεαλογία) and "quarrels about the law" (μάχας νομικάς), which in the context one can assume means the Mosaic law, or Torah.[11] Even though there is a Jewish element to the Cretan opposition, there does not seem to be the same problems one witnesses in other of Paul's letters, especially Romans and Galatians.[12] The similarities are much greater with

treatment of a possible timeline, see Köstenberger, *1–2 Timothy and Titus*, 293–95.

8. See Johnson, *Letters to Paul's Delegates*, 211–12, for reasons why the church may have been young, including such a short visit by Paul in Acts to make establishing a church difficult, and in contrast to the church at Ephesus that already had elders who should not be "recent converts" (1 Tim 3:6), Titus was to appoint elders in every city (Titus 1:5). Also, though not especially important for the present study because of the assumed canonical nature of Titus, see Köstenberger, *1–2 Timothy and Titus*, 293–95, on a possible timeline for Paul's dealings with both Titus and Crete. See also Mounce, *Pastoral Epistles*, lix–lxii.

9. For example, see Mounce, *Pastoral Epistles*, lxix. The heading is titled "The Ephesian Heresy," but he highlights passages only found in Titus in the subsection, "Jewish Elements" (Titus 1:10, 14). In fact, he asks in the beginning of his next section, "How then were Timothy and Titus to respond to these issues in their churches?" Mounce, *Pastoral Epistles*, lxxvi. Certainly, the characterization of the opponents in 1 Timothy and Titus do share remarkable similarity of style and vocabulary, but the two are not identical.

10. For a similar use of the phrase by Paul, see Rom 4:12; Gal 2:12; Col 4:11.

11. The word "dispute" (μάκη) is used only in 2 Cor 7:5; 2 Tim 2:23; Titus 3:8. Νομικός is used primarily in Luke (Luke 7:30; 10:25; 11:45, 46, 52; 14:3), but it is used once in Matthew (Matt 22:35; a textual variant) and twice in Titus (Titus 3:9, 13). In all the cases in Luke, the word refers to "lawyers," being those who were experts in the law, which would also be the case in Matthew if one accepts the textual variant (the variant is the addition of the word "lawyer" [νομικός] as an explanation of who is asking Jesus a question). In each of these cases, including Titus, the object to which the word refers is the Torah. Interestingly enough, these "disputes about the law" Paul calls unprofitable opposed to the profitability of "good works" (Titus 3:8–9) directly follows the passage in consideration (Titus 3:3–8). For a more thorough investigation, see Mounce, *Pastoral Epistles*, 453.

12. It should be noted that L. T. Johnson compares Titus to Galatians. Johnson seeks to compare the PE as individual letters with other letters in the Pauline corpus (1 Timothy and 1 Corinthians; 2 Timothy and Philippians). See Johnson, *Letters to Paul's Delegates*, 214. Among the PE, Johnson points out the obvious similarities between 1 Timothy and Titus. Johnson, *1 Timothy, 2 Timothy, Titus*, 112. The nature and style of

1 Timothy and the Ephesian heresy than with other of Paul's letters. One also must keep in mind that the issues of myths and genealogies are not simply issues regarding ancestry but what were characterized in chapter 3 of this work as proto-gnostic speculative myths and genealogies similar to 1 *Enoch*.[13] One does not get the impression from the overall argumentation of the letter that Paul is combating those concerned with Jewish privilege. However, there was some Jewish influence akin to the influence of the Ephesians in 1 Timothy.[14] Important for this study with regard to the NPP is reference to the "circumcision," which is a moniker used by Paul to speak of the Jews (Rom 4:9; 15:8; Gal 2:8; Eph 2:11) and the fact that there must have been some arguments akin to the "Judaizers" of Galatians (Titus 1:15–16)[15] or those who forbade eating meat sacrificed to idols in Romans and 1 Corinthians (cf. Rom 14:20; 1 Cor 10:24–33).[16] There is more evidence in Titus than 1 Timothy of ethnic Jewish influence and obedience to some nationalistic elements of the law.[17] However, Andreas Köstenberger states

---

Titus, though sharing vocabulary and fundamental Pauline theology, is not the same type of letter as Galatians, which evidences the lack of distinctive qualities among the opposition. Otherwise, one would expect more comparable qualities between them. On the other hand, E. F. Scott writes, "The passage reminds us more of the Paul who wrote Romans and Galatians than anything else in the Pastoral Epistles; but the outward resemblance only brings out the differences more significantly." Scott, *Pastoral Epistles*, 177. Similarly, W. Hulitt Gloer writes, "This statement is pure Paul, echoing his discussions with the Judaizers in Romans and Galatians." Gloer, *1 & 2 Timothy–Titus*, 83. Though the statement and theology are similar, the immediate context is not sufficiently similar to make a perfect comparison.

13. See Dunn, "First and Second Letters," 866; Quinn, *Letter to Titus*, 109–10. The phrase used is "Jewish myths and commandments of men (Ἰουδαϊκοῖς μύθοις καὶ ἐντολαῖς ἀνθρώπων)," which may draw to one's mind both the mythological aspect as well as the *halakhah*. See Quinn, *Letter to Titus*, 109.

14. The influence in Titus is not the influence of false knowledge (γνῶσις; this word is not used in Titus or the rest of the PE) in 1 Tim 6:20, but the "knowledge of the truth" contrasted with quarreling and divisiveness (e.g., Titus 1:1, 10, 13–16; 3:1–2, 8–11). The phrase "knowledge of the truth" (ἐπίγνωσιν ἀληθείας) is used in both 1 Tim 2:4 and Titus 1:1.

15. "To the pure, all things are pure; but to those who are defiled and unbelieving, nothing is pure, but both their mind and their conscience are defiled. They profess to know God, but by *their* deeds they deny *Him*, being detestable and disobedient, and worthless for any good deed" (NASB, italics original).

Andreas Köstenberger also notes the similarity with Galatians and the use of the moniker "circumcision." See Köstenberger, *1–2 Timothy and Titus*, 301.

16. Rom 14:20 is the only Pauline use of the word "pure" (καθαρός) outside the PE (cf. 1 Tim 1:5; 3:9; 2 Tim 1:3; 2:22; Titus 1:15).

17. Cf. Titus 1:10, 14–15; 3:9. Also note that Zenas is called a "lawyer," which everywhere in the NT refers to experts in the Jewish law (cf. Luke 7:30; 10:25; 11:45, 46, 52; 14:3). It is also significant that the Cretan church seemed to possess a level of

that, "The message of Titus cannot be simply reduced to a polemic against a set of opponents."[18] This statement is especially true of Titus 3:3–7. Though there were Jewish elements among Paul's opponents (some elements similar to that found in Galatia), Titus 3:3–7 does not seem to be addressing these specific issues. Instead, this passage is not a polemic at all. Rather, it is a positive statement of salvation that Paul uses to justify the behavior he tells Titus to remind the Cretans to be engaged. In sum, Titus is similar in style, structure, and vocabulary with 1 Timothy. However, though the opponents may share certain qualities with 1 Timothy, one gets a better picture of the Jewish influence of the Cretan church from the outside and the "harsh misanthropic character of its converts"[19] from the inside.

Titus 3:3–7

What follows is a translation of Titus 3:3–7 as well as an investigation into its most significant aspects in relation to the NPP. These aspects will be compared and contrasted with the NPP hermeneutic, which will test the NPP's validity outside of Romans and Galatians.

"incivility" and that the church represented a "very raw form of Christianity" without elders and deacons, and those appointed do not face the same stipulations of 1 Tim 3:6 of not being "new converts." All quotations taken from Johnson, *Letters to Paul's Delegates*, 212–13.

18. Köstenberger, *1–2 Timothy and Titus*, 301. Roberts Cara states, "This teaching is a not-too-well-defined combination of proto-gnostic (maybe just generic Hellenistic ideas) and Jewish-Christian elements. Maybe the false teaching was not a combination of views into one group, but false teachings of several groups, or maybe, a continuum of views." Cara, *Cracking the Foundation of the New Perspective*, 156.

19. Johnson, *Letters to Paul's Delegates*, 213.

Translation[20]

(3) For we ourselves were once foolish,[21] disobedient,[22] deceived,[23] enslaved to desires and various pleasures,[24] living[25] in badness and envy, despicable,[26] hating one another. (4) But, when the goodness[27] and lovingkindness[28] of God our Savior[29] appeared, (5) not from works we did that were from righteousness but according to his mercy, he saved us through the washing[30] of regeneration[31]

20. Titus 3:8 has not been added to the translation. The most significant portion of Titus 3:8 is the characterization of Titus 3:4–7 as a "faithful saying" (πιστὸς ὁ λόγος). Paul follows with a charge to Titus to speak confidently of these things, "so that those who believe God may take care to engage in good works."

21. This word (ἀνόητος) can also mean "senseless" ("ἀνόητος," BDAG, 84; cf. Rom 1:14; Gal 3:1, 3; 1 Tim 6:9).

22. Cf. Ro 1:30; 2 Tim 3:2; Titus 1:16. Rom 1:30 and 2 Tim 3:2 both use the term in connection with parents.

23. Each time this term (πλανάω) is used by Paul outside the PE, the phrase is the same (μὴ πλανᾶσθε; 1 Cor 6:9; 15:33; Gal 6:7). This usage reinforces Paul's focus on knowledge and truth (Titus 1:1).

24. This word is used by Paul only in 2 Tim 3:6 (ἐπιθυμίαις ποικίλαις) and Titus 3:3 (ἐπιθυμίαις καὶ ἡδοναῖς ποικίλαις). The former usage refers to those who were captivating women and were led by various pleasures "always learning and never able to come to the knowledge of the truth" (2 Tim 3:7).

25. The term διάγω ("to live, spend") is used only in the PE ("διάγω," BDAG, 227; 1 Tim 2:2; Titus 3:3).

26. This word, στυγητός ("loathsome, despicable"), is a NT *hapax legomenon*. See "στυγητός," BDAG, 949.

27. κρηστότης ("kindness") is a thoroughly Pauline word, used in the NT only by Paul (Rom 2:4; 3:12; 11:22; 2 Cor 6:6; Gal 5:22; Eph 2:7; Col 3:12; Titus 3:4). What is significant in this case is not Paul's usage elsewhere regarding man's kindness (Rom 3:12), but God's kindness as witnessed in his sending his son (Rom 11:22).

28. φιλανθρωπία ("affectionate concern for and interest in humanity, lovingkindness") is used only here (Titus 3:4) and Acts 28:2 in the NT. See "φιλανθρωπία," BDAG, 1055–56.

29. Here God is called "Our Savior," which is done regularly within the PE (e.g., 1 Tim 1:1; 2:3; Titus 1:2–4; 2:10).

30. "Washing" (λουτρόν) is used only one other time in the NT (Eph 5:26). The term likely refers both to spiritual washing (as in Eph 5:26), but may also reflect a baptismal "washing." In fact, in Eph 5:26 the term is modified by "water" (ὕδωρ; "the washing of water with the word").

31. The word παλιγγενεσία ("regeneration/rebirth") is used only one other time in the NT (Matt 19:28; see "παλιγγενεσία," BDAG, 752). It is not a reference to the resurrection *per se*, but when Jesus will sit on the throne along with the Twelve. One gets the impression what is being emphasized in Titus 3:5 is the new life and regeneration brought about through cleansing, not the resurrection. However, it could be a reference to both regeneration and the resurrection in that the resurrection and spiritual renewal

and the renewal[32] of the Holy Spirit (6) which has been richly[33] spilled out[34] on us through Jesus Christ our Savior, (7) so that being justified by the grace of that one[35] we might become heirs[36] according to the hope[37] of eternal life.[38]

Foolishness and Goodness

In Titus 3:1–2, Paul tells Titus to "remind them (Ὑπομίμνῃσκε αὐτοὺς)[39] *to be subject* (ὑποτάσσεσθαι) to rulers, to authorities, *to be obedient* (πειθαρχεῖν), *to be* (εἶναι) ready for every good deed, *to malign* (βλασφημεῖν) no one, *to be* (εἶναι) uncontentious, gentle, showing every consideration for all men." This string of infinitives all have to do with the way in which the Cretan

---

are interconnected. See Bird, *Saving Righteousness of God*, 53–56.

32. ἀνακαίνωσις is used by Paul only one other time (Rom 12:2) in which he refers to the "renewal of your mind." See "ἀνακαίνωσις," BDAG, 64–65.

33. "Richly" (πλουσίως) is used by Paul only once outside the PE (Col 3:16; 1 Tim 6:17; Titus 3:6). Each time the word is used by Paul it refers to the abundance of God (cf. also 2 Pet 1:11).

34. This word (ἐκχέω; "poured out, spilled") is used only three times by Paul (Rom 3:15; 5:5; Titus 3:6), one of which (Rom 3:15) is a quotation from the OT/LXX (Isa 59:7). See "ἐκχέω," BDAG, 312.

35. "That" (ἐκεῖνος) is translated as "his" in some translations (e.g., NRSV, NASB, KJV). Paul uses this term elsewhere (Rom 6:21; 14:14–15; 1 Cor 9:25; 10:11, 28; 15:11; 2 Cor 7:8; 8:9, 14; 10:18; Eph 2:2; 2 Thess 1:10; Titus 3:7), but 2 Timothy has a higher frequency of usage (2 Tim 1:12, 18; 2:13, 26; 3:9; 4:8). Paul never uses "that" with "grace" anywhere else. The closest parallel is 2 Cor 8:9, wherein Paul uses ἐκεῖνος with πτωχεία ("poverty"). If Paul does not mean "his" grace, he may be referring to the closest antecedent, which is Titus 2:11, wherein Paul writes a similar statement, "For the grace (χάρις) of God appeared (ἐπιφαίνω), bringing salvation to all men." Also, see Knight, *Pastoral Epistles*, 346, who thinks the appearing of God in 3:5 may be the antecedent. However, one must also note that "that" is here used in the genitive case (ἐκείνου), which may be why "his" is preferred in some translations. The translation "by the grace of that one" here is meant to highlight Paul's use of "that." As noted above, Paul uses a similar construction in 2 Cor 8:9 (τῇ ἐκείνου πτωχείᾳ).

36. "Heir" (κληρονόμος) is a common term for Paul in Romans and Galatians (Rom 4:13–14; 8:17; Gal 3:29; 4:1, 7). The only other time the word is used by Paul is here, in Titus 3:7.

37. "Hope" (ἐλπίς) is a thoroughly Pauline word used in every Pauline letter except Philemon and 2 Timothy (Rom 5:5 is an especially significant usage in which the term ἐκχέω, "pour out," is also found).

38. The phrase "hope of eternal life" (ἐλπίδα ζωῆς αἰωνίου) is also found in Titus 1:2.

39. Paul does not use this term (ὑπομιμνῄσκω, "remind") outside the PE, and only twice within them (2 Tim 2:14; Titus 3:1). Αὐτούς likely refers to the Cretan converts.

Christians interact with society.[40] Beginning in Titus 3:3, Paul transitions from the third-person plural to the first-person plural. This transition does not seem to be simply a rhetorical device, but a way for Paul to engage his audience and articulate the gospel in a way that included himself.[41] In other words, Paul shifts from a command to Titus for "them," by including himself ("we").[42] By including himself, Paul is acknowledging the universality of the gospel. Paul, an apostle, was not exempt from conversion, nor was he exempt from a life of sinfulness from which he was saved because of God's initiative. The sinfulness of man and God's initiative lie at the heart of Titus 3:3–7. However, even though Paul includes himself among the "foolish," it does not necessarily mean he identifies with each of these sins listed. Instead, Paul is engaging the Cretan Christians by identifying with them in their previously sinful state.

The former life Paul discusses is not characterized by such gross sinfulness as that found in 1 Timothy 1:9–10 (those for whom the law is used). Instead, the focus is on what creates dissention as well as foolishness and enslavement to lust and pleasure.[43] Paul, from any perspective (NPP, or otherwise), could have characterized himself in many of these terms. However, Paul's aim is not to focus on his own conversion (as in 1 Tim 1:12–16),[44] but to identify himself with these sinful acts and "foolishness" in order to highlight the foundational truth of salvation and renewal—a former life that gives way to a new life and unprofitable works replaced by profitable ones (cf. Titus 3:8–9). So, though similar to 1 Timothy 1:12–16 in that Paul does include himself in the "conversion," Titus 3:3–7 contrasts with 1 Timothy 1:12–16, in that he does not use his conversion as the epitome of God's mercy in salvation. His conversion is assumed here, but remains relatively anonymous. In fact, the list of "who we formerly were" is not random, but is likely focused on the issues present within the Cretan community.[45]

40. Civility and behavior acceptable to society for the sake of the early Christian's reputation is a consistent Pauline theme (Rom 13:1–8; Col 4:5; 1 Thess 4:12; 1 Tim 3:7).

41. In contrast, see Quinn, *Letter to Titus*, 201 wherein he argues, "It was not the regular practice of the Paul of history to accuse himself of the vices that he was adducing in a list." Cf. 1 Tim 1:6–16. Quinn calls the device employed by the first-person plural the "relational aspect" (201).

42. This shift is highlighted by Paul's use of an emphatic καί, "even, as well, too."

43. Johnson points out that the vice list is in contradistinction to the reminders of Titus 3:1–2. See Johnson, *Letters to Paul's Delegates*, 247.

44. Marshall does not see great continuity in this list with Paul's prior life. He states, "The list of characteristics here is a stereotyped one that is generally true of non-believers as a group but does not appear to fit, for example, Paul's pre-conversion life too well." Marshall and Towner, *Critical and Exegetical Commentary on the Pastoral Epistles*, 306.

45. Many of the words used in this list are either words used only in the PE or

The goodness and kindness of God is set in contrast to the septuple vices listed in Titus 3:3. The word "goodness/kindness" (χρηστότης) in the NT is only used by Paul. In Galatians 5:22, it is one of the fruit of the Spirit. In Romans 2:4, Paul rhetorically demonstrates that it is the kindness of God that leads to repentance. In Romans 11:22, Paul contrasts God's kindness to God's severity, stating, "But to you, God's kindness, if you continue in his kindness; otherwise, you will also be cut off." This statement is important in seeing that God's kindness, even to Paul, has its limits and must be "continued in" (ἐὰν ἐπιμένῃς), which, by way of the following verse, seems to insinuate that faith is what maintains that kindness (Rom 11:23). The word is also used of God (and salvation) in Ephesians 2:7.[46] In Titus 3:4, this kindness is the kindness of God demonstrated through the renewal of the Holy Spirit poured out through Christ.[47] The word "lovingkindness" (φιλανθρωπία) is only used one other time in the NT (Acts 28:2). The idea behind both words is to describe the reason for God's intervention on behalf of the disobedient—God is kind and a lover of mankind.

He Saved Us

One of the major discussions revolving around the verb ἔσωσεν[48] among commentators of Titus 3:5 is whether this usage represents a salvation-historical view of salvation or that of individual salvation, what Cara calls "existential."[49] It seems that Paul is incorporating both the historical *and*

---

hapax legomenon. Even words that are used outside the PE are used elsewhere in Paul and Luke/Acts. Paul does often use the former life of believers in contrast to new life (1 Cor 6:9–11; Gal 4:8–10; Eph 2:1–10; Col 1:21–25). See Quinn, *Letter to Titus*, 201. Also, Quinn calls attention to some significant parallels of this vice list with that of the Qumran Rule. Quinn, *Letter to Titus*, 208–9.

46. At this point, it should have become clear how similar Eph 2:1–10 is to the theology of 2 Tim 1:8–12 and Titus 3:3–7, even though Ephesians is outside the purview of this specific study.

47. The word "to appear" (ἐπιφαίνω) is used only in Titus (2:11; 3:4), Luke 1:79, and Acts 27:20. There is a striking similarity to the usage in Titus 2:11. Both instances in Titus are mentioned in connection with proper behavior (cf. Titus 2:12; 3:8).

48. One might recall that often salvation is regarded as a future event. That is not the case in Titus 3:5. The verb here is in the aorist indicative. However, N. T. Wright regards justification in three tenses (past, present, and future), which demonstrates the complexity of his position. See Wright, *Pauline Perspectives*, 423.

49. See Cara, *Cracking the Foundation*, 161. Cara argues that either way one understands the thrust of the statement, individual salvation is naturally embedded within it. In addition, James Dunn writes, "Here again the verb ἐπιφαίνω refers to the first appearance of divine grace (as in 2:11), but in this case the thought is not so immediately focused on the action of Christ as on the impact of saving grace in human experience."

existential views of salvation in that he refers to the appearance of kindness and mercy (i.e., God breaking forth into the world in some way in history, but also, quite obviously, in a personal, individual way to the Cretans and Paul himself).[50] This passage as a whole (Titus 3:3–7) is comparable to Titus 2:11–15, in which the focus is more on God's overarching plan of salvation and how that salvation affects social interaction and civility. Both Titus 2:1–15 and 3:1–8 contain Pauline directives followed by Paul's justification for these directives.[51] In the former case, Paul looks to familial/household social interaction as that which provides a good reputation, "for the grace of God has appeared, bringing salvation to all men" (Titus 2:11). In other words, proper treatment of one another, and even the way in which slaves were to serve, was meant to exhibit proof that God had redeemed a people "zealous for good works" (Titus 2:14). Similarly, Titus 3:3–7 is a statement of the gospel in response to how the Cretans were to behave toward rulers and authorities. This is the only time the verb σώζω is used in Titus. The significance of Paul's usage here is his appeal to their own conversion from a life of foolishness to a life of good deeds. Just as God was kind and loved humanity, which resulted in their salvation, they must also exhibit kindness to humanity. The kindness and love of God for the salvation of the Cretans is significant for the present study in that this statement by Paul is not used as a stand-alone statement (even if it could stand alone as a hymnic/creedal statement or baptismal liturgy),[52] but it is used to defend the

See Dunn, "First and Second Letters," 876. See also Bassler, 1 Timothy, 2 Timothy, Titus, 208 wherein Bassler argues that the use of "saved" in contrast to works is contrary to Paul who uses "justified." I. Howard Marshall writes, "If the thought in ch. 2 was more salvation-historical in that it described God's saving intervention in the world and its purpose, here the thought is expressed more in terms of the individual experience of conversion and salvation through which people are enabled to live a new life." Marshall with Towner, Pastoral Epistles, 305.

50. The word ὅτε is temporal, hinting at a time when God's goodness and lovingkindness had not appeared. This appearance may be in reference to Christ's appearing, but could also refer to God revealing himself in the lives of Christians, since Paul is not speaking only of humanity, generally, but of himself, Titus, and the Cretans, specifically. See Marshall with Towner, Pastoral Epistles, 312, and Lau, Manifest in Flesh, 160–76. If this is a hymnic formula, it may account for both meanings, the coming of Christ encompassing the individual conversion. Outside of Titus 3:4, the phrase "but when" (ὅτε δέ) only appears in Galatians within the Pauline corpus (Gal 1:15; 2:11, 12; 4:4). Two significant passages are Gal 1:15–16 and 4:4. The first refers to Paul's own conversion, while the second references the coming of Christ.

51. Most commentators point out the similarities between Titus 2:11–14 and Titus 3:4–7. For example, see Gloer, 1 & 2 Timothy–Titus, 79; Fee, 1 and 2 Timothy, Titus, 202; Bassler, 1 Timothy, 2 Timothy, Titus, 206; Collins, I & II Timothy and Titus, 359–60; and Yarbrough, Letters to Timothy and Titus, 536.

52. For example, see Collins, I & II Timothy and Titus, 359–61 and Hanson, Studies

efficacy of Paul's instructions. In other words, beginning in Titus 3:4, Paul may be alluding to, or even quoting, a well-known, standard statement of soteriology in order to demonstrate the need for Christians to be obedient, subject, and ready for every good work.

There is no indication of a Jewish "works-righteous" element prompting Paul's statement, though there may have been a developing sense of Christian superiority, similar to, but not equivalent to what now may be called "legalism." In Philippians 3:6, Paul characterizes his life in Judaism, "as to righteousness found in the Law, blameless." This is not a statement of sinlessness, but that within the confines of the law, Paul was blameless.[53] For the NPP, Jewish "legalism" is not the direct opposing idea for Paul in Romans and Galatians (or Philippians), which also seems to be the case in Titus 3:3–7. With this statement, Paul is not opposing Jewish "legalism," or even Judaism itself.[54] Instead, Paul is affirming subjection, civility, and the doing of good deeds by virtue of the nature of the Cretan's (and his) own salvation. Paul's argument in this instance is similar to that of Romans 4:6–8 wherein Paul argues that blessedness is "reckoned" (λογίζομαι) to those whose lawless deeds have been forgiven. Paul writes, "Just as David speaks of the blessing upon the man upon whom God reckons righteousness *apart from works*: 'Blessed are those whose lawless deeds have been forgiven and whose sins have been covered'" (Rom 4:6–7). In other words, even in Romans 4, the issue is not that righteous deeds cannot make one righteous, but that blessedness is reckoned when lawless deeds are forgiven. The difference in these two passages is that "works" in Romans 4 refers undoubtedly to sinful acts (4:8), whereas Paul qualifies "works" in

---

in the Pastoral Epistles, 78–96. See also Robert Cara who calls Titus 3:4–7 (and Titus 2:11–14) a "wonderful theological motivation" that followed the practical instruction of 3:1–2. Cara, *Cracking the Foundation*, 157. He identifies Titus 3:4–7, along with the other "faithful sayings," as "'standard mini-speeches' he used often in his ministry" (157). He also states of the creedal statement in Titus 3:4–7, "Whether Paul was the absolute originator of the sayings or not, he still used them" (158). On the other hand, I. Howard Marshall does not think the statement is a hymn or a creed. Marshall with Towner, *Pastoral Epistles*, 306–7.

53. Philippians 3:3–6 is an important passage for the NPP in that they argue the passage demonstrates Paul's robust conscience prior to his conversion and that it also demonstrates the validity of Sanders's covenantal nomism. For a few examples see, Wright, *Paul: In Fresh Perspective*, 115–16; Dunn, *New Perspective on Paul*, 463–84; Sanders, *Paul and Palestinian Judaism*, 550. Wright attempts to provide more nuance to the discussion in Wright, *Justification*, 141–53.

54. As noted above, certainly there were Jewish elements to some of the opponents of Titus, but it does not seem Jewish opponents make this iteration of the gospel necessary. Instead, this articulation of the gospel as a "faithful saying" is more universal in its scope.

Titus 3:5 with works that are done in righteousness (i.e., "good" works). The comparable quality of both arguments is that works (whether good or bad) are not that which make one righteous. In the previous two chapters of the present work, the focus of the passages (1 Tim 1:6–16; 2:3–7; 2 Tim 1:8–12) has been on salvation and so it is here. However, what is significant is the addition of the Pauline metaphor of justification as part of the articulation of the appearing of God's kindness and his love for humanity. As in 2 Timothy 1:8–12, God saves apart from works, but in Titus 3:3–7 there is also the added element of how one is "justified."

Works of Righteousness[55] and Good Deeds

Though "he saved" (ἔσωσεν) is the primary verb, the phrase "not from works we did that were from righteousness but according to his mercy," is emphasized by its position in the sentence ahead of the verb.[56] As already discussed, "works" is a primary category of Pauline theology and the NPP. The NPP has focused on the specific phrase "works of law," the meaning of which was outlined more fully in the last chapter. Basically, "works of law" are understood by the NPP to be specific works that separate Jew from gentile, what James Dunn defines as "covenantal identifiers."[57] Obviously, that exact phrase, "works of law" is not used here, and by that omission, the NPP (or, at least, Dunn) assumes a different definition of "works," as well as a different argument being made by Paul. The exact phrase used by Paul

---

55. The word "righteousness" (δικαιοσύνη) is used often by Paul in the undisputed letters. It is used five times in the PE with the greatest number of usages being in 2 Timothy (2:22; 3:16; 4:8). δικ- language generally is not prevalent in the primary passages undertaken in this study (only once in 1 Tim 1:9, and now Titus 3:5, 7). However, Titus 3:3–7 contains two words from this word group (δικαιοσύνη/δικαιόω), which some commentators point out is significant in that Paul is contrasting "works we did in righteousness" and "justified by grace of that one." For example, see Wall and Steele, *1 & 2 Timothy and Titus*, 366; Wieland, *Significance of Salvation*, 232.

56. The position of emphasis is demonstrated in the translation above.

57. For example, see Dunn, *New Perspective on Paul*, 455–60. Wright expresses about the phrase "works of Law" in Gal 2:16, "Here it is: the first statement of the Christian doctrine of justification by faith. Or rather, the first statement of its negative pole, that one cannot be justified by works of 'the Law'—which, by the way, for Paul, *always* means 'the Jewish Law, the Torah.'" Wright, *Justification*, 116, italics original. He explains further, "They are not, in other words, the moral 'good works' which the Reformation tradition loves to hate. They are the things that divide Jew from Gentile." Wright, *Justification*, 117. Although this characterization may be true of Gal 2:16, the "works" in question in Titus 3:5 are not "works of Law," but "works we did in righteousness."

in Titus 3:5 is οὐκ ἐξ ἔργων τῶν ἐν δικαιοσύνη ἃ ἐποιήσαμεν,[58] a phrase used nowhere else in Pauline literature.[59]

James Dunn states that Titus 3:5 is "one of the clearest statements in all the Bible that the implementation of God's saving purpose is wholly at the initiative of God."[60] However, he also seeks to defend the underlying elements of the NPP. He points out, "It is not an anti-Jewish statement" and "It is not a direct repetition of what Paul said; he spoke of righteousness as a gift from God (as in Rom 4:3) and of works of the law, not of righteous works."[61] He also explains, "It is not a disparagement of good works or righteous deeds."[62] N. T. Wright, though commenting on the idea of salvation apart from works of righteousness, does not overtly engage NPP thought.[63] What is clear is that (1) Dunn does not adhere to Pauline authorship, so this passage does not interfere with his articulation of the NPP, and that (2) his addition of these caveats uncovers the potential danger Titus 3:5–7 poses to the NPP. In all fairness, the NPP is not opposed to Paul being against legalism, but that Paul's primary polemic is not against legalism, or a plagued Western conscience.[64] His polemic is against Jew-

58. George Knight states of these "works we did in righteousness," "But it is evident from the Greek, nevertheless, that the saying is depicting the works or deeds as being righteousness, that is (up)right and good in a moral sense." Knight, *Faithful Sayings in the Pastoral Epistles*, 93. I. Howard Marshall defines the "works" in a similar way, but conflates these "works done in righteousness" with the doctrine of justification pointing to Titus 3:7. He writes, "The process of justification (cf. 3:7, δικαιόω) is the recognition by God of people as righteous, regardless of their past actions, on the basis of the work of Christ; it is the conferring of a status which must then be demonstrated in practice in righteous living (cf. adv. δικαίως)." Marshall with Towner, *Pastoral Epistles*, 314. Surprisingly, Cara states, "It is certainly possible that a *part* of the broad 'works' in context included Jewish nationality markers and Jewish works righteousness." Cara, *Cracking the Foundation*, 161, italics original. See also n67 below.

59. One may be tempted to compare Titus 3:5 to Phil 3:6. However, there is not enough commonality in vocabulary, or even context, to make a proper comparison. The only significant parallel is Paul's use of the word "righteousness." However, in Phil 3:6, the righteousness is specifically that which comes from the law, concerning which Paul calls himself "blameless" (ἄμεμπτος).

60. Dunn, "First and Second Letters," 876.

61. Dunn, "First and Second Letters," 876.

62. Dunn, "First and Second Letters," 877.

63. See Wright, *Paul for Everyone*, 159–62.

64. For example, see Dunn, *New Perspective on Paul*, 26–27. He states, "For my own part, I have *no* desire to diminish the seriousness of the charges which Paul levels against humankind, particularly in the devastating analysis of Rom 1:18–3:20, as I hope my earlier work made clear. . . . All I want to do is to remind those interested that there is *also* a social and ethnic dimension to Paul's own understanding and expression of the gospel." Dunn, *New Perspective on Paul*, 27, italics original.

ish ethnic superiority. One could argue that, in many ways, the issue in Titus 3:3–7 is similar to that found in Galatians and Romans in that Paul is combating *Christian* superiority over against those in authority and "all men" (πάντας ἀνθρώπους; Titus 3:2), a superiority garnered in retrospect from their presently-saved position.

Paul uses the phrase "good deeds/works" (Titus 2:7, 14; 3:1, 8, 14)[65] five times in Titus.[66] Thus, just from sheer frequency, one cannot argue that Paul was opposed to "works," even in a general sense. In fact, in the case of Titus, good works play an important role in Paul's theology. However, what is just as clear, is that Paul intends the focus to be on God as the one who saves and that good works come from a life in Christ. "Works,"[67] even righteous ones, are not the catalyst for salvation, but mercy is. It is hard to imagine anyone would deny that Paul's point is in response to a form of "works-righteousness," or, better put, a superiority based on an already-received salvation.[68] From the context, it does not seem that Paul thought Titus, or even the Cretans, believed they had earned their salvation through righteous works. By his list of who they used to be (Titus 3:3), Paul is demonstrating that salvation was granted despite bad works, not as a reward for good works. Paul is stating another axiomatic truth of the gospel to strengthen his commands in Titus 3:1–2. Just as the Cretan Christians were told to submit to authorities that may have exhibited bad deeds, these works did not disqualify these leaders from salvation (or from the submission and obedience of the Cretans). He reminds them, "We also were foolish" (Titus 3:3). So, the axiomatic truth that God saves apart from righteous works was not a reminder of the good works the Cretans had done that did not save them, but a reminder of the good works the Cretans had not done, yet they had been saved anyway.[69]

65. Each of the usages are καλῶν ἔργων, except Titus 3:1 (ἔργον ἀγαθόν).

66. Titus 1:16; 2:7, 14; 3:8, 14.

67. It should be noted that although Dunn and Wright do not attempt to include Jewish identity markers within the meaning of "works we did in righteousness" in Titus 3:5, Robert Cara does. As expressed in n58, he states, "It is certainly possible that a *part* of the broad 'works' in context included Jewish nationality markers and Jewish works-righteousness." Cara, *Cracking the Foundation*, 161, italics original. See also Dunn, "First and Second Letters," 876–77, and Wright, *Pastoral Letters*, 160.

68. This superiority is similar to the Jewish superiority of Romans and Galatians, but instead of Paul opposing "works of law," he is opposing "works done in righteousness," which further solidifies the truth that no matter the work, it is God who both saves and justifies.

69. L. T. Johnson explains that the qualification, "works we did in righteousness," "has a double edge" by reminding the Cretans of their past behavior and by rebutting "the claims of the opponents that a pure life can be established by the observance of laws of purity—works of human 'righteousness.'" Johnson, *1 Timothy, 2 Timothy, Titus*, 135.

Now that justification had come by grace, they were to engage in good works (Titus 3:8; cf. Titus 2:11–14).[70]

Paul's specific definition of "works" in Titus 3:5 presents a few problems to the NPP: (1) The NPP's definition of "works" often coincides, not with salvation, but with justification. In 2 Timothy 1:8–12, this definition presents a major problem in that no words from the διχ- word group are used. However, even here in Titus 3:3–7, "justified by grace" is part of the process (or another metaphor to explain the process), not the primary polemic against works-righteousness. (2) The "works" described here should not be understood to be "covenantal identifiers,"[71] but must be understood as "righteous" works, more generally speaking. (3) Similarly, because of the lack of discussion of "the Law,"[72] one can assume that Paul is *not* speaking to Jewish-legalism instigated by obedience to the law.

Mercy

Rather than a salvation from works, God saved us "according to his mercy." All three occurrences of ἔλεος in Romans are directly concerned with the inclusion of both Jew and gentile in the gospel (Rom 9:23; 11:31; 15:9).[73] The word is used only once in the closing statements of Galatians (Gal 6:16), and once in Ephesians (Eph 2:4). The other five instances of the word in Pauline literature are in the PE (1 Tim 1:2; 2 Tim 1:2, 16, 18; Titus 3:5). Paul also uses the cognate verb ἐλεέω often in Romans.[74]

70. As he does in Titus 2:11–14, Paul is using this "creedal" statement in Titus 3:4–7 to strengthen his command to obey these ungodly authorities. He is demonstrating the veracity of this instruction through a universally accepted Christian statement: salvation does not come by works, but through the mercy of God.

There are significant parallels to Titus 3:3–7 in other Pauline letters. E.g., see Rom 4:2–6; 9:11, 32; 11:6; 13:3 (authorities are not a cause for fear of good works); 2 Cor 9:8; 11:15 ("end according to their works"); Gal 2:16; 3:2, 5; 5:19; 6:4; Eph 2:9–10. Outside of Romans and Galatians, "works" are usually regarded as a good thing, save for Paul's statements in Eph 2:10, Titus 3:5 and 2 Tim 1:8–12. Paul's emphasis on "good works" speaks to the nature of his argument and theology. The gospel is always at God's initiative. But, only in certain situations does Paul need to make clear that works are not the reason for God's salvation (or calling), whether good or bad. One also needs to be aware within this debate that Paul also espouses the statement that one's deeds do matter, and that God sometimes punishes those who practice bad deeds (Rom 2:5–8; 2 Cor 11:15).

71. For example, see Dunn, "First and Second Letters," 876–77.

72. It should be noted that Paul does mention that "disputes about the law" (μάκας νομικὰς) should be avoided in Titus 3:9 and that these disputes stand in contrast to maintaining good works (Titus 3:8).

73. Cf. the OT usage in Exod 34:6–7; Ps 85:15 (LXX).

74. Rom 9:15, 18; 11:30–32. Cf. also 1 Tim 1:13–16 where the verb is used twice in

The closest parallels to Titus 3:5 are Romans 11:30–32 and Ephesians 2:4–5, both of which juxtapose disobedience with undeserved mercy.[75] However, in Titus 3:5, Paul contrasts righteous works with mercy. The similarity is thematic. In both cases Paul is appealing to disobedience that gives way to God's mercy. Just as the Greeks received mercy, so too, the Jews received mercy. Paul concludes, "For God has shut up all in disobedience that he might be merciful to all" (Rom 11:32). In Titus 3, the Cretans were to obey the authorities, because they had themselves been saved by God's mercy, and not by righteous works. The use of "mercy" is significant because one might expect the word "grace" since it is a more prolific term in Paul (used in Titus 3:7 with the verb "justified" [διακιόω]). As for connection with the NPP, "mercy" has not been at the fore of the primary debates. In fact, whether speaking of Jew/gentile relations or salvation generally, it is clear that salvation is a merciful, gracious act. What the NPP may not articulate quite well enough is how, once the Jew/gentile relations settled and Christians began interacting with pagans, that might influence Paul's articulation of his theology. In other words, although the mercy of God is evidently needed for Jew and gentile alike, Paul may also use this socio-logical statement to speak also of Christians and non-Christians, which is a sub-set of the prior category of Jew/gentile.

Washing and Renewal

The terms here are not overly significant for the present study, but for the sake of thoroughness, there are a few issues to address. The term for "washing" (λουτρόν) is attested only one other time in the NT (Eph 5:26). There is some debate as to whether or not this "washing" is a reference to baptism.[76] Quinn points out that the term may have been a clever way for Paul to borrow the ubiquity of the Roman baths and to reinvent its

---

reference to Paul's own conversion.

75. "For just as you once were disobedient to God, but now have been shown mercy because of their disobedience, so these also now have been disobedient, that because of the mercy shown to you they also may now be shown mercy. For God has shut up all in disobedience so that He may show mercy to all" (Rom 11:30–32).

"But God, being rich in mercy, because of His great love with which He loved us even when we were dead in our transgressions made us alive together with Christ (by grace you have been saved)" (Eph 2:4).

76. For example, see Dunn, "First and Second Letters," 877; Quinn, Letter to Titus, 220; Marshall with Towner, Pastoral Epistles, 317–18; Towner, Letters to Timothy and Titus, 781; Fee, 1 and 2 Timothy, Titus, 205; Kelly, Pastoral Epistles, 252.

ambience for the Christian *polis*.[77] Although this reference likely has baptism in mind, both the Jews and Greeks were well-acquainted with washing as a means of physical and ritual cleanliness. Also, if Titus 3:4–7 is a creedal (or liturgical) statement, it would make sense to make reference to baptism, which was a common practice in early Christianity.[78] "Regeneration" is a Pauline *hapax legomenon*, but in Matthew 19:28 it appears as a reference to the resurrection.[79] As for "renewal" (ἀνακαίνωσις)," Paul uses the word in Romans 12:2 in reference to the "renewal of the mind" in contrast to conformity with the world.

Justified by Grace: Justification and the NPP

The focal point of most debates revolving around the NPP is the definition and articulation of Paul's use of δικ- vocabulary, primarily "righteousness" (δικαιοσύνη) and "justified" (δικαιόω).[80] Although Titus 3:3–7 is similar to 1 Timothy 1:12–16; 2:3–7, and 2 Timothy 1:8–12, the presence of the verb "justified" (δικαιόω) adds special significance. Although one may be inclined not to compare this passage with the NPP because the polemical situation is different, or because of the letter's disputed Pauline pedigree, there are simply too many tenets of the NPP outlined in chapter 1 present

77. See Quinn, *Letter to Titus*, 220–21.

78. It is worth noting that Paul's usual description of baptism is not in reference to water or washing, or even cleanliness, but to death and resurrection (Rom 6:3–4; Col 2:12–13). However, in Acts 22:16, Paul's baptism is connected with the washing away of sins. Paul also uses this same term (ἀπολούω) in 1 Cor 6:11, but there is no direct connection with baptism.

79. N. T. Wright argues that "'regeneration' is not a term that occurs in any of Paul's discussions of justification. 'Regeneration' is primarily a Johannine concept, and we should be wary of superimposing it on Paul's careful language and categories." See Wright, *Paul and the Faithfulness of God*, 954. One may also note the connection these two verses make to the resurrection. In other words, Matt 19:28 obviously refers to the resurrection, so this "washing of regeneration" in Titus 3:5 may also refer tangentially to the resurrection, and in close proximity to "justification" (Titus 3:5–7; cf. 1 Tim 3:16, the only other reference to δικαιόω in the PE that likely also refers to the resurrection). See also Bird, *Saving Righteousness of God*, 53–59.

80. For example, see Waters, *Justification and the New Perspectives on Paul*; Spence, *Justification*; Piper, *Future of Justification*; Husbands and Treier, *Justification*; Westerholm, *Justification Reconsidered*; McCormack, *Justification in Perspective*; Hays, "Justification," 3:1129–33; Irons, *Righteousness of God*; Wright, *Justification*. All of these works engage the NPP and the theology of justification. As noted below, the major passages discussed outside of Romans and Galatians are Phil 3:3–12 and 2 Cor 5:21, neither of which mention "justified" (δικαιόω), but "righteousness" (δικαιόσυνη). See also Dunn, *Theology of Paul the Apostle*, 334–89.

not to do so. Paul includes himself in the characterization of their former life ("us," ἡμεῖς), uses the word "works" (οὐκ ἐξ ἔργων) in contrast to
"mercy" (ἀλλὰ κατὰ τὸ αὐτοῦ ἔλεος), and this is the only time the word
"justified" (δικαιωθέντες) is used in the PE in a similar situation as its use
in Romans and Galatians.[81] And, the specific terminology of "justified"
being qualified by "grace" (χάρις) is done by Paul only in Romans 3:24
(δικαιούμενοι δωρεὰν τῇ αὐτοῦ χάριτι).[82]

The NPP has had a relatively consistent view of justification since the
time of E. P. Sanders.[83] In his seminal work, *Paul and Palestinian Judaism*,
Sanders was not completely set on one usage of the term "justified" and
"righteousness."[84] In fact, he even states that "'righteousness' does not have
any one fixed meaning."[85] He continues, "'Righteousness by faith,' in other

---

81. The only other time the word is used at all in the PE is 1 Tim 3:16. As noted
above in n79, see Bird, *Saving Righteousness of God*, 53–56, who deals with this verse
specifically, stating "What is implicit in several texts elsewhere is made explicit here,
viz., that Jesus's resurrection constitutes his justification by God." Bird, *Saving Righteousness of God*, 53.

82. Gal 5:4 is similar, but instead of "grace" modifying justified, falling from "grace"
is the result of seeking to be justified by law (κατηργήθητε ἀπὸ Χριστοῦ, οἵτινες ἐν
νόμῳ δικαιοῦσθε, τῆς χάριτος ἐξεπέσατε).

83. Robert Cara argues that the consistency within the NPP is its articulation of
what justification "is not." He states, "NPP is clear and unified on what justification does
not mean." However, he does admit "one standard NPP view" advocated by Wright
and Dunn, which is that "*Initial justification is by faith and recognizes covenant status
(ecclesiology), while final justification is partially by works, albeit works produced by the
Spirit.*" See Cara, *Cracking the Foundation*, 23–25, italics original. Michael Bird maintains that the NPP is correct in that "imputed" righteousness cannot be demonstrated
from a single text. However, he also insists that systematic theology does indeed prove
the veracity of the theology of imputed righteousness. See Bird, *Saving Righteousness
of God*, 182.

84. The terms "justified," "righteousness," "righteous," etc. are all related words, the
relation of which is the genesis of much of the debate surrounding Pauline theology.
For example, if one is "made righteous" as an attribute, and that is what Paul means
when he uses the word "justified," that definition carries a different theological emphasis than justification as judicial acquittal. There are several works that detail the
meaning of justification, and righteousness, that may be consulted. One of the most
comprehensive is McGrath, *Iustitia Dei*.

85. Sanders, *Paul and Palestinian Judaism*, 491. He makes this statement regarding
only Rom 4. He would no doubt hold this statement to be true throughout the rest of
Pauline literature. In fact, he does state, "It seems to me that in fact the verb does not
always bear the same meaning in Paul" (471). This variegated use of "righteousness"
is also pointed out by John Ziesler in *Meaning of Righteousness in Paul*. He states of
the δικ- word group, "If we take the verb as essentially relational or forensic, and the
noun and adjective as describing behavior within relationship, and if we also make full
use of the corporate Christ idea, we arrive at an exegesis which satisfies the concerns
of both traditional Catholicism and traditional Protestantism. . . . The relationship

words, is not any *one* doctrine. It is the heuristic category employed by Paul against the notion that obedience to the law is necessary. We should repeat here the observation that 'righteousness by faith' receives very little *positive* working out by Paul."[86] Sanders's characterization of justification, then, draws not upon the definition of the word *per se*, but Paul's use of the word in his polemics against the law and Judaism. Dunn describes "justified" as "predominantly Paul's word in the NT"[87] because, of the thirty-five uses of the word, twenty-seven are in Paul.[88] He defines δικαιόω, more rigidly than Sanders, as a "metaphor drawn from the lawcourt to describe the judge's responsibility to give a fair verdict and to 'justify,' that is, acquit the innocent, as in typically Jewish usage."[89] This "typically Jewish usage" is in keeping with the NPP's view that Paul had more continuity with Judaism[90] and that justification did not actually grant anyone righteousness as a quality to be possessed, or even that somehow God's (or Christ's) righteousness stood in the gap.[91] Instead, Paul's metaphor of justification was born from Jew/gentile disputes about who is part of the people of God. Wright, too, emphasizes the "forensic," Jewish, law-court nature of the "righteous" word group as opposed to the Greek and English meaning of the word which "carried moralistic overtones."[92] Wright cuts to the center of the debate: "If

between justification and righteousness is not uniform" (212). It should be noted that Ziesler does not come to this conclusion based solely on Romans and Galatians, but he includes Philippians, Colossians, Thessalonians, Ephesians, Corinthians, and the PE. Ziesler, *Meaning of Righteousness in Paul*, 147–63. In fact, with regard to Titus 3:3–7, Ziesler argues, "It is true that from this passage alone, a 'make righteous' meaning is possible, but a declaratory (not a demonstrative) one is equally possible, and it is to be preferred as following the usual meaning in other literature. God accepts, or acquits us, purely by his grace" (155).

86. Sanders, *Paul and Palestinian Judaism*, 492, italics original.

87. Dunn, *Epistle to the Galatians*, 134.

88. Of these twenty-seven occurrences, twenty-three are found in Romans and Galatians. First Corinthians contains two occurrences (1 Cor 4:4; 6:11). Interestingly, Dunn's count also includes the two occurrences in the PE (1 Tim 3:16; Titus 3:7).

89. Dunn, *Galatians*, 134. See also Dunn, *Theology of Paul the Apostle*, 335–40.

90. The primary argument of Dunn and Wright is not that Paul and Judaism are the same, but that Paul thought in Jewish terms and that Paul saw the gospel as a continuation of God's promise to the Jews, which also has to do with his "conversion." They do not see the Jews, or at least the Jews to whom Paul is writing, as "legalistic." Thus, as has been pointed out already, the issue for the NPP is whether or not some traditional readings of Pauline justification frame Paul's polemic in the wrong way. For example, see Dunn, *Theology of Paul the Apostle*, 335–38 and Wright, *Jesus, Paul and the People of God*, 235–61. Examples like these could be demonstrated many times over.

91. Dunn discusses the NPP's problems with the Lutheran position despite its positive outcomes in *New Perspective on Paul*, 187–205.

92. Wright, *What Saint Paul Really Said*, 98. Also see Wright, *Justification*, 68–70.

we use the language of the law court, it makes no sense whatever to say that the judge imputes, imparts, bequeaths, conveys, or otherwise transfers his righteousness to either the plaintiff or the defendant."[93] Wright directly challenges the notion that righteousness is imputed, what has been traditionally the Reformed position.[94] Wright also describes Paul's theology of justification as past, present, and in some sense, future.[95] Wright explains further that the "context of Paul's major 'justification' passages is not the individual search for a gracious God but the question of how you know who belongs to God's people."[96] With Dunn and Wright, there is a move from a

93. Wright, *What Saint Paul Really Said*, 98.

94. The Reformed view of the δικ- word group (specifically δικαιόω) is what has been called "imputed righteousness." In essence, "imputed righteousness" is the belief that in justification God's righteousness stands in place of the sinfulness of the individual. Or, as R. K. Johnston puts it, "Imputation has ultimately to do with salvation, with our 'alien righteousness,' with being reckoned *as if* we were righteous." Johnston, "Imputation," 600, italics original. It is important to note, that what also is at stake in this definition is whether or not justification was part of Paul's overarching articulation of the gospel, rather than simply a polemical doctrine, as argued by the NPP.

Similarly, though not necessarily important for testing the NPP in Titus 3:3–7 is 2 Cor 5:21 and Phil 3:9. The traditional understanding is that Paul is arguing that the law does not make one righteous, but that God does. However, the NPP, especially N. T. Wright, takes issue with this understanding, arguing that one receives God's righteousness, not as a quality, but as a status. This characterization has to do with Wright's belief that justification has more to do with ecclesiology than obedience to the gospel. For example, see Wight, *What Saint Paul Really Said*, 119, 122. He writes concerning Phil 3:9, "This status of 'righteousness,' Paul insists, is something he has 'in the Messiah.' 'Righteousness' here is not, despite multiple attempts to assert such a thing, the status which God himself possesses, and somehow grants or reckons or passes over to the believer. It is 'the righteousness *from* God' (the Greek is *ek theou*); it is not God's own righteousness, but rather the status that is given by God. (The contrasting phrase, *dikaiosynē ek nomou*, hardly denotes a righteousness which the law itself possesses and which is imputed to the law-observant Jew!)." See Wright, *Justification*, 150. It is worth noting that Sanders argues that the meaning of "righteousness" in Phil 3:9 means "having, attaining or being given righteousness." Sanders, *Paul and Palestinian Judaism*, 470–71. Dunn also discusses Phil 3:2–14 in detail. See Dunn, *New Perspective on Paul*, 463–87; Dunn, *Theology of Paul the Apostle*, 369–79. Also, see his discussion of 2 Cor 5:21 wherein Wright argues that the traditional interpretation does not properly take into account the larger context and the Jewish meaning of the "righteousness of God" (Wrights argues that the phrase means "covenantal faithfulness" rather than a quality to be had or given). Wright, *Justification*, 158–67.

95. See Wright, *Pauline Perspectives*, 423.

96. Wright, *Pauline Perspectives*, 429. This is the position of both Dunn and Wright. Also see Dunn, *New Perspective on Paul*, 190. In another articulation Wright explains, "'Justification' is thus the declaration of God, the just judge, that someone is (a) in the right, that their sins are forgiven, and (b) a true member of the covenant family, the people belonging to Abraham. That is how the word works in Paul's writings. It doesn't describe how people get in to God's forgiven family; it declares that they are in." Wright,

variegated complexity of the terms (Sanders) to a more consistent, uniform definition of righteousness.[97] The problem with this "consistency" is that it seems to flatten Paul's positive theology into a theology of polemics. It is clear, especially within Galatians, that Paul's theology of justification is primarily polemical. However, in Titus 3:3–7, this definition fails to account for the nuanced way in which Paul uses δικ- language.

The problem that arises with the use of "justified" in Titus 3:7 is whether or not the articulation of Pauline justification by the NPP fits. Although disagreeing with the NPP on many levels, even Robert Cara states, "This is termed 'justification,' which is a sinner declared to be righteous based on the work of Christ."[98] So, even Cara acknowledges the declarative way in which δικαιόω functions. What this agreement in definition demonstrates is not that the definition of the word is an insurmountable problem, but the circumstances in which the word is used dictate its meaning. For example, Cara points out that the NPP defines justification in two ways: initial and final. Initial justification is by faith.[99] Final justification is, at least partially, by works.[100] The objective of this study is not to identify whether or not the NPP is right with regard to their definition in specific exegesis

---

Pauline Perspectives, 218.

97. As already discussed in previous chapters, the δικ- word group (especially the word δίκαιος) has a variegated usage even within undisputed Paul. So, even within the PE "righteous" can be moral or forensic (e.g., 1 Tim 1:9; 2 Tim 4:8). For example, Michael Bird writes, "First, 'righteousness' in Paul is a complex and multivalent concept that evokes a wide range of ideas, thoughts, and echoes of Scripture. I have maintained that 'justification' in Paul is forensic and not transformative." Bird, *Saving Righteousness of God*, 181.

98. Cara, *Cracking the Foundation*, 162. Although this statement may at first seem to coincide with NPP theology because of Cara's use of the word "declared," which calls to mind acquittal, earlier in his work he explicitly adheres to the Reformed definition of justification from the Westminster Shorter Catechism 33. He states, "As is clear from this definition, a believer is justified based on the work of Christ and not his own works. The sin of the believer is imputed to Christ, and Christ's righteousness is imputed to the believer. . . . Hence, a believer has nothing to fear at the final judgment because the legal judgment has already been made when she put her faith in Christ." Cara, *Cracking the Foundation*, 54.

99. The word "faith" (πίστις) is not used in this passage. However, in 3:8, "those who have believed God" (οἱ πεπιστευκότες θεῷ) are to engage in good works.

100. For example, see Dunn, *New Perspective on Paul*, 67–80. Wright defines justification in the glossary of *Paul for Everyone*: "God's declaration, from his position as judge of the world, that someone is in the right, despite universal sin. This declaration will be made on the last day on the basis of an entire life (Rom 2:1–16), but it is brought forward into the present on the basis of Jesus's achievement, because sin has been dealt with through his cross (Rom 3:21–4:25); the means of this present justification is simply faith. This means, particularly, that Jews and Gentiles alike are full members of the family promised by God to Abraham (Gal 3; Rom 4)." Wright, *Pastoral Letters*, 174.

in undisputed Paul. The objective is to identify whether or not the NPP's definitions work within Titus 3:3–7. It seems the NPP's definition *can* work, but the circumstances in Titus 3:3–7 do not match those of Galatians and Romans—the two letters in which Dunn (following Schweitzer and Wrede) says the doctrine of justification is "confined."[101]

Further, the use of the word "heir" (κληρονόμος)[102] is significant for this study in that every Pauline usage other than Titus 3:7 is in Romans and Galatians and, other than Rom 8:17–18,[103] revolves around a discussion of Abraham, law, and justification.[104] So, once again, even though the situation of Titus is different than that of Galatians and Romans, they share similar vocabulary and theology. Even though one could maintain that "justified by grace" is negative because of its contrast to "works," (per Sanders) it would be difficult to argue that the "works" being envisioned in Titus 3:5 refer to Jewish covenantal works. Instead, it seems that Paul's primary, very specific polemic of Romans and Galatians is being expanded to include "works" of any kind, and that being justified is in direct contrast to the supposed "works we did in righteousness." Paul is purposefully contrasting salvation apart from "works we did righteousness" to being "justified" through grace. It is this "grace" that gives one the righteous status of heir.[105]

Regarding the meaning of "justified" in this passage, it is clear that justification comes via God's work in Christ, the Holy Spirit,[106] and grace.[107]

---

101. Dunn, *New Perspective on Paul*, 193. However, though the usage of the word δικαιόω in Romans and Galatians is more prevalent, Paul does also use the word twice in 1 Corinthians (4:4; 6:11) and twice in the PE (1 Tim 3:16; Titus 3:7).

102. It should be pointed out that the cognate terms "inheritance" (κληρονομία) and "to be appointed by lot" (κληρόω; NT hapax legomenon; Eph 1:11;) are also used by Paul (Gal 3:18, Eph 1:14, 18; 5:5; Col 3:24). See "κληρονομία" and "κληρόω," BDAG, 548–49.

103. Note the connection between Rom 8:17–18 and 2 Tim 1:8–12 and "suffering."

104. Rom 4:13–14; Gal 3:29—4:7.

105. "Being justified" (δικαιωθέντες) is connected with being saved and is what qualifies one to be an heir (ἵνα δικαιωθέντες τῇ ἐκείνου χάριτι κληρονόμοι γενηθῶμεν).

106. Several commentators point out the overt Trinitarian element in this passage. For example, see Fee, *1 and 2 Timothy, Titus*, 206; Clark, *Pastoral Epistles*, 237; Guthrie, *Pastoral Epistles*, 218.

107. Though his thoughts will be discussed more fully in the concluding chapter of the present work, for now one should note, as John Barclay points out, that with regard to Romans 11, "works" are not "culturally specific." He argues that Paul's statement about God's grace held true in his own day, as well as in Elijah's day (Rom 11:5–6). He states, "But since the Christ-event defines his understanding of God, this rule can hardly be limited to time and culture." Barclay, *Paul and the Gift*, 546. In a footnote, he explains, "In this regard, the subsequent Pauline tradition (e.g., Eph 2:8–10; Titus 3:4–6) did not misinterpret Paul in its generalized statements that

This righteous (and saved) status, though already given, also provides future hope for eternal life.[108] Sanders's multivalent definition of the righteous word group holds true even in Titus 3:3–7 in that, although not dealing with Torah, being justified by grace is in contrast to salvation by works. In other words, in attempts to define the δικ- word group consistently, the NPP has failed to appreciate the complexity of the term and its use outside the Jew/gentile dispute.

Conclusions: Titus 3:3–7—A Faithful Saying

The language of Titus 3:3–7 incorporates copious Pauline theological terminology, and by that, incorporates much of the language of the NPP. Though Paul's reference to Judaism is only by way of his specific opponents and the implicit connection of his former life, the major categories of "works," "righteousness," "justification," "salvation," "mercy," and "grace" remain. In contrast to the characterization of δικαιόω as a primarily polemical term in the NPP, "justified" in this case is viewed more positively and not directly in response to the Jew/gentile relations prevalent in Romans and Galatians.[109] Contrary to Dunn and Wright's characterization in undisputed Paul, the term "righteousness" bears a moralistic tone (Titus 3:5).[110] So, it seems Titus 3:3–7 does stand in contrast to "works-righteousness." An argument

---

'works' are irrelevant for the operation of grace." Barclay, *Paul and the Gift*, 546n57. In other words, Paul can be both specific and more generalized in his articulation of God's grace in contrast to works.

108. Once again, the starkest comparisons are drawn from Galatians and Romans (Rom 5:5; 8:23–25; Gal 4:1–7; 5:5).

109. It is also closely tied to salvation as in Rom 5:9, "Much more then, having been justified (δικαιωθέντες) by his blood, we shall be saved (σωθησοόμεθα) by the wrath of God through Him."

110. For example, see Wright, *Paul and the Faithfulness of God*, 798–801, wherein he argues from Daniel, Isaiah, and even an interchange between David and Saul (1 Sam 24:1–17) that "the verdict 'righteous,' 'in the right,' is a matter of *the status conferred by the court's verdict*, rather than overall moral character." Wright, *Paul and the Faithfulness of God*, 799, italics original. Although "righteousness" may often bear this connotation, in Titus 3:5–7, that does not seem to be the case. See also Dunn, *Theology of Paul the Apostle*, 341–42. He argues similarly that both δικαιόω and δικαιοσύνη have different meanings in Greek and Hebrew thought. In Greek thought, "'righteousness' is an idea or ideal against which the individual's action can be measured." However, Hebrew thought (צדיק) focuses on the "relational concept." He points to the same passage as Wright as proof (1 Sam 24:17). Like Wright, he argues, "This recognition that the thought world which comes to expression in the English term ('justification') is through and through Hebraic/biblical/Jewish in character is a key factor in gaining a secure hold on Paul's teaching on justification." Dunn, *Theology of Paul the Apostle*, 342.

could be made that Paul was not actively combatting works-righteousness, but that he was anticipating a notion of superiority by Christians who had been saved and subsequently engaged in good works (which would become "legalism"/"works-righteousness"). Even if "legalism" was Paul's primary polemic, the delineation of salvation in Titus 3:3–7 is comparable to the Jew/gentile issues of Romans and Galatians. But, instead of ethnic (or, Jewish covenantal/Torah-observing) superiority, in Titus 3:3–7 one detects a "Christian" superiority, which originated in retrospect. In other words, the Cretan Christians may have considered themselves superior only after their conversion. Just as the Jews were in danger of assuming a special relationship with God based on their ethnicity and the works that status required, so too, the early Christians inherited a morphed form of this same mentality. After having been saved and now living a more "righteous" life, they undoubtedly were prone to forgetting their own salvation was predicated upon mercy, and that their righteous state was granted through grace.

Titus 3:3–7 resembles a coupling of 1 Timothy 1:6–16 and 2:3–7, wherein Paul urges Timothy to pray for kings and rulers, because God wishes that all would come to repentance. In being subject and kind to all men, Paul reminds Titus to tell the Cretans, that they also were once foolish and that "we were saved" (Titus 3:5) apart from works done in righteousness. His point is that in spite of evil deeds, and not because of those done in righteousness, salvation was granted, and this principle is lived out in showing kindness and subjection and by doing good works (Titus 3:1–2, 8).[111] The natural inclination, both here and 1 Timothy 2:3–7, is that once someone has been saved, they begin to see others negatively, as if somehow one deserves salvation more than another. Paul looks to prevent that thinking.

This distinction is important to make in relation to the NPP. The NPP does not believe Paul is combating "works-righteousness" in Romans and Galatians. Instead, Paul is opposed to "righteousness" based on Jewish merit, or better, acceptance into the people of God by way of works of Torah (or, ethnic identity markers). But, the type of thinking in Titus 3:3–7 is a form of "works-righteousness," which forces one to consider how the NPP might incorporate this into their hermeneutic. This will be taken up more fully in the next chapter. However, for the present, in order for the hermeneutic of the NPP to work in this case, one must consider "righteousness" in a more textured, variegated way—as both moralistic and covenantal.[112] Also, the

---

111. This emphasis is also pointed out by Cara. Cara, *Cracking the Foundation*, 161–62. He states as well, "Hence, human works are the soteriological opposite of God's salvation-mercy-justification-grace, that is, human effort is here considered works righteousness." Cara, *Cracking the Foundation*, 162.

112. For example, Robert Wall explains, "The expression is a judicial metaphor: a

NPP must envision a Pauline justification theology capable of encompassing both incorporation into the people of God and as a personal acquittal. As noted above, even James Dunn admits of this passage, "In fact, what we have is one of the clearest statements in all the Bible that the implementation of God's saving purpose is wholly at the initiative of God—'not from works in righteousness which we have done, but according to his own mercy' (v. 5)."[113] However, he does provide a few caveats, all with regard to the NPP, although not stated so outrightly. He states something similar to what was stated in the last chapter regarding 2 Timothy 1:8–12, "The more specific case made by Paul (that gentile believers should not be required to take on a Jewish life-style/works) is broadened into a restatement of the original principle behind God's saving act (as in Eph 2:8–9)."[114]

The findings of this chapter with regard to the hermeneutic of the NPP may be summed up by Colin Kruse. He makes these observations concerning Titus 3:4–7:

> First, works of righteousness in this context has nothing to do with national identity and privileges of Israel. Second, the theme of justification by grace without human works of righteousness is introduced here in a passage which has no direct application to the problem of Judaizing. . . . Third, there is a parallel to this passage in 1 Corinthians 6:9–11, where Paul reminds the Corinthians that some of them too had once been enslaved in all sorts of sinful behavior, "but," he says, "you were washed, you were sanctified, you were justified in the name of the Lord Jesus Christ and in the Spirit of our God" (6:11).[115]

The next chapter will summarize the findings of this study and make some final observations about the viability of the NPP hermeneutic in the PE, paying special attention to the four categories outlined in chapter 1.

---

judge renders a verdict of acquittal based on evidence of innocence. Here God gives the verdict of 'not guilty' on the sole basis of Christ's faithfulness (Rom 3:21–31). But if this verdict is then applied individualistically as an internal matter of the heart and thereby detached from any real change in the way one lives, then we would suggest that it is far wide of the mark. . . . While a righteousness of works is not a precondition for God's rescue operation of sinners (so 3:5a), a righteousness of works is its certain outcome." Wall and Steele, *1 & 2 Timothy and Titus*, 366.

113. Dunn, "First and Second Letters," 876.

114. Dunn, "First and Second Letters," 876.

115. Kruse, *Paul, the Law, and Justification*, 268. Sanders points to 1 Cor 6:9–11 (and Rom 5:6–9) in order to demonstrate the complexity of translating the term δικαιόω consistently. Sanders, *Paul and Palestinian Judaism*, 471.

6

Some Conclusions Regarding the New Perspective on Paul and the Pastoral Epistles

Restatement of Problem, Thesis, and Method

THE PE AND THE NPP have existed alongside one another as separate fields of study, though rarely crossing paths primarily due to long-standing, unquestioned assumptions about the authorship of the PE—that Paul did not write them. This dissertation has aimed to bridge this gap between Paul and the PE by testing the validity of the NPP in the PE by way of the canonical perspective. By approaching this study from the canonical perspective, this study has been able to focus on the historical opponents of the PE as individual letters written for specific situations in Ephesus, Crete, and in preparation for Paul's "departure" (2 Tim 4:6) but still in relative continuity with the rest of the Pauline canon. Chapter 1 of this work stated the problem, thesis, and detailed method for the research. Chapter 2 traced the two research trajectories—Paul and the PE—which have culminated in this work.[1] Chapter 3 focused on the opponents of 1 Timothy as well as an interpretation of 1 Timothy 1:6–16 and 2:3–7 in conversation with the NPP. These two passages demonstrated that (1) one function of the law was that it was not for the "righteous" but for the "lawless and rebellious," (2) that Paul retrospectively understood himself as the "foremost sinner," who served as the example *par excellence* of God's mercy in salvation, and that (3) Paul's

---

1. As demonstrated in Chapter 2, there have been prior studies done to help bridge this gap. For example, see Aageson, *Paul, the Pastoral Epistles, and the Early Church*; Anderson, *Paul's New Perspective*; Beker, *Heirs of Paul*; Barclay, *Paul and the Gift*; Watson, *Paul, Judaism, and the Gentiles*; Kruse, *Paul, the Law, and Justification*; Vaughan, "Investigation of the Authenticity of the Pastoral Epistles"; Venema, *Gospel of Free Acceptance in Christ*; Lash, "New Perspective and Good Deeds."

apostleship to the gentiles extended beyond Jew/gentile relations within the church (1 Tim 2:3–7). Chapter 4 interpreted 2 Timothy 1:3, 8–12. The study of these passages found that Paul shared a "clean conscience" with his Jewish forebears (2 Tim 1:3), and made a correlation between himself and Timothy, who also inherited (in a way) his faith from his mother and grandmother (2 Tim 1:5). Chapter 4 also found that Paul knew that there was a great danger in the ministry he shared with Timothy—that it somehow might lead to the notion that they had earned, or deserved, their position based on works (2 Tim 1:8–12). Chapter 5 identified the opponents of Titus, making sure to highlight both the comparable as well as distinctive qualities of the Cretan opposition with the Ephesian opposition. This chapter also studied Titus 3:3–7, a passage sharing remarkable vocabulary with the Pauline theology of Romans and Galatians. The study of this passage found that despite the NPP's best efforts to define δικ- language succinctly and consistently, the nature of the context of Titus 3:1–10 requires a more nuanced, less rigid definition of Pauline justification theology.

Essentially, by testing the NPP in the PE, one is testing undisputed Paul with the Paul of the PE.[2] As the history of research demonstrates, the NPP has focused attention on Romans and Galatians and the polemics found within them. More precisely, although the NPP has incorporated all of undisputed Paul in their theologies, Romans and Galatians have taken center stage in most of the current debates because of the NPP's reaction to traditional, Lutheran readings of Paul that have focused on first-century Judaism as legalistic and on individual salvation from a plagued conscience.[3] Ironically, the NPP has itself become a polemical hermeneutic seeking to set right the wrongs of the traditional perspective.[4] Because of the polemical nature of the

2. Guy Prentiss Waters explains the dilemma Titus 3:5, Eph 2:9, and 2 Tim 1:9 presents to the NPP: "This state of affairs raises two questions: (1) Students of Scripture who ascribe all thirteen epistles to Paul are faced *either* with two irreconcilable Pauline teachings of works (the one in the undisputed and the other in the disputed letters), *or* with a recognition that the view represented in Titus, Ephesians, and 2 Timothy should govern our view of the passages discussed in Galatians, Romans, and Philippians. (2) But there is also a problem for NPP proponents. How is it that these supposedly post-Pauline documents so quickly came to misunderstand what NPP proponents argue is a fundamental and organizing doctrine not only for Romans, but for Pauline thought as whole? While some explanation of this understanding is required, it has not been forthcoming." Waters, *Justification and the New Perspectives on Paul*, 167.

3. For example, one of Wright's earliest books, *Climax of the Covenant*, devotes a chapter to several Pauline letters, one among the "disputed" category (Phlm 6; Col 1:15–20; 1 Cor 8; 2 Cor 3). However, the majority of the book focuses on Galatians, Romans, and Phil 3:5–11. See Wright, *Climax of the Covenant*.

4. This phrase is reminiscent of a new book by Griffiths, *When Wright Is Wrong*. In this work he primarily deals with only Wright's position and confines himself to Romans

NPP's roots and the reaction it provoked, one might expect that the NPP and the traditional perspective to be incompatible. However, it seems, based on this study of the several passages in the PE, that the NPP and the traditional perspectives represent two aspects of Paul's theology, and that, if definitions are more nuanced and the lines of contention redrawn, the theology of Paul is robust enough to incorporate both. What follows are some general conclusions drawn from the study of 1 Timothy 1:1–16, 2:3–7; 2 Timothy 1:3, 8–12; Titus 3:3–7 in conversation with the NPP.

This project has not spent a great deal of time discussing "covenantal nomism," even though it is the primary aspect and assumption of the NPP. As stated in chapter 1, covenantal nomism as defined by E. P. Sanders is "the view that one's place in God's plan is established on the basis of the covenant and that the covenant requires as the proper response of man his obedience to its commandments, while providing a means of atonement for transgression."[5] The relative omission of discussion of covenantal nomism is due to the absence in the passages examined in the PE of the type of polemic found in Romans and Galatians. Thus, a proper comparison and analysis could be somewhat artificial. The "works" Paul mentions in the PE are not the "works of Law" that may be restricted to covenantal identifiers. Instead, Paul seems to be reacting against, or anticipating, a legalistic mindset, which is precisely what Sanders argues Paul is not dong in Romans, Galatians, and Philippians.[6] In the passages of the PE studied in the previous pages, one may catch glimpses of this "pre-conversion" thought in Paul. For example, in 1 Timothy 1:6–16, Paul did not seem interested in being "saved," until his encounter with Christ on the road to Damascus. It is only then, in retrospect, he can see himself as a "blasphemer and a persecutor and a violent aggressor" (1 Tim 1:13). In fact, even after his conversion, he is still able to look back at his former life (and the worship of his "forebears" [πρόγονος]; 2 Tim 1:3) with a "clean conscience." However, though

---

and Galatians and approaches the critique from a "Reformed Baptist covenantal position" (3). See also Vanhoozer, "Wrighting the Wrongs of the Reformation?," 235–59.

5. Sanders, *Paul and Palestinian Judaism*, 75. Sanders prefers the term "covenantal nomism" over "soteriology," because soteriology is concerned with the "other-world." He argues that rabbinic Judaism is not concerned with the question of "What must I do to be saved?" (75). Cara's entire work, including his discussion of the deutero-Pauline epistles is written to undermine Sanders's characterization of first-century Judaism. See Cara, *Cracking the Foundation*.

6. See Sanders, *Paul and Palestinian Judaism*, 550, wherein he concludes, "Our analysis of Rabbinic and other Palestinian Jewish literature did not reveal the kind of religion best characterized as legalistic works-righteousness. But more important for the present point, is the observation that in any case that charge is not the heart of Paul's critique."

(rabbinic) Judaism may have not been interested in soteriology as such, in the PE, Paul certainly was. This soteriology is demonstrated in 1 Timothy 1:6–16; 2:3–7; 2 Timothy 1:9–10; and Titus 3:4–7.[7] Whether or not he was concerned with "salvation" in his previous life as a Jew, he now was concerned with the "salvation of all men," using himself and his apostleship to the gentiles as an example (1 Tim 2:4; Titus 2:11). Similarly, as justification by faith played such a prominent role in Galatians and Romans, opposed not so much to legalism as to "covenantal nomism," Paul's focus on soteriology in the PE relegates justification to a role within, and as part of, salvation (Titus 3:5–7) because of the nature of the situation, and not to justification's overall theological significance.[8]

The New Perspective on Paul in the Pastoral Epistles

As stated in the first chapter of this work, this project has not been designed to validate, invalidate, or otherwise apologize for the NPP, or the traditional perspective, for that matter. Instead, this project is designed to test the basic hermeneutic of the NPP within the PE by way of the canonical perspective. The four tenets of the NPP outlined in the methodology have provided a rubric by which the specific passages within the PE were chosen. So, from the start there was a certain degree of commonality because of the similarity of subject matter. What follows is a summary of the findings of this study using these categories as a guide.

Justification and Salvation

What stands out in studying the PE is the focus on "salvation" language and the relative paucity of "justification" language and how the statements of salvation in the passages studied (called creeds, hymns, "faithful sayings,"[9] or "standard mini-speeches"[10]) are used to validate Paul's directives or premises.

7. Two of the passages are referred to as "faithful sayings" (πιστὸς ὁ λόγος; 1 Tim 1:15; Titus 3:8). Although denying Pauline authorship, Beker argues that the use of δικαιόω in Titus 3:7 refers back to "early Christian liturgical tradition." Beker, *Heirs of Paul*, 42.

8. Garwood Anderson states, "Besides these texts [Romans, Galatians and the cognate expression in Phil 3:2–11], thick with the language of justification, we find only passing references in 1 Corinthians 6:11 and Titus 3:7, where 'justification' is coordinate with, we might even say diluted by, other soteriological language." Anderson, *Paul's New Perspective*, 283.

9. 1 Tim 1:15; Titus 1:8.

10. Cara, *Cracking the Foundation*, 157.

The verb σώζω is used seven times within the PE and eight times within Romans,[11] but it is not used at all in Galatians, Philippians, or Colossians. On the other hand, the verb δικαιόω is used fifteen times in Romans, seven times in Galatians, twice in 1 Corinthians, and twice in the PE.[12] With these statistics, one can see very easily why discussions of justification (and salvation, for that matter) have revolved around Romans and Galatians among the undisputed epistles.[13] As noted early on, this project is not an attempt to define salvation and justification as they are used by Paul. This, in many ways, has been done and remains a subject of current debate.[14] The assumption underlying this project is that the meaning of either of these word groups, the δικ- word group especially, is not easily captured in a single polemic, but that the language is complex and subject to its context.

The importance of salvation in the PE in relation to the NPP is complex, in part, because of the mixing of Pauline categories. For example, in Romans and Galatians, "not by works" is often coupled with "justified," as opposed to "saved."[15] In contrast, in 2 Timothy 1:9 and Titus 3:5, "not by works" is coupled with "saved."[16] This emphasis on being "saved" apart from "works" (rather than "justified") demonstrates both the polemical, special

---

11. 1 Tim 1:15; 2:4; 4:16; 2 Tim 1:9; 4:18; Titus 3:5 (only once in Titus); cf. Rom 5:9–10; 8:24; 9:27; 10:9, 13; 11:14, 26.

12. Rom 2:13; 3:4, 20, 24, 26, 28, 30; 4:2, 5; 5:1, 9; 6:7; 8:30, 33; 1 Cor 4:4; 6:11; Gal 2:16–17; 3:8, 11, 24; 5:4; 1 Tim 3:16; Titus 3:7. It should be observed that the word is clustered in Romans 3 and Galatians 2–3.

13. The warning of Garwood Anderson should here be emphasized: "Given the structure of the following argument, it is necessary to reiterate that neither exegesis nor biblical theology can be reduced to word counts or usage statistics. When in what follows I note that certain words are used here and not there, I introduce a datum; I do not suppose that the datum is self-interpreting, that its implications are self-evident. . . . I state these caveats up front precisely because, while tracking the lexical usage through the (inclusive) Pauline corpus—hard data, as it were—we should not suppose that graphing such data amounts to an argument in itself." Anderson, *Paul's New Perspective*, 284–85. For the rebuke by James Barr of Kittel for making such similar mistakes, see Barr, *Semantics of Biblical Language*, 206–62.

14. A few examples (some noted elsewhere in this work) are: Wieland, *Significance of Salvation*; Seifrid, *Christ, Our Righteousness*; Ziesler, *Meaning of Righteousness in Paul*; Bates, *Salvation by Allegiance Alone*; Malherbe, "'Christ Jesus Came Into the World To Save Sinners,'" 331–58; Marshall, "Salvation, Grace, and Works in the Later Writings in the Pauline Corpus," 3–29; Ratzlaff, "Salvation: Individualistic or Communal?," 108–17.

15. Rom 3:20, 28; Gal 2:16.

16. 1 Tim 1:9 reads, "Who saved us (τοῦ σώσαντος ἡμᾶς) and called us with a holy calling, not according to our works (οὐ κατὰ τὰ ἔργα ἡμῶν)," whereas Titus 3:5, "not from works (οὐκ ἐξ ἔργων) we did in righteousness but according to his mercy he saved us (ἔσωσεν ἡμᾶς)." 1 Tim 1:6–16 also serves as an implicit example, even though the contrast between "works" and "saved" is not made outright.

significance of justification witnessed in Galatians, for example, and the more overarching category of salvation of which justification plays a part (Rom 5:9).[17] In other words, salvation in these two cases is not polemical, but is seen as a positive statement of the gospel of mercy.

The use of "justified" in 1 Timothy 3:16 is not the common Pauline usage,[18] which leaves the isolated use in Titus 3:7 in the PE. In most contexts, and in debates within the NPP, "justified" is understood to address the specific polemic of Jew/gentile relations with regard to the gospel of faith. In Titus 3:7, that element is not present. In fact, rather than a statement like that made in Galatians 2:16 wherein "justified by faith" is contrasted with "justified by works of Law," in Titus 3:7 salvation and justified are more interchangeable and interconnected.[19] Thus, justified, if even in this one example, does not seem to function polemically.[20]

The cognate terms among the δικ- word group (δίκαιος, δικαιοσύνη, δικαιόω) are used prolifically in Paul, and the PE are representative of the spectrum of Pauline usage.[21] However, in the specific passages chosen, the term "righteous" (δίκαιος) is used in 1 Timothy 1:9 and refers to righteous behavior, which is also observed in Romans 5:7, for example.[22] Similarly, "righteousness" (δικαιοσύνη) as used in Titus 3:5 bears a tone of moral

---

17. It is worth noting, as well, that "saved" does not necessarily mean salvation from a "plagued conscience," nor does it always mean "salvation" in a historical-ecclesiastical sense (cf. 2 Tim 1:9; Titus 3:5).

18. In 1 Tim 1:16, Jesus himself is justified, or "vindicated" by the Spirit. See Bird, *Saving Righteousness of God*, 53–56. Bird argues that Christ's justification by the Spirit refers to his resurrection, and that it is both in the death and resurrection that believers are found in Christ and receive justification. Although not dealing with the justification of mankind directly, this passage does provide another aspect of Paul's use of the word δικαιόω. However, because the use is found in a doxology of sorts ("and by common confession great is the mystery of godliness," καὶ ὁμολογουμένως μέγα ἐστὶν τὸ τῆς εὐσεβείας μυστήριον), it was not considered for the present study. A thorough study of the passage in deciphering a Pauline definition of justification may be another avenue of further research. Bird connects the passage to Isa 52–53 and the Suffering Servant, summing up his own findings, "It is union with Christ in his death *and resurrection* that constitutes the material cause of justification." Bird, *Saving Righteousness of God*, 56, italics original.

19. One is saved, not by "works of righteousness" *and* also "justified by grace."

20. The use of "justified" in a non-polemical context is also demonstrated by 1 Cor 6:9–11.

21. δίκαιος (Rom 1:17; 2:13; 3:10, 26; 5:7, 19; 7:12; Gal 3:11; Eph 6:1; Phil 1:7; 4:8; Col 4:1; 2 Thess 1:5–6; 1 Tim 1:9; 2 Tim 4:8; Titus 1:8); δικαιοσύνη (Rom 1:17; 3:5, 21–22, 25–26; 4:3–6, 9, 11, 13, 22; 5:17, 21; 6:13, 16, 18–20; 8:10; 9:30–31; 10:3–6, 10; 14:17; 1 Cor 1:30; 2 Cor 3:9; 5:21; 6:7, 14; 9:9–10; 11:15; Gal 2:21; 3:6, 21; 5:5; Eph 4:24; 5:9; 6:14; Phil 1:11; 3:6, 9; 1 Tim 6:11; 2 Tim 2:22; 3:16; 4:8; Titus 3:5).

22. Rom 5:7 states, "For one will hardly die for a righteous man (ὑπὲρ δικαίου)."

or ethical righteousness, rather than relational, or covenantal, righteousness—the definition espoused by the NPP. What the PE have demonstrated is that an attempt to narrowly define Paul's usage of a word, or word group, does not do justice to the nature of the language nor his use of it. In sum, as far the language of salvation and δικ- language are concerned, the PE present the complexity of Pauline usage which the NPP, in some cases, has flattened because of the way it is used in the polemical situations of Romans and Galatians.

Law and Works

The dual ideas of "law" and "works" are generally contrasted with "faith" or "Spirit" in Romans and Galatians.[23] The law in Romans, Galatians, and 1 and 2 Corinthians is not cast in a positive light.[24] For the most part, in Romans and Galatians, works are treated as part of the law, or as works associated with Jewishness. The NPP understands "law" as almost always referring to the Torah. Thus, much of the NPP's discussion of law and works has not revolved around "works" or "law" in a general sense (or, in a legalistic sense). The PE maintains this pattern with regard to the law. The uses of "law" all likely refer to the Torah or the OT (1 Tim 1:7–9; Titus 3:9).[25] So, there were no real inconsistencies found in these uses between the NPP and the PE. In fact, 1 Timothy 1:8 is remarkably similar to Romans 7:12, 16.

However, the use of "works" in the PE is quite different than that of Romans and Galatians. In undisputed Paul, the phrase "good works" is not used at all.[26] In the PE, the phrase is prevalent and good works are encouraged.[27] Interestingly, even though good works are commended and encouraged as part of the Christian life and witness, they are not the catalyst for salvation (2 Tim 1:9; Titus 3:5). So, both the NPP, the traditional

---

23. Also, this contrast is found in other places in different terms, though the underlying contrast is the same (e.g., 2 Cor 3:6).

24. Though, even here, there are exceptions (e.g., Rom 7:12, 16; 13:10; Gal 3:24).

25. There are other examples of this focus on law, even though the term "law" is not used. For example, Paul speaks of "Scripture" (2 Tim 3:16–17), genealogical disputes (1 Tim 1:4; Titus 3:9), Jewish myths (Titus 1:14), all of which in one way or another are connected to the OT.

26. Cf. 2 Cor 5:10, which states, "For we must all appear before the judgment seat of Christ, that each one may be recompensed for his deeds in the body (τὰ δία τοῦ σώματος), according to what he has done (πρὸς ἃ ἔπραξεν), whether good or bad." The word ἔργον is not used. This passage is similar to Rom 2:6–10.

27. Good works are also encouraged in Eph 2:8–10, even though salvation does not come by them.

perspective, and the PE agree that salvation comes "not by works." However, what these "works" are shifts from Galatians (and, possibly, Romans) to the PE. If one assumes that the NPP is correct in their articulation of "works of law" and the primary polemic found in both of these letters, one is still left to reckon with the use of the phrase in 2 Timothy 1:9 and Titus 3:5. In both cases, "works" are not qualified by law, but instead, they are either not qualified at all (2 Tim 1:9) or by "works we did in righteousness" (Titus 3:5). In either case, the NPP hermeneutic must account for the different emphasis and the reason for this different emphasis. Dunn states as much, even though he argues that 2 Timothy 1:9 and Titus 3:5 do not express the author's "fresh perspective,"[28] but that they state an already confirmed truth. He explains, "In other words, here are further examples of what we have already found in Eph 2:8–9—that is, a restatement of the more fundamental principle of human acceptability before God, rather than a restatement of Paul's more narrowly directed polemic." For Dunn, these statements in the PE are fundamental and important, but they are not the fresh, polemical perspective of Paul. It is this gap between the PE and Paul that this study has sought to bridge. All that remains to be admitted by the NPP is that a fresh thinker like Paul could have alluded to previously established fundamental theological principles rather than (re)articulate his own "fresh" theology (e.g., Rom 2:2; 3:19; 7:14; 8:22; Gal 2:16).

Paul's View of Judaism

Paul's view of Judaism and his polemic against it is the core of NPP thought. In the NPP, E. P. Sanders's "covenantal nomism" has remained the standard way of characterizing the Judaism against which Paul is reacting. Once again, this study is not concerned with whether or not the NPP's, or the traditional perspective's characterizations are correct. For this study, what is important is whether or not Judaism as characterized by the NPP can be demonstrated in the PE. Both 1 Timothy 1:12–16 and 2 Timothy 1:3 do find resonance with the NPP's description of Judaism, and in that, Paul's "conversion." Paul found relative resonance with his forebears (2 Tim 1:3) and maintains the veracity and efficacy of the Scriptures (2 Tim 3:16–17). Paul explains that he worships God with a "clean conscience the way my forebears did" (2 Tim 1:3), and James Dunn points out that when Paul looks to "mercy" in 2 Timothy 1:9 and Titus 3:5, he is looking back to the fundamental insights of Israel.[29]

28. Dunn, *New Perspective on Paul*, 385.

29. Dunn points to Exod 34:6–7 and God's calling of Israel (Rom 9:7–11, 24). See

However, in the PE there were certain sects within Judaism, what seems to be Jewish-Christians espousing some Jewish ideas, against which Paul reacts.[30] Within Titus, Paul identifies some of the opposition as "those from the circumcision" (Titus 1:10), which is a familiar Pauline way of identifying his Jewish opponents. The problem with the NPP in the PE does not seem to be Paul's description of Judaism. In fact, there is a great deal of resonance between the NPP and the PE. The problem is the fact that Paul does not address his theological polemic against these opponents in the same way he does in Romans and Galatians. This different emphasis in polemic speaks both to the opposition being faced as well as Paul's articulation of his theology. The first problems within the church (Jew/gentile relations) seem to be giving way to newer, similar problems that do not require a different theology, but different emphasis and argumentation.

Opponents

It should now be relatively clear that although there was a Jewish influence of sorts within 1 Timothy and Titus, the passages reviewed are not written in response to issues significantly comparable to that of Romans and Galatians. Certainly, there is a degree of commonality between the PE and the rest of Pauline literature. However, just as Philippians and Galatians are written for different reasons, there is also a different agenda behind the writing of each of the PE. The opposition does not seem to be "Judaizers" of the sort found in Galatians. Instead, Paul is writing to contextualize the new faith for life within their own communities *and* for the articulation of the gospel for those on the outside.[31]

It seems with the identification of the opponents in the PE as quite distinct from those in Romans and Galatians, established (and even fledgling) gentile churches had more of a problem with "works-based" salvation than their Jewish counter-parts, or these gentile churches had a problem with a *different type* of "works-based" religiosity. The NPP argues from the undisputed letters of Paul that the problem with Judaism was not meritorious works (or, "legalism"), but works based on Jewish identity and distinction. However, in 1 Timothy and Titus, the opponents are not interested in the same Jewish privilege or use of the law to that end. Instead, justification language is

---

Dunn, *New Perspective on Paul*, 386.

30. E.g., 1 Tim 1:4, 7–9; Titus 1:10, 15; 3:9.

31. For example, see Ho, "Mission in the Pastoral Epistles," 241–67. Of the passages covered in this project he specifically mentions 1 Tim 1:12–16; 2:1–7 and Titus 3:4–7 as being written with "mission" in mind.

replaced by salvation language (in every case but one), and "works of law" are replaced by "works," generally speaking—both good and bad, though in both 2 Timothy and Titus, the works discussed are works seen even in a positive sense (i.e., "good" works, even though the term "good" is not used).[32] In the case of 2 Timothy, Paul seems to be reiterating the point so that Timothy understands that both he and Paul were not called and saved based on their own work. In this way, 2 Timothy 1:8–12 is reminiscent of Romans 9:11, which, of course, has implications for the calling of other believers, as does Paul's example of his own conversion in 1 Timothy 1:12–16. With the change of emphasis comes a nuancing of theology. To use Wright's terminology to a different end, Paul's concern in the PE was not on how one can tell who is in, but on how one gets in.[33] What is represented in these passages is Paul's foundational, adaptive, not a polemical theology. While it seems that most of the time "undisputed" Paul is using justification by faith in a polemical way, Paul's instruction on being "saved" is more positive, and like justification, comes at the initiative of God.

A Contextual Shift

In order to understand properly the implications of the canonical perspective for this study, it is necessary to make a short return to the "canonical forest" of chapter 1. The analogy was that of a forest, not defined by its center only, but also by its boundaries—the thing by which the forest is separated, and distinct, from the meadow. Pauline theology, although finite and distinctive (from, say, the theology of James or John) is also quite adaptive. In other words, the Pauline forest, always forest and not part of the glade, does not always look the same. So, if one defines the Pauline center by Romans, everything that does not resemble Romans is measured by the degree to which it errs from it. Even Romans, as Paul's most extensive theological treatise, is not "center" in that way. Even so, Colossians, Ephesians, and even 1 Corinthians have a different purpose, though they are no less Pauline.

32. This shift is noted by Garwood Anderson. He explains, "As I will argue, (1) the notion of justification proved especially fitting for the targeted contexts to which Paul applied it, but (2) it would soon coexist with and eventually give way to other soteriological concepts, (3) which were conceptually broader in scope but also continuous with justification. Finally, I will argue that this transition marks a development of Pauline soteriology that corresponds to his appropriation of 'works' and grace surveyed in the previous chapter." Anderson, *Paul's New Perspective*, 284 (see also 18).

33. Wright writes, "Justification in this setting, then, is not a matter of *how someone enters the community of the true people of God*, but of *how you tell who belongs to the community*." Wright, *What Saint Paul Really Said*, 119, italics original.

Similarly, the situation of each of the PE is quite different than the situation of Romans and Galatians. So, too, the PE have been shown to share considerable commonality with undisputed Paul, while also demonstrating a shift of focus. The forest, as seen from the meadow, looks quite different than the view from its center. And, canonically speaking, the PE via their place at the end of the canonical Pauline letters likely take into account what has already been articulated in previous letters (like Romans and Galatians). In other words, the PE are not epistles isolated by themselves. Instead, they represent a normalized, adaptable Pauline theology.

This shift of focus has been defined in various ways. J. Christiaan Beker has defined Paul's theology as that of *coherence* and *contingency*,[34] the language of which shifts when speaking of the PE to *tradition* and *traditum*, though the underlying assumptions are the same.[35] Similarly, James Aageson argues for a Pauline "development" in the PE—Paul (in Aageson's case, the church or Paulinists) developing his theology through time.[36] However, a better way to articulate this "development" as witnessed through this study may be to call it a "contextual shift."[37] Paul did not so much change, amend, or develop his theology, as the context with which his theology was faced shifted. John M. G. Barclay explains this shift:[38]

34. See Beker, *Triumph of God*, 15–19, 39–103. He defines *coherence* as "the unchanging components of Paul's gospel, which contain the fundamental convictions of his gospel." Beker, *Triumph of God*, 15. Contingency is "the changing, situational part of the gospel, that is, the diversity and particularity of sociological, economical, and psychological factors that confront Paul in his churches and in his missionary work and to which he had to respond" (15–16). Even Childs uses this terminology to refer to both Romans and the PE. See Childs, *Church's Guide for Reading Paul*, 254–55.

35. Although Beker does not think Paul wrote the PE, he adapts his *coherence* and *contingency* method for "subsequent historical periods," which includes the PE. He explains this subsequent adaptation of Paul's theology as the *traditum* (the deposit of the tradition) and the *traditio* (the transmission of the tradition). Beker, *Heirs of Paul*, 27–34.

36. Aageson argues this development was not Paul's own development, but the development of Paul's image. See Aageson, *Paul, the Pastoral Epistles, and the Early Church*, 2–5.

37. Barclay, *Paul and the Gift*, 571.

38. Even though he makes only a few statements concerning the PE in connection with the NPP, Barclay seems to have a firm grasp on the canonical continuity of the PE with Pauline theology. Whether or not Paul wrote these letters, inevitably the church (or Paul) would have to address "legalism" or "works-righteousness." Even if legalism was not Paul's polemic in the "undisputed" letters, history witnessed the rise of legalism and moral superiority *within* the church. These legalistic tendencies are that against which Luther responded. The PE, especially 2 Tim 1:8–12 and Titus 3:3–7, addressed this problem many centuries earlier. The NPP has provided a proper balance to the characterization of first-century Judaism. However, in the meantime, historical Paul has been excised

The shift that takes place here is not the particular to the universal (Paul himself covers both, working from particularity of the
Christ-event to its universal implications), nor from the specific
to the abstract (like Paul, his interpreters have specific targets
for their theology), nor from the communal to the individual
(Paul's own theology of grace has both communal and individual dimensions). What changes, rather, is the social context.
The critical theology of a new social movement, by which it
formulated its identity and clarified its boundaries, becomes the
self-critical theology of an established tradition: its missionary
theology is turned inwards.[39]

Although this study cannot completely agree with all of the above statements (e.g., that the PE represent "interpreters"), what the PE bear out is
that with the churches of Crete and Ephesus and the imminence of Paul's
death there is a shift of context that requires a shift of theological emphasis.[40] "Works of law" are broadened to "works" more generally speaking.
Justification theology in response to Jew/gentile tension gives way to
standardized soteriology as reminders, or support, of an already-received
salvation. In other words, if one allows the NPP's basic premises as laid out
through the study of Romans, Galatians, and Phil 3:1–11 (Jew/gentile relations), the theology of the PE represent a shift in context, not a maturation
of theology. What one is left with is that the NPP, if too rigidly dependent
upon Romans and Galatians alone, is not able to incorporate the theology
of the PE. There are too many words and phrases defined so sharply based
on those situations to account properly for the nuance of words and phrases shared in the PE. What has become clear in this study is that the more

from canonical Paul, and by that, "legalism" has no Pauline combatant.

39. Barclay explains that this same shift continued until Luther, who himself turned
to the "inward mission." He explains, "Paul's polemics against 'works of the law' are
taken to be directed not against an external (and no longer valid) definition of worth
(Torah-practice) but against the subjective evaluation of one's own good works as effec-
tive for salvation. This change in focus fostered a regrettable tendency to figure "Jews"
as exemplars of human self-righteousness, but it constituted a brilliant re-contextualization of Pauline theology in the conditions of the sixteenth century church." Barclay,
Paul and the Gift, 571–72.

40. Similarly, when Brevard Childs questions how these two different literary
genres (Romans and the PE) are related, he concludes, "The solution is not one of har-
monization. . . . Rather, the canonical structures sets up a dialectical interaction within
the context of the corpus between the general and the specific, between the universal
content of the gospel and the unique needs of each congregation, between the sound
doctrine of Paul and the particularity of its application by the apostle who labored to
target the continuing theological crises with the gospel of Jesus Christ." Childs, *Church's
Guide for Reading Paul*, 76.

closely tied to the polemic of Romans, and especially the more narrowly focused Galatians, justification (or even salvation) becomes, the harder it is to maintain that position outside them.

For example, though the phrase "works of law" is not used in the PE, the terms "works" (2 Tim 1:9) and "works we did in righteousness" (Titus 3:5) are both used. Thus, if one rigidly defines "works" in Paul as Torah-keeping, then the more universal aspect of God's initiative apart from general works (of any kind) is missed, or understood as second-century early Catholic dogmatism. Paul is able to state that one is saved not from "our works" (2 Tim 1:9) *and* that "by works of law no flesh is justified" (Rom 3:20; Gal 2:16). In other words, Paul's theology was adaptive and able to accommodate a variety of problems the early church faced. Understanding Paul's theology to "develop," as if it was not yet fully formed, is to mischaracterize it. The same theology that did away with gentile exclusion of the gospel based on "covenantal identifiers," was the same theology that argued Paul and Timothy had not themselves earned their calling by works (2 Tim 1:8–12) or that the Cretan Christians were not saved by works of righteousness. In studying the NPP and the PE, what seems to come to the surface is that Paul was not developing his theology through time. If the PE are taken seriously as representing Pauline thought, it was not so much the temporal element that affected Paul's theology as the situational elements, though one must admit the temporal element cannot be completely dismissed—the progression of the church inevitably brought new situations.

The findings of this study do not invalidate the hermeneutic of the NPP as delineated through the study of undisputed Paul. In fact, there is a great deal of continuity between the NPP and the PE—all of the primary elements of the NPP are present in the PE.[41] The either/or readings of the NPP and traditional perspective are not always helpful. That Paul's theology forbade Jewish privilege should be obvious by now. However, Paul was not always obliged to articulate his theology in those terms—a fact evidenced even within undisputed Paul.[42] Although these findings could be interpreted as a "cop-out," it seems the reality is that Paul's theology was big enough to incorporate both of what is now called the NPP and the traditional perspective.[43] Romans itself, though sometimes quite specific, seems

41. In fact, there have been many correlations between the passages studied in the PE and Romans 9–11, which coincides with Wright's assessment that Romans 9–11 is the crux (or climax) of Paul's argument in Romans. See Wright, *Climax of the Covenant*, 231–57.

42. E.g., Rom 5:6–9; 1 Cor 6:11.

43. Barclay puts it this way, "Thus the reading of Paul offered in this book may be interpreted *either* as a re-contextualization of the Augustinian-Lutheran tradition,

to encompass most of Paul's primary theological categories, Galatians is principally polemical, and the PE represent encompassing, fundamental statements of faith to encourage his delegates and their mission. In the case of 1 Timothy 1:6–16, Paul's view is perfectly compatible with the NPP, in that the view of the law is quite positive, and it resonates with Paul's statements in Romans 7:12, 16. Within this same passage, Paul's conscience is bothered by the retrospective look into his former life. He was not displeased, or shameful, about his Jewish pedigree, and he does not bemoan a legalistic mindset. Instead, his sinfulness is highlighted in his blasphemy, persecution, and violence. In 1 Timothy 2:3–7, Paul's articulation of the universality of the gospel is highlighted in his designation as "apostle to the Gentiles." As for 2 Timothy 1:3 and 1:8–12, Paul finds continuity with his forebears rather than outright rejection. He points out to Timothy that their salvation and calling are not "according to our works," which would likely include any works at all—good or bad. However, it should be noted that Timothy is not an opponent and Paul's words are a proclamation and protection, not a polemic. Finally, in Titus 3:3–7, Paul incorporates much of his theological jargon used in other of his letters, and by that, he articulates a full theology of God's salvation and justification that come via mercy and grace, opposed to righteous deeds.

The NPP represents a sociological problem while the PE represent an early Christian problem. The problem Paul faces according to the NPP is how faith in Christ connected with the law and Judaism, Jew and Greek. The PE are more about how Christians saw outsiders and their individual salvation. Paul had to remind them that they, too, were once sinful. This new Christian life was characterized by good works, but Paul did not want them to assume these good works of righteousness were what saved them or instigated God's mercy and grace. This was a church versus the world problem, not a Jew versus gentile problem, even though, as 2 Timothy 2:3–7 demonstrates, that Paul's mission to the gentiles extended beyond sociological issues and into the gospel offered to everyone (cf. Gal 3:28; Col 3:11).[44]

If the PE are to be engaged as canonical Pauline documents, then the proponents of the NPP must continue to wrestle with Paul's complex usage

---

returning the dynamic of the incongruity of grace to its original mission environment where it accompanied the formation of new communities, *or* as a reconfiguration of the 'new perspective,' placing its best historical and exegetical insights within the frame of Paul's theology of grace." Barclay, *Paul and the Gift*, 573.

44. Colin Kruse states, "If we allow that Paul was the author of the letter, or at least the Pauline basis of the passage, then it follows that Paul's doctrine of justification by grace through faith was not merely a fighting doctrine introduced to refute the teaching of the Judaizers, but was at the heart of his understanding of what God has done in Christ for the salvation of humankind." Kruse, *Paul, the Law, and Justification*, 268.

of the δικ- word group, with the function of justification *outside* discussions of gentiles inclusion, and with the Pauline definition of salvation that comes apart from works (of any kind). The NPP must also wrestle with the reality of a context within which Paul does combat legalism and works-righteousness, even if that legalism is formed retrospectively by Christians (Titus 3:3–7). The NPP, by rejecting the PE, or pushing them to the side, is missing a deeper, fuller expression of Pauline theology. In fact, this study is aware of only a few who mention 1 Timothy 2:3–7 and 2 Timothy 1:3 with regard to the NPP, including opponents of the NPP.[45] Yet, both 1 Timothy 1:6–16 and 2:3–7 are significantly resonant with the NPP hermeneutic (and undisputed Paul). Though Paul clearly sees himself as the foremost sinner *after* his conversion, there is no indication that prior to his conversion he thought the same. Instead, he classified himself in a similar way in 1 Corinthians 15:8–9 regarding his apostleship and self-designation as "least of the apostles." The traditional perspective needs also to reckon how the early sociological issue of gentile inclusion into the people of God influenced Paul's articulation of his theology.

Ideas for Further Research

This study has not dealt with the PE, as a whole. Instead, passages bearing similarity to NPP characteristics were purposely chosen. So, further research remains to be done in the rest of the PE in comparison with the NPP. In fact, one of the major contributions of this study was the inclusion of 1 Timothy 6–16, 2:3–7, and 2 Timothy 1:3 into the discussion. The NPP and non-NPP alike, do not deal with these passages in the current debates regarding the NPP (the passages usually focused on are 2 Timothy 1:9 and Titus 3:4–7). There may be more passages that this study overlooked as well. There may also be implications for the authorship of the PE based on the findings of this study. There was a great degree of commonality of language from undisputed Paul to the PE, especially in Romans and 1 Corinthians, and a great deal of continuity between the PE and the NPP (despite the significant differences). Also, when the vocabulary was not Pauline, one could often find the vocabulary in Luke, Acts, and Hebrews. The majority of current discussions of Pauline

---

45. For example, although not an opponent of the NPP, Michael Bird cites 1 Tim 2:7 as an example of Paul as apostle to the gentiles in "disputed" Paul in Appendix I in *Anomalous Jew*, 105. See also Vaughan, "Investigation of the Authenticity of the Pastoral Epistles," 151–54, who, although pointing out how the works/salvation contrast in 2 Tim 1:8–10 contrasts with the view of the NPP, seems unaware that the comments he makes about Paul's continuity with his "forebears" are resonant with the NPP's view of Judaism and Paul's continuity with it.

theology revolve around being "in Christ," salvation, or justification. However, the study of 2 Timothy 1:9 demonstrated that both the verbs "saved" and "justified" have limited use in the Pauline corpus. The verb "called" (καλέω) is just as prevalent in Pauline literature and may need to be incorporated more fully into the debates.[46] The PE also demonstrate that justification, at least not "justification" language, is not Paul's primary theological category. Further implications of the study may include a more robust characterization of each of the opponents of the PE and how these opponents affected Paul's articulation of theology. Finally, more study needs to be done on ways in which the NPP can better incorporate "disputed," or canonical, Paul as a way to better understand Paul himself. Similarly, there is more work to be done regarding the canonical perspective, the Pauline canon specifically, and the NPP in that little work has been done to consider the whole of Pauline theology as witnessed in the canonical structure of the NT (canonical ordering) with a mind to the hermeneutical lens of the NPP.

46. Wright mentions this Pauline emphasis on "calling" and "election" with regard to the people of God. Wright, *Paul and the Faithfulness of God*, 1026–27.

Bibliography

Aageson, James W. "The Pastoral Epistles and the Acts of Paul: A Multiplex Approach to Authority in Paul's Legacy." *LTQ* 40 (2005) 237–48.

———. "The Pastoral Epistles, Apostolic Authority, and the Development of the Pauline Scriptures." In *The Pauline Canon*, edited by Stanley E. Porter, 5–26. Leiden: Brill, 2004.

———. *Paul, the Pastoral Epistles, and the Early Church*. Peabody: Hendrickson, 2008.

Abegg, Martin. "Paul, 'Works of the Law' and MMT." *BAR* 20.6 (1994) 53–55.

Aland, K. "The Problem of Anonymity and Pseudonymity in Christian Literature of the First Two Centuries." *JTS* 12 (1961) 39–49.

Alford. Henry. *The Greek Testament*. 4th ed. 4 volumes. London: Rivington, 1865.

Allison, Gregg R. "Theological Interpretation of Scripture: An Introduction and Preliminary Evaluation." *Southern Baptist Theological Journal* 14 (2010) 28–36.

Allman, James E. "Gaining Perspective on the New Perspective on Paul." *Bibliotheca Sacra* 170.677 (2013) 51–68.

Anderson, Garwood P. *Paul's New Perspective: Charting a Soteriological Journey*. Downers Grove: InterVarsity, 2016.

Arnold, G. Philip. "Pauline Perspectives: A Summary and Critique of the New Perspective on Paul." *Wisconsin Lutheran Quarterly* 112.3 (2015) 184–94.

Avemarie, Friedrich. "Die Werke des Gesetzes im Spiegel des Jakobusbriefs: A Very Old Perspective on Paul." *Zeitschrift für Theologie und Kirche* 98.3 (2001) 282–309.

———. "Erwählung und Vergeltung: Zur optionalen Struktur rabbinischer Soteriologie." *NTS* 45.1 (1999) 108–25.

———. *Tora und Leben: Untersuchungen zur Heilsbedeutung der Tora in der frühen rabbinischen Literatur*. Tübingen: Mohr Siebeck, 1996.

Badenas, Robert. *Christ and the End of the Law: Romans 10.4 in Pauline Perspective*. Sheffield: Sheffield Academic, 1985.

Bachmann, Michael, and Johannes Woyke, eds. *Lutherische und Neue Paulusperspektive: Beiträge zu einem Schlüsselproblem der gegenwärtigen exegetischen Diskussion*. Tübingen: Mohr Siebeck, 2005.

Bahr, G. J. "Paul and Letter Writing in the First Century." *CBQ* 28 (1966) 465–77.

Balz, Horst, and Gerhard Schneider. *Exegetical Dictionary of the New Testament*. 3 vols. Grand Rapids: Eerdmans, 1990.

Barclay, John M. G. *Paul and the Gift*. Grand Rapids: Eerdmans, 2015.

Barclay, William B., and Ligon J. Duncan. *Gospel Clarity: Challenging the New Perspective on Paul.* Carlisle: EP Books, 2010.

Barr, James. *The Semantics of Biblical Language.* London: Oxford University Press, 1961.

Barrett, C. K. *The Pastoral Epistles.* Oxford: Clarendon, 1963.

————. *Signs of an Apostle.* London: Epworth, 1970.

————. "Titus." In *Neotestamentica et Semitica: Studies in Honour of Matthew Black*, edited by E. Earle Ellis and M. Wilcox, 1–14. Edinburgh: T. & T. Clark, 1969.

Barnett, Albert E. *Paul Becomes a Literary Influence.* Chicago: Chicago University, 1941.

Bartholomew, Craig, et al., eds. *Canon and Biblical Interpretation.* Scripture and Hermeneutics Series 7. Grand Rapids: Zondervan, 2006.

Barton, John. *Reading the Old Testament: Method in Biblical Study.* London: Dartman, Longman & Todd, 1984.

Bassler, Jouette M. *1 Timothy, 2 Timothy, Titus.* ANTC. Nashville: Abingdon, 1996.

————. "A Plethora of Epiphanies: Christology in the Pastoral Epistles." *Princeton Seminary Bulletin* 17.3 (1996) 310–25.

Bates, Matthew. *Salvation by Allegiance Alone: Rethinking Faith, Works, and the Gospel of Jesus the King.* Grand Rapids: Baker, 2017.

Bauer, Walter. *Heresy and Orthodoxy in Earliest Christianity.* Philadelphia: Fortress, 1971.

Bauer, Walter, et al. *A Greek-English Lexicon of the New Testament and Other Christian Literature.* 3rd ed. Chicago: University of Chicago, 2000.

Baugh, S. M. "1 Timothy." In *Zondervan Illustrated Bible Background Commentary*, edited by C. E. Arnold, 3:444–511. 4 vols. Grand Rapids: Zondervan, 2001.

Baur, Ferdinand Christian. *Die sogenannten Pastoralbriefe des Apostels Paulus auf neue kritisch untersucht.* Stuttgart: Cotta'sche, 1835.

————. *Paul the Apostle of Jesus Christ; His Life and Works, His Epistles and Teachings.* Grand Rapids: Baker, 2011.

Beale, G. K., and Benjamin L. Gladd. *Hidden But Now Revealed: A Biblical Theology of Mystery.* Downers Grove: InterVarsity, 2014.

Beale, G. K., and D. A. Carson. *Commentary on the New Testament Use of the Old Testament.* Grand Rapids: Baker, 2007.

Beker, J. Christiaan. "The Authority of Scripture: Normative or Incidental?" *ThTo* 49.3 (1992) 376–82.

————. *Heirs of Paul: Paul's Legacy in the New Testament and in the Church Today.* Minneapolis: Fortress, 1991.

————. *Paul the Apostle: The Triumph of God in Life and Thought.* 2nd ed. Philadelphia: Fortress, 1984.

————. "Paul's Theology: Consistent or Inconsistent?" *NTS* 34 (1988) 364–77.

————. *The Triumph of God: The Essence of Paul's Thought.* Translated by Loren T. Stuckenbruck. Minneapolis: Fortress, 1990.

Benetreau, S. *Les Epitres Pastorales: 1 et 2 Timothee, Tite.* Commentaires Evangeliques de la Bible. Vaux-sur-Seine: EDIFAC, 2008.

Bird, Michael F. *An Anomalous Jew: Paul Among Jews, Greeks, and Romans.* Grand Rapids: Eerdmans, 2016.

————. "Salvation in Paul's Judaism." In *Paul and Judaism: Crosscurrents in Pauline Exegesis and the Study of Jewish-Christian Relations*, edited by Reimund Bieringer and Didier Pollefeyt, 15–40. Library of New Testament Studies 463. New York: T. & T. Clark, 2012.

———. *The Saving Righteousness of God: Studies on Paul, Justification, and the New Perspective*. Paternoster Biblical Monographs. Eugene, OR: Wipf & Stock, 2007.

Blasi, Anthony J. *Making Charisma: The Construction of Paul's Public Image*. New Brunswick: Transactions, 1991.

Boer, Martinus C. de. "Images of Paul in the Post-Apostolic Period." *CBQ* 42 (1980) 359–80.

Bonhoeffer, Dietrich. *Letters and Papers from Prison*. Fontana Books. 5th Impression. London: SCM, 1963.

Boyarin, Daniel. *Border Lines: The Partitioning of Judeao-Christianity*. Philadelphia: University of Pennsylvania, 2004.

———. *A Radical Jew: Paul and the Politics of Identity*. Berkeley: University of California Press, 1994.

Bray, Gerald L. *The Pastoral Epistles*. The International Theological Commentary. London: T. & T. Clark, 2019.

Brown, Raymond E. *The Churches the Apostles Left Behind*. New York: Paulinist, 1984.

Brox, Norbert. *Die Pastoralbriefe*. Regensburg: Friedrich Pustet, 1969.

———. *Falsche Verfasserangaben: Zur Erklärung der frühchristlichen Pseudepigraphie*. Stuttgart: KBW Verlag, 1975.

Bultmann, Rudolf. "πιστεύω." *TDNT* 6:174–228.

———. *Theology of the New Testament*. Translated by Kendrick Grobel. New York: Scribner's, 1955.

Byrne, Brendan. "Interpreting Romans: The New Perspective and Beyond." *Int* 58 (2004) 241–52.

Campbell, Constantine R. *Advances in the Study of Greek: New Insights for Reading the New Testament*. Grand Rapids: Zondervan, 2015.

Campbell, Douglas A. *The Deliverance of God: An Apocalyptic Rereading of Justification in Paul*. Grand Rapids: Eerdmans, 2009.

———. "Locating Titus and 1 and 2 Timothy." In *Framing Paul: An Epistolary Biography*, 339–403. Grand Rapids: Eerdmans, 2014.

———. *Paul: An Apostle's Journey*. Grand Rapids: Eerdmans, 2018.

———. "Foreword." In *Paul, Apostle of Liberty*, by Richard N. Longenecker, xi–xx. 2nd ed. Grand Rapids: Eerdmans, 2015.

Cara, Robert J. *Cracking the Foundation of the New Perspective on Paul: Covenantal Nomism Versus Reformed Covenantal Theology*. Reformed, Exegetical, and Doctrinal Studies. Fearn, Ross-Shire, UK: Christian Focus, 2017.

Carson, D. A., et al. *Justification and Variegated Nomism*. 2 vols. Grand Rapids: Baker, 2004.

Caulley, Thomas Scott. "Fighting the Good Fight: the Pastoral Epistles in Canonical Perspective." Society of Biblical Literature Seminar Papers 26 (1987) 550–64.

Chandler, Tertius, and Gerald Fox. *Three Thousand Years of Urban Growth*. New York: Academic Press, 1974.

Childs, Brevard S. *Biblical Theology: A Proposal*. Minneapolis: Fortress, 2002.

———. *Biblical Theology in Crisis*. Philadelphia: Westminster, 1970.

———. *Biblical Theology of the Old and New Testaments: Theological Reflection on the Christian Bible*. Minneapolis: Fortress, 1992.

———. *The Book of Exodus: A Critical, Theological Commentary*. Philadelphia: Westminster, 1974.

———. "The Canonical Shape of the Prophetic Literature." *Int* 32.1 (1978) 46–55.

———. *The Church's Guide for Reading Paul: The Canonical Shaping of the Pauline Corpus*. Grand Rapids: Eerdmans, 2008.

———. *Introduction to the Old Testament as Scripture*. Philadelphia: Fortress, 1979.

———. *The New Testament as Canon: An Introduction*. Philadelphia: Fortress, 1984.

———. *Old Testament in a Canonical Context*. Philadelphia: Fortress, 1986.

Chilton, Bruce D. *Rabbi Paul: An Intellectual Biography*. New York: Doubleday, 2004.

Clark, D. J. "Discourse Structure in Titus." *Bible Translator: Technical Papers* 53.1 (2002) 101–17.

Clark, Gordon H. *The Pastoral Epistles*. Jefferson: The Trinity Foundation, 1983.

Collins, John J., and Daniel C. Harrow. *Early Judaism: A Comprehensive Overview*. Grand Rapids: Eerdmans, 2012.

Collins, Raymond F. *I & II Timothy and Titus: A Commentary*. The New Testament Library. Louisville: Westminster John Knox, 2002.

———. "The Image of Paul in the Pastorals." *Laval Théologique et philosophique* 31 (1975) 147–73.

———. "The Theology of the Epistle to Titus." *Ephemerides theologicae lovanienses* 76 (2000) 56–72.

Colson, F. H. "'Myths and Genealogies' A Note in the Polemic of the Pastoral Epistles." *JTS* 19 (1917–18) 265–71.

Couser, Greg A. "God and Christian Existence in the Pastoral Epistles: Toward Theological Method and Meaning." *NovT* 42 (2000) 262–83.

Cranfield, C. E. B. *A Critical and Exegetical Commentary on the Epistle to the Romans*. 2 vols. The International Critical Commentary. Edinburgh: T. & T. Clark, 1979.

———. "St. Paul and the Law." *SJT* 17 (1964) 43–68.

———. "'The Works of the Law' in the Epistle to the Romans." *JSNT* 43 (1991) 89–101.

Cranford, Michael. "The Possibility of Perfect Obedience: Paul and an Implied Premise in Galatians 3:10 and 5:3." *NovT* 36 (1994) 242–58.

Crossan, John Dominic. *The Birth of Christianity*. New York: HarperSanFrancisco, 1998.

Crossan, John Dominic, and Jonathan L. Reed. *In Search of Paul: How Jesus's Apostle Opposed Rome's Empire with God's Kingdom: A New Vision of Paul's Word and World*. New York: HarperCollins, 2004.

Dahl, Nils Alstrup. *Studies in Paul: Theology for the Early Christian Mission*. Minneapolis: Augsburg, 1977

Das, A. Andrew. *Beyond Covenantal Nomism: A "Newer Perspective on Paul and the Law*. PhD diss., Union Theological Seminary, 1999.

———. "Beyond Covenantal Nomism: Paul, Judaism, and Perfect Obedience." *Concordia Journal* 27 (2001) 234–52.

———. *Paul and the Jews*. Peabody: Hendrickson, 2003.

———. *Paul, the Law, and the Covenant*. Peabody: Hendrickson, 2001.

———. "Paul and Works of Obedience in Second Temple Judaism: Romans 4:4–5 as a 'New Perspective' Case Study." *CBQ* 71 (2009) 795–812.

Davies, Margaret. *The Pastoral Epistles*. New Testament Guides. Sheffield: Sheffield Academic, 1996.

Davies, W. D. *Christian Origins and Judaism*. London: Dartman, Longman & Todd, 1962.

———. *Paul and Rabbinic Judaism: Some Rabbinic Elements in Pauline Theology*. 4th ed. Philadelphia: Fortress, 1980. Originally published London: SPCK, 1955.

De Roo, Jacqueline. *"Works of the Law" at Qumran and in Paul.* New Testament Monographs 13. Sheffield: Sheffield Phoenix, 2007.

De Wette, Wilhelm M. L. *An Historico-Critical Introduction to the Canonical Books of the New Testament.* 5th ed. Translated by F. Frothingham. Boston: Crosby & Nichols, 1858.

———. *Kurze Erklärung der Brief an Titus, Timotheus und die Hebräer.* Kurzgefasstes exegetisches Handbuch zum Neuen Testament 20. Leipzig: Weidmann's Buchhandlung, 1844.

Dibelius, Martin, and Hans Conzelmann. *The Pastoral Epistles.* Translated by Philip Buttolph and Adela Yarbro. Hermeneia. Philadelphia: Fortress, 1972.

Dodd, C. H. *According to the Scriptures: The Sub-Structure of New Testament Theology.* London: Nisbet, 1953.

———. *The Old Testament in the New.* Facet Books Biblical Series 3. Philadelphia: Fortress, 1963.

Donaldson, Terrence L. *Paul and the Gentiles: Remapping the Apostle's Convictional World.* Minneapolis: Fortress, 1997.

———. "Zealot and Convert: The Origin of Paul's Christ-Torah Antithesis." *CBQ* 51 (1989) 655–82.

Donelson, Lewis L. *Pseuepigraphy and Ethical Argument in The Pastoral Epistles.* Hermeneutische undersuchungen zur Theologie 22. Tübingen: Mohr Siebeck, 1986.

Donfried, Karl P., ed. *1 Timothy Reconsidered.* Colloquium Oecumenicum Paulinum 18. Lueven: Peeters, 2008.

Downs, D. J. "'Early Catholicism' and Apocalypticism in the Pastoral Epistles." *CBQ* 67 (2005) 641–61.

Drane, John W. *Paul, Libertine or Legalist? A Study in the Theology of the Major Pauline Epistles.* London: SPCK, 1975.

Driver, Daniel R. *Brevard Childs, Biblical Theologian: For the Church's One Bible.* Forschugen zum Alten Testament 2. Reihe 46. Tübignen: Mohr Siebeck, 2010.

Drury, C. "The Pastoral Epistles." In *The Oxford Bible Commentary,* edited by J. Barton and J. Muddiman, 1220–23. Oxford: Oxford University Press, 2001.

Duff, J. N. "A Reconsideration of Pseudepigraphy in Early Christianity." PhD diss., University of Oxford, 1998.

Dunn, James D. G. "The First and Second Letters to Timothy and the Letter to Titus: Introduction, Commentary, and Reflections." In *The New Interpreter's Bible,* 11:773–880. 12 vols. Nashville: Abingdon, 2000.

———. *Galatians.* Black's New Testament Commentary. London: A. & C. Black, 1993.

———. *Jesus and the Spirit: A Study of the Religious and Charismatic Experience of Jesus and the First Christians as Reflected in the New Testament.* London: SCM, 1997.

———. *Neither Jew nor Greek: A Contested Identity.* Grand Rapids: Eerdmans, 2015.

———. "A New Perspective on the New Perspective on Paul." *EC* 4.2 (2013) 157–82.

———. "The New Perspective on Paul." In *The New Perspective on Paul: Revised Edition,* 99–120. Grand Rapids: Eerdmans, 2008.

———. *The New Perspective on Paul: Collected Essays.* WUNT 185. Tübingen: Mohr Siebeck, 2005.

———, ed. *Paul and the Mosaic Law.* WUNT 89. Tübingen: Mohr Siebeck, 1996.

———. *Romans.* 2 vols. WBC. Nashville: Thomas Nelson, 1988.

———. *The Theology of Paul the Apostle.* Grand Rapids: Eerdmans, 1998.

————. *The Theology of Paul's Letter to the Galatians.* New Testament Theology. Cambridge: Cambridge University Press, 1993.

————. *Unity and Diversity in the New Testament: An Inquiry into the Character of Earliest Christianity.* 3rd ed. London: SCM, 2006.

————. "Whatever Happened to 'Works of Law'?" In *The New Perspective on Paul: Revised Edition,* 381–94. Grand Rapids: Eerdmans, 2008.

Easton, Burton Scott. *The Pastoral Epistles.* New York: Scribner's, 1947.

Ehrman, Bart D. *The New Testament: A Historical Introduction to the Early Christian Writings.* 3rd ed. Oxford: Oxford University Press, 2004.

Eichhorn, Johann Gottfried. *Einleitung in das Neue Testament* 3.1. Leipzig: Weidmann, 1812.

Ellicott, Charles J. *A Critical and Grammatical Commentary on the Pastoral Epistles with a Revised Translation.* Eugene, OR: Wipf & Stock, 1998.

Ellis, E. Earle. *Paul's Use of the Old Testament.* Edinburgh: Oliver and Boyd, 1957.

————. "Traditions in the Pastoral Epistles." In *Early Jewish and Christian Exegesis: Studies in Honor of William Hugh Brownlee,* edited by Craig A. Evans and William F. Stinespring, 237–53. Atlanta: Scholars, 1987.

Emerson, Matthew. *Christ and the New Creation: A Canonical Approach to the Theology of the New Testament.* Eugene, OR: Wipf & Stock, 2013.

————. "Paul's Eschatological Outlook in the Pastoral Epistles." *CTR* 12.2 (2015) 83–98.

————. "Victory, Atonement, Restoration, and Response: The Shape of the New Testament Canon and the Holistic Gospel Message." *STR* 3.2 (2012) 177–94.

Engberg-Pederson, Troels. *Paul and the Stoics.* Louisville: Westminster John Knox, 2000.

Enslin, Morton S. *Letters to the Churches: 1 and 2 Timothy, Titus.* Bible Guides 18. London: Abingdon, 1963.

Fee, Gordon. *1 and 2 Timothy, Titus.* NIBC. Peabody: Hendrickson, 1988.

————. "Christology in the Pastoral Epistles." In *Pauline Christology: An Exegetical-Theological Study,* 418–72. Peabody: Hendrickson, 2007.

Fesko, J. V. "A Critical Examination of N. T. Wright's Doctrine of Justification." *CP* 1 (2005) 102–15.

Fiore, Benjamin. *The Function of Personal Example in the Socratic and Pastoral Epistles.* Abib 105. Rome: Biblical Institute, 1986.

————. *The Pastoral Epistles: 1 Timothy, 2 Timothy, Titus.* Sacra Pagina. Collegeville: Liturgical, 2007.

Fowl, Stephen E. *Theological Interpretation of Scripture.* Eugene, OR: Cascade, 2009.

Fuller, Daniel. "Paul and the 'Works of the Law.'" *WTJ* 38 (1975) 28–42.

Furnish, Victor Paul, and Leander Keck. *The Pauline Letters.* Nashville: Abingdon, 1984.

Gager, John G. *The Origins of Anti-Semitism: Attitudes Toward Judaism in Pagan and Christian Antiquity.* New York: Oxford University Press, 1983.

Garlington, Don B. *An Exposition of Galatians: A Reading from the New Perspective.* 3rd ed. Eugene, OR: Wipf & Stock, 2007.

————. *Faith, Obedience, and Perseverance: Aspects of Paul's Letter to the Romans.* Wissenschaftliche Untersuchungen zum Neuen Testament 79. Tübingen: Mohr Siebeck, 1994.

————. *In Defense of the New Perspective on Paul: Essays and Reviews.* Eugene, OR: Wipf & Stock, 2005.

———. *"The Obedience of Faith": A Pauline Phrase in Historical Context.* WUNT 38. Tübingen: Mohr Siebeck, 1991.

———. "The Obedience of Faith in the letter to the Romans: Part 1: The Meaning of ὑπακοὴ πίστεως (Rom 1:5; 16:26)." *WTJ* 52 (1990) 201–24.

———. "The Obedience of Faith in the Letter to the Romans: Part III: The Obedience of Christ and the Obedience of the Christian." *WTJ* 55 (1993) 281–97.

———. "The New Perspective on Paul: An Appraisal Two Decades Later." *Criswell Theological Review* 2.2 (2005) 17–38.

Gaston, Lloyd. *Paul and the Torah.* Vancouver: The University of British Columbia Press, 1987.

Gathercole, Simon. "The Doctrine of Justification and Beyond: Some Proposals." In *Justification in Perspective*, edited by Bruce L. McCormack, 219–42. Grand Rapids: Baker, 2006.

———. *Where Is Boasting? Early Jewish Soteriology and Paul's Response in Romans 1–5.* Grand Rapids: Eerdmans, 2002.

Gehring, Roger W. *House Church and Mission: The Importance of Household Structures in Early Christianity.* Peabody: Hendrickson, 2004.

Gignilliat, Mark S. *A Brief History of Old Testament Criticism: From Benedict Spinoza to Brevard Childs.* Grand Rapids: Zondervan, 2012.

Gloer, W. Hulitt. *1 & 2 Timothy–Titus.* Smyth & Helwys Bible Commentary. Macon, GA: Smyth & Helwys, 2010.

Gorday, P. *Colossians, 1–2 Thessalonians, 1–2 Timothy, Titus, Philemon.* Ancient Christian Commentary on Scripture. Downers Grove: InterVarsity, 2000.

Goswell, Gregory. "The Order of the Books of the Greek Old Testament." *JETS* 52.3 (2009) 449–66.

———. "The Order of the Books of the Hebrew Bible." *JETS* 51.4 (2008) 673–88.

———. "The Order of the Books of the New Testament." *JETS* 53.2 (2010) 225–41.

———. "The Ordering of the Books of the Canon and the Theological Interpretation of the Old Testament." *JTI* 13.1 (2019) 1–20.

Gray, Patrick. "Perspectives on Paul the Sinner." *BBR* 24 (2014) 45–55.

Griffiths, Philip D. R. *When Wright Is Wrong: A Reformed Baptist Critique of N. T. Wright's New Perspective on Paul.* Eugene, OR: Wipf & Stock, 2019.

Gritz, Sharin Hodgin. *Paul, Women Teachers, and the Mother Goddess at Ephesus: A Study of 1 Timothy 2:9–15 in Light of the Religious and Cultural Milieu of the First Century.* Lanham: University Press of America, 1991.

Gundry, Robert N. "The Inferiority of the New Perspective on Paul." In *The Old Is Better: New Testament Essays in Support of Traditional Interpretations*, edited by Robert N. Gundry, 195–224. WUNT 178. Tübingen: Mohr Siebeck, 2005.

Gundry, Robert N., ed. *The Old Is Better: New Testament Essays in Support of Traditional Interpretations.* Wissenschaftliche Untersuchungen zum Neuen Testament 178. Tübingen: Mohr Siebeck, 2005.

Guthrie, Donald. *The Pastoral Epistles: An Introduction and Commentary.* TNTC. Grand Rapids: Eerdmans, 1990.

———. *The Pastoral Epistles and the Mind of Paul.* London: Tyndale, 1955.

———. *New Testament Introduction: Revised Edition.* 4th ed. Downers Grove: InterVarsity, 1990.

Hagner, Donald. "Paul and Judaism: Testing the New Perspective." In *Revisiting Paul's Doctrine of Justification: A Challenge to the New Perspective*, 76–105. Downers Grove: InterVarsity, 2001.

Hanson, A. T. "The Domestication of Paul: A Study in the Development of Early Christian Theology." *BJRL* 63 (1981) 402–18.

———. *The Pastoral Epistles*. New Century Bible Commentary. Grand Rapids, MI: Eerdmans; London: Marshall, Morgan & Scott, 1982.

———. *The Pastoral Letters: Commentary on the First and Second Letters to Timothy and the Letter to Titus*. CBC. Cambridge: Cambridge University Press, 1966.

———. *Studies in the Pastoral Epistles*. London: SPCK, 1968.

———. "The Use of the Old Testament in the Pastoral Epistles." *Irish Biblical Studies* 3 (1981) 203–19.

Harding, Mark. *Tradition and Rhetoric in the Pastoral Epistles*. SBLit 3. New York: Peter Lang, 1998.

———. *What Are They Saying About the Pastoral Epistles?* New York: Paulist, 2001.

Harrison, P. N. *Paulines and Pastorals*. London: Villiers, 1964.

———. *The Problem of the Pastoral Epistles*. London: Oxford University Press, 1921.

Hasler, V. *Die Briefe an Timotheus and Titus*. Zürcher Bibelkommentar. Zürich: Theologischer, 1978.

Hassler, Andrew. "Ethnocentric Legalism and the Justification of the Individual: Rethinking Some New Perspective Assumptions." *JETS* 54.2 (2011) 311–27.

Hays, Richard B. *The Conversion of Imagination: Paul as Interpreter of Israel's Scripture*. Grand Rapids: Eerdmans, 2005.

———. *Echoes of Scripture in the Letters of Paul*. New Haven: Yale University Press, 1989.

———. "Galatians." In *New Interpreter's Bible: Corinthians–Philippians*, 11:181–348. 12 vols. Nashville: Abingdon, 2000.

———. "Justification." In *ABD*, edited by David Noel Freedman, 3:1129–33. 6 vols. New York: Doubleday, 1992.

———. "Three Dramatic Roles: The Law in Romans 3–4." In *Paul and the Mosaic Law*, edited by James D. G. Dunn, 151–64. Tübingen: Mohr Siebeck, 1996.

Herzer, Jens. "Rearranging the 'House of God': A New Perspective on the Pastoral Epistles." In *Empsychoi Logoi—Religious Innovations in Antiquity: Studies in Honour of Pieter Willem van Der Horst*, 547–66. Boston: Brill, 2008.

———. "Zwischen Mythos und Warheit: Neue Perspektiven auf de sogenannten Pastoralbriefe." *NTS* 63.3 (2017) 428–50.

Ho, Chiao Ek. "Mission in the Pastoral Epistles." In *Entrusted with the Gospel: Paul's Theology in the Pastoral Epistles*, edited by Andreas Köstenberger and Terry Wilder, 241–67. Nashville: B&H, 2010.

Holtzmann, Heinrich. *Die Pastoralbriefe kritische und exegetisch untersucht*. Leipzig: Wilhelm Engelmann, 1880.

Houlden, J. L. *The Pastoral Epistles: 1 and 2 Timothy, Titus*. Pelican New Testament Commentaries. Harmonsworth: Penguin, 1976.

Hübner, Hans. *Das Gesetz bei Paulus: Ein Beitrag zum Werden der paulinischen Theologie*. Gottingen: Vandenhoeck & Ruprecht, 1978.

———. *Law in Paul's Thought*. Edinburgh: T. & T. Clark, 1984.

Huizenga, Annette Bourland. *1–2 Timothy and Titus*. Wisdom Commentary 53. Collegeville: Liturgical, 2016.

Hultgren, Arland J. *1–2 Timothy, Titus*. ACNT. Minneapolis: Augsburg, 1984.

———. *The Rise of Normative Christianity*. Minneapolis: Fortress, 1994.

Husbands, Mark, and Daniel J. Treier. *Justification: What's at Stake in the Current Debates*. Downers Grove: InterVarsity, 2004.

Irons, Charles Lee. *The Righteousness of God: A Lexical Examination of the Covenant-Faithfulness Interpretation*. WUNT 2. Volume 386. Tübingen: Mohr Siebeck, 2015.

Jensen, Robert W. *Canon and Creed*. Louisville: Westminster John Knox, 2010.

Jeremias, Joachim, and Hermann Strathmann. *Die Briefe an Thimotheus und Titus, Der Brief an die Hebräer*. Göttingen: Dandendorf & Ruprecht, 1968.

Johnson, Luke Timothy. "First Timothy 1,1–20: The Shape of the Struggle." In *1 Timothy Reconsidered*, edited by Karl Paul Donfried, 19–39. Leuven: Peeters, 2008.

———. *The First and Second Letters to Timothy: A New Translation and Commentary*. AYB. New Haven, CT: Yale University Press, 2001

———. *I Timothy, 2 Timothy, Titus*. Knox Preaching Guides. Atlanta: John Knox, 1987.

———. *Letters to Paul's Delegates: 1 Timothy, 2 Timothy, Titus*. NTC. Valley Forge, PA: Trinity Press International, 1996.

———. "*Oikonomia Theou*: The Theological Voice of 1 Timothy from the Perspective of Pauline Authorship." *Horizons in Biblical Theology* 21 (1999) 87–104.

Johnston, R. K. "Imputation." In *EDT*, edited by Walter A. Elwell, 600–601. Grand Rapids: Baker, 2001.

Karris, Robert J. "The Background and Significance of the Polemic of the Pastoral Epistles." *JBL* 92 (1973) 549–64.

———. *The Pastoral Epistles*. NTM 17. Wilmington: Glazier, 1979.

Käsemann, Ernst. "The Righteousness of God in Paul." In *New Testament Questions of Today*, 168–82. Philadelphia: Fortress, 1969.

Keck, Leander. "Faith Seeking Canonical Understanding: Childs' Guide to the Pauline Letters." In *The Bible as Christian Scripture: The Work of Brevard Childs*, edited by Christopher Seitz and Kent Harold Richards, 103–17. Atlanta: Society of Biblical Literature, 2013.

Keegan, T. J. *First and Second Timothy, Titus, Philemon*. New Collegeville Bible Commentary. Collegeville: Liturgical, 2006.

Kelly, J. N. D. *The Pastoral Epistles*. London: A. & C. Black, 1963.

Kenney, Anthony J. P. *A Stylometric Study of the New Testament*. Oxford: Oxford University Press, 1986.

Kereszty, Roch. "The Unity of the Church in Theology." *Second Century* 4 (1984) 202–18.

Kertlege, Karl. *Rechtfertigung bei Paulus: Studien zur Struktur und zum Bedeuntungsgehalt des paulinischen Rechtfertigungsbegriffs*. Münster: Verlag Aschendorff, 1966.

Kidd, Reggie M. "Titus as *Apologia*: Grace for Liars, Beasts, and Bellies." *HBT* 21 (1999) 185–209.

———. *Wealth and Beneficence in the Pastoral Epistles: A "Bourgeois" Form of Early Christianity*. SBLDS 122. Atlanta: Scholars, 1990.

Kim, Seyoon. *Paul and the New Perspective: Second Thoughts on the Origins of Paul's Gospel*. Grand Rapids: Eerdmans, 2002.

Kittel, Gerhard. "Die γενεαλογίαι der Pastoralbriefe." *ZNW* 20 (1921) 49–69.

Klinker-De Klerck, M. "The Pastoral Epistles: Authentic Pauline Writings." *European Journal of Theology* 17.2 (2008) 101–8.

Knight, George W., III. *Commentary on the Pastoral Epistles*. New International Greek Testament Commentary. Grand Rapids: Eerdmans, 1992.

———. *The Faithful Sayings in the Pastoral Letters*. Grand Rapids: Baker, 1979.

Köstenberger, Andreas J. "1 Timothy," "2 Timothy," "Titus." In *The Expositor's Bible Commentary*, edited by Tremper Longman III and D. E. Garland, 12:487–625. Rev. ed. 13 vols. Grand Rapids: Zondervan, 2006.

———. *Commentary on 1–2 Timothy and Titus*. Biblical Theology for Christian Proclamation. Edited by T. Desmond Alexander et al. Nashville: B&H, 2017.

———. "Hermeneutical and Exegetical Challenges in Interpreting the Pastoral Epistles." In *Entrusted with the Gospel: Paul's Theology in the Pastorals*, edited by Andreas J. Köstenberger and Terry L. Wilder, 1–27. Nashville: B&H, 2010.

Köstenberger, Andreas J., and Terry L. Wilder, eds. *Entrusted with the Gospel: Paul's Theology in the Pastoral Epistles*. Nashville: B&H, 2010.

Köstenberger, Andreas J., and Thomas R. Schreiner. *Women in the Church: An Interpretation and Application of 1 Timothy 2:9–15*. 3rd ed. Wheaton: Crossway, 2016.

Kruse, Colin G. *Paul, the Law, and Justification*. Peabody: Hendrickson, 1997.

Ladd, George Eldon. *A Theology of the New Testament*. Grand Rapids: Eerdmans, 1993.

Lash, Jeff. "The New Perspective and Good Deeds: A Contextual Comparison of 'Works' in Paul from Galatians and the Pastoral Epistles." MA thesis, Grand Rapids Baptist Seminary, 2012.

Lau, Andrew Y. *Manifest in Flesh: The Epiphany Christology of the Pastoral Epistles*. Tübingen: Mohr, 1996.

Lemcio, C. C. "Images of the Church in 1 Corinthians and 1 Timothy: An Exercise in Canonical Hermeneutics." *Asbury Theological Journal* 56 (2001) 45–59.

Liefeld, W. L. *1 and 2 Timothy, Titus*. The NIV Application Commentary. Grand Rapids: Zondervan, 1999.

Lock, Walter. *The Pastoral Epistles: Critical and Exegetical Commentary*. ICC. Edinburgh: T. & T. Clark, 1924.

Lohfink, Gerhard. "Paulinische Theologie in der Rezeption der Pastoralbriefe." In *Paulus in den neutestamentlichen Spätschriften: zur Paulusrezeption im Neuen Testament*, 50–121. Freiburg: Herder, 1981.

Lohmeyer, Ernst. *Probleme Paulinischer Theologie*. Stuttgart: W. Kohlhammer Verlag, 1961.

Longenecker, Richard N. *Galatians*. WBC 41. Nashville: Nelson, 1990.

———. *Paul, Apostle of Liberty*. 2nd ed. Grand Rapids: Eerdmans, 2015.

———, ed. *The Road From Damascus: The Impact of Paul's Conversion on His Life, Thought, and Ministry*. Grand Rapids: Eerdmans, 1997.

Luther, Martin. *Commentary on Romans*. Kregel Classics. Translated by J. Theodore Mueller. Grand Rapids: Kregel, 1976.

MacDonald, Margaret Y. "Beyond Identification of the Topos of Household Management: Reading the Household Codes in Light of Recent Methodologies and Theoretical Perspectives in the Study of the New Testament." *NTS* 57.1 (2011) 65–90.

———. *The Pauline Churches: A Socio-Historical Study of Institutionalization of the Pauline and Deutero-Pauline Writings*. SNTSMS 60. Cambridge: Cambridge University Press, 1988.

Macleod, Donald. "The New Perspective: Paul, Luther, and Judaism." *Scottish Bulletin of Evangelical Theology* 22.1 (2004) 4–31.

Malherbe, Abraham J. "'Christ Jesus Came into the World to Save Sinners': Soteriology in the Pastoral Epistles." In *Salvation in the New Testament: Perspectives on Soteriology*, 331–58. Leiden: Brill, 2005.

———. *Moral Exhortation: A Greco-Roman Sourcebook.* LEC 4. Philadelphia: Westminster, 1986.

Malina, Bruce J., and John J. Pilch. *Social-Science Commentary on the Deutero-Pauline Letters.* Minneapolis: Fortress, 2013.

Mappes, D. A. "The Heresy Paul Opposed in 1 Timothy." *Bibliotheca Sacra* 156 (1999) 452–58.

Marshall, I. Howard. "The Christian Life in 1 Timothy." *Reformed Theological Review* 49 (1990) 81–90.

———. "Faith and Works in the Pastoral Epistles." SNTSU 9 (1984) 203–18.

———. "The Pastoral Epistles in Recent Study." In *Entrusted with the Gospel: Paul's Theology in the Pastorals*, edited by Andreas J. Köstenberger and Terry L. Wilder, 268–324. Nashville: B&H, 2010.

———. "Recent Study of the Pastoral Epistles." *Them* 23 (1997) 3–21.

———. "Salvation, Grace, and Works in the Later Writings in the Pauline Corpus." *NTS* 42 (1996) 3–29.

Marshall, I. Howard, with Philip Towner. *A Critical and Exegetical Commentary on the Pastoral Epistles.* ICC. Edinburgh: T. & T. Clark, 1999.

Martin, Brice L. *Christ and the Law in Paul.* Eugene, OR: Wipf & Stock, 2001.

Martin, Dale B. *Pedagogy of the Bible: An Analysis and Proposal.* Louisville: Westminster John Knox, 2008.

Martyn, J. Louis. *Galatians: A New Translation with Introduction and Commentary.* Anchor Bible 33A. New York: Doubleday, 1997.

Matlock, R. Barry. "Almost Cultural Studies? Reflections on the 'New Perspective' on Paul." In *Biblical Studies/Cultural Studies*, edited by J. Cheryl Exum and Stephen D. Moore, 433–59. Sheffield: Sheffield Academic Press, 1998.

Maxwell, Paul C. "Analyzing the Apostle Paul's 'Robust Conscience:' Identifying and Engaging the Psychological Concerns of Krister Stendahl's Inceptive Article." *WTJ* 75 (2013) 145–64.

McCormack, Bruce L. *Justification in Perspective: Historical Developments and Contemporary Challenges.* Grand Rapids: Baker, 2006.

McDonald, Ian. "The New Perspective on Paul." *ExpT* 114 (2003) 208–33.

McGrath, Alister E. *Iustitia Dei: A History of the Christian Doctrine of Justification.* 3rd ed. Cambridge: Cambridge University Press, 2005.

Meade, David G. *Pseudonymity and Canon: An Investigation of the Relationship of Authorship and Authority in Jewish and Earliest Christian Tradition.* WUNT 39. Tübingen: Mohr Siebeck, 1986.

Meek, James A. "The New Perspective on Paul: An Introduction for the Uninitiated." *CJ* 27 (2001) 208–33.

Meinardus, Otto F.A. *In the Footsteps of the Saints: St. Paul is Greece.* New Rochelle: Caratzas, 1979.

Merkle, Benjamin L. *The Elder and Overseer: One Office in the Early Church.* SBL 57. New York: Lang, 2003.

Merz, A. "The Fictitious Self-Exposition of Paul: How Might Intertextual Theory Suggest a Reformulation of the Hermeneutics of Pseudepigraphy?" In *The Intertextuality of the Epistles: Explorations of Theory and Practice*, edited by T. L. Brodie et al., 113–32. Sheffield: Sheffield Phoenix, 2006.

Michel, O. "*Grundfragen der Pastoralbriefe.*" In *Auf dem Grunde der Apostel und Propheten. Festgabe für Theophil Wurm*, edited by M. Loeser, 83–99. Stuttgart: Quell, 1948.

Mijoga, H. B. P. *The Pauline Notion of Deeds of the Law*. San Francisco: International Scholars Publications, 1999.

Miller, J. D. *The Pastoral Letters as Composite Documents*. SNTSM 93. Cambridge: Cambridge University Press, 1997.

Mitchell, M. M. "New Testament Envoys in the Context of Greco-Roman Diplomatic and Epistolary Conventions: The Example of Timothy and Titus." *JBL* 111 (1992) 641–62.

Mitton, C. Leslie. *The Formation of the Pauline Corpus of Letters*. London: Epworth, 1955.

Moffatt, James. *Paul and Paulinism*. Boston: Pilgrim, 1910.

Montefiore, C. G. *Judaism and St. Paul*. London: Goschen, 1914.

———. *Liberal Judaism: An Essay*. New York: MacMillan, 1903.

———. "Rabbinic Judaism and the Epistles of St. Paul." *Jewish Quarterly Review* 13 (1900–1901) 61–217.

———. *Rabbinic Literature and Gospel Teachings*. London: MacMillan, 1930.

Moo, Douglas J. "Israel and the Law in Romans 5–11: Interaction with the New Perspective." In *Justification and Variegated Nomism*, edited by D. A. Carson et al., 2:185–216. 2 vols. Grand Rapids: Baker, 2004.

———. "John Barclay's *Paul and the Gift* and The New Perspective on Paul." *Them* 41.2 (2016) 279–88.

———. "'Law,' 'Works of the Law,' and Legalism in Paul." *WTJ* 45 (1983) 73–100.

Moore, George F. "Christian Writers on Judaism." *HTR* 14 (1921) 197–254.

———. *Judaism in the First Centuries of the Christian Era: The Age of the Tannaim*. 3 vols. Harvard: Harvard University Press, 1930.

Montague, G. T. *First and Second Timothy, Titus*. Catholic Commentary on Sacred Scripture. Grand Rapids: Baker Academic, 2008.

Mounce, William D. *Pastoral Epistles*. WBC 46. Nashville: Word, 2000.

Moule, C. F. D. *An Idiom Book of New Testament Greek*. 2nd ed. Cambridge: Cambridge University Press, 1959.

———. "The Problem of the Pastoral Epistles: A Reappraisal." *Bulletin of the John Rylands University Library of Manchester* 47 (1965) 430–52.

Moule, H. C. G. *The Second Epistle to Timothy: Short Devotional Studies on the Dying Letter of St. Paul*. 1905. Reprint, Grand Rapids: Baker, 1952.

Moyise, Steve. *The Old Testament in the New: An Introduction*. 2nd ed. Revised and expanded. London: Bloomsbury, 2015.

Murphy-O'Connor, Jerome. "2 Timothy Contrasted with 1 Timothy and Titus." *RevBib* 98 (1991) 403–18.

———. "Pastoral Epistles." *RevBib* 108 (2001) 630–35.

———. *Paul: A Critical Life*. Oxford: Clarendon, 1996.

Mutschler, Bernhard. *Glaube in den Pastoralbriefe: Pistis als Mitte christlicher Existenz*. WUNT 256. Tübingen: Mohr Siebeck, 2010.

Nes, Jermo van. "On the Origin of the Pastorals' Authenticity Criticism: A 'New' Perspective." *NTS* 62.2 (2016) 315–20.

———. *Pauline Language and the Pastoral Epistles: A Study of Linguistic Variation in the Corpus Paulinum.* Leiden: Brill, 2018.

Neudorfer, H. W. *Der erste Brief des Paulus an Timotheus.* Historisch Theologische Auslegung. Wuppertal: Brockhaus/Geissen: Brunnen, 2004.

Neumann, Kenneth J. *The Authenticity of the Pauline Epistles in Light of Stylostatistical Analysis.* SBLDS 120. Atlanta: Scholars, 1990.

Ngewa, Samuel M. *1 & 2 Timothy and Titus.* African Bible Commentary. Grand Rapids: Zondervan, 2009.

Noble, Paul R. *The Canonical Approach: A Critical Reconstruction of the Hermeneutics of Brevard S. Childs.* Leiden: Brill, 1995.

Perkins, P. "Pastoral Epistles." In *Eerdmans Commentary on the Bible,* edited by J. D. G. Dunn and J. W. Rogerson, 1428–46. Grand Rapids: Eerdmans, 2003.

Perrin, Nicholas and Richard B. Hays, eds. *Jesus, Paul and the People of God: A Theological Dialogue with N. T. Wright.* Downers Grove: IVP Academic, 2011.

Pietersen, Lloyd K. *The Polemic of the Pastorals: A Sociological Examination of the Development of Pauline Christianity.* JSNTSup 264. London: T. & T. Clark, 2004.

Piper, John. *Counted Righteous in Christ: Should We Abandon the Imputation of Christ's Righteousness?* Wheaton: Crossway, 2002.

———. *The Future of Justification: A Response to N. T. Wright.* Downers Grove: InterVarsity, 2008.

Porter, Stanley E. "Pauline Authorship and the Pastoral Epistles: Implications for Canon." *BBR* 5 (1995) 105–23.

Porter, Stanley E., and Gregory P. Fewster, eds. *Paul and Pseudepigraphy.* Pauline Studies 8. Leiden: Brill, 2013.

Price, Robert M. "The Evolution of the Pauline Canon." *Hervomde Teologiese Studies* 53 (1997) 36–65.

Prior, Michael. *Paul the Letter-Writer and the Second Letter to Timothy.* JSNTSup 23. Sheffield: Sheffield, 1989.

———. "Revisiting the Pastoral Epistles." *Scripture Bulletin* 31 (2001) 2–19.

Quarles, Charles L. "The Soteriology of R. Akiba and E. P. Sanders' *Paul and Palestinian Judaism*," *NTS* 42 (1996) 185–95.

Quinn, Jerome D. *The Letter to Titus: A New Translation with Notes and Commentary and An Introduction to Titus, I and II Timothy, the Pastoral Epistles.* AYB. New Haven: Yale University Press, 1990.

Quinn, Jerome D., and William C. Wacker. *The First and Second Letters to Timothy: A New Translation with Notes and Commentary.* ECC. Grand Rapids: Eerdmans, 2000.

Rainbow, Paul A. *The Way of Salvation: The Role of Christian Obedience in Justification.* Paternoster Biblical Monographs. Milton Keynes: Paternoster, 2005.

Räisänen, Heikki. *Jesus, Paul, and Torah: Collected Essays.* Sheffield: Sheffield Academic Press, 1992.

———. *Paul and the Law.* WUNT 29. Tübingen: Mohr Siebeck, 1983.

Rapa, Robert Keith. *The Meaning of "Works of the Law" in Galatians and Romans.* SBLit 31. Edited by Hemchand Gossai. New York: Lang, 2001.

Ratzlaff, Lloyd W. "Salvation: Individualistic or Communal?" *Journal of Psychology and Theology* 4.2 (1976) 108–17.

Reicke, Bo. *The New Testament Era: The World of the Bible from 500 B. C. to A. D. 100.* Translated by David E. Green. Philadelphia: Fortress, 1974.

Reuss, Joseph. *Der Brief an Titus.* Düsseldorf: Patmos-Verlag, 1966.

Richards, E. Randolph. *Paul and First-Century Letter Writing: Secretaries, Compositions, and Collection.* Downers Grove: InterVarsity, 2004.

Richards, William A. *Difference and Distance in Post-Pauline Christianity: An Epistolary Analysis of the Pastorals.* SBLit 44. New York: Lang, 2002.

Robinson, James M., and Helmut Koester. *Trajectories through Early Christianity.* Philadelphia: Fortress, 1971.

Roetzel, Calvin. *Paul: The Man and the Myth.* Minneapolis: Fortress, 1999.

Rosner, Brian S. *Paul and the Law: Keeping the Commandments of God.* New Studies in Biblical Theology 31. Downers Grove: Intervarsity, 2013.

Saarinen, R. *The Pastoral Epistles with Philemon and Jude.* Brazos Theological Commentary on the Bible. Grand Rapids: Brazos, 2008.

Sailhamer, John. *Introduction to Old Testament Theology: A Canonical Approach.* Grand Rapids: Zondervan, 1995.

Sanders, E. P. "The Covenant as a Soteriological Category and the Nature of Salvation in Palestinian and Hellenistic Judaism." In *Jews, Greeks and Christians,* edited by Robert Hamerton Kelly and Robin Scroggs, 11–44. Leiden: Brill, 1976.

———. "On the Question of Fulfilling the Law in Paul and Rabbinic Judaism." In *Donum Gentilicium: New Testament Studies in Honour of David Daube,* edited by C. K. Barrett et al., 103–26. Oxford: Clarendon, 1978.

———. "Patterns of Religion in Paul and Rabbinic Judaism: A Holistic Method of Comparison." *HTR* 66 (1973) 455–78.

———. *Paul.* Oxford: Oxford University Press, 1991.

———. *Paul: The Apostle's Life, Letters, and Thought.* Minneapolis: Fortress, 2015.

———. *Paul, the Law, and the Jewish People.* Philadelphia: Fortress, 1973.

———. *Paul and Palestinian Judaism: A Comparison of Patterns of Religion.* Minneapolis: Fortress, 1977.

———. "Paul's Attitude Toward the Jewish People." *Union Seminary Quarterly Review* 33 (1978) 175–87.

Sanders, James. *Canon and Community: A Guide to Canonical Criticism.* Philadelphia: Fortress, 1984.

———. *Torah and Canon.* Philadelphia: Fortress, 1972.

Sandmel, Samuel. "Myths, Genealogies, Jewish Myths and the Writing of the Gospels." In *Two Living Traditions: Essays on Religion and the Bible,* 158–65. Detroit: Wayne State University Press, 1972.

Sandys-Wunsch, J., and L. Eldredge. "J. P. Gabler and the Distinction between Biblical and Dogmatic Theology: Translation, Commentary, and Discussion of His Originality." *SJT* 33 (1980) 133–80.

Schechter, Solomon. *Aspects of Rabbinic Theology.* 1909. Reprint, New York: Schoken, 1961.

Scherbenske, Eric W. *Canonizing Paul: Ancient Editorial Practice and the Corpus Paulinum.* New York: Oxford University Press, 2013.

Schlatter, Adolf. *Die Kirche der Griechen im Urteil des Paulus: Eine Auslegung Seiner Briefe an Timotheus und Titus.* Stuttgart: Calver Verlag, 1958.

Schleiermacher, Friedrich. *Über den sogenannten ersten Brief des Paulus an den Timotheos.* Berlin: Sendscriben an J. C. Glass, 1807.

Schmidt, Johann Ernst Christian. *Historisch-kritische Einleitung in's Neue Testament.* Giessen: Tasche und Muller, 1804.

Schnabel, E. J. *Paul and the Early Church.* Early Christian Mission 2. Downers Grove: InterVarsity, 2004.

Schoeps, H. Joachim. *The Jewish-Christian Argument: A History of Theologies in Conflict.* Translated by David Green. London: Faber & Faber, 1963.

———. *The Theology of Paul the Apostle in the Light of Jewish Religious History.* Translated by H. Knight. London: Lutterworth, 1961.

Schreiner, Thomas R., "Is Perfect Obedience to the Law Possible? A Re-examination of Galatians 3:10." *JETS* 27 (1984) 151–60.

———. *The Law and Its Fulfillment: A Pauline Theology of Law.* Grand Rapids: Baker, 1993.

———. *Paul: Apostle of God's Glory in Christ.* Downers Grove: InterVarsity, 2001.

———. "'Works of Law' in Paul" *NovT* 33.3 (1991) 217–44.

Schubert, Paul. *Form and Function of the Pauline Thanksgiving.* Berlin: Verlag von Alfred Töpelmann, 1939.

Schürmann, Heinz. "Das Testament des Paulus für die Kirche." In *Traditionsgeschichtliche Untersuchung zu den synoptischen Evangelien*, 310–40. Düsseldorf: Patmos-Verlag, 1968.

Schütz, J. H. *Paul and the Anatomy of Apostolic Authority.* Cambridge: Cambridge University Press, 1975.

Schweitzer, Albert. *The Mysticism of Paul the Apostle.* Translated by W. Montgomery. London: A. & C. Black, 1931.

———. *Paul and His Interpreters: A Critical History.* Translated by W. Montgomery. London: A. & C. Black, 1912.

Scott, Ernest F. *The Pastoral Epistles.* MNTC. New York: Harper, 1936.

Segal, Alan F. *Paul the Convert: The Apostolate and Apostasy of Saul the Pharisee.* New Haven: Yale University Press, 1990.

Seifrid, Mark A. *Christ, Our Righteousness: Paul's Theology of Justification.* New Studies in Biblical Theology 9. Downers Grove: InterVarsity, 2000.

———. *Justification by Faith: The Origin and Development of a Central Pauline Theme.* Leiden: Brill, 1992.

———. "The 'New Perspective on Paul' and Its Problems." *Them* 25.2 (2000) 4–18.

Silva, Moisés. "The Law and Christianity: Dunn's New Synthesis." *WTJ* 53 (1991) 339–53.

Smith, James E. "The New Perspective on Paul: A Select and Annotated Bibliography." *CTR* 2.2 (2005) 91–111.

Smith, Jeffrey. "An Overview and Critique of the New Perspective on Paul's Doctrine of Justification." *RBTR* 3.1 (2006) 118–33.

Soulen, Richard N., and R. Kendall Soulen. *Handbook of Biblical Criticism.* 4th ed. Louisville: Westminster John Knox, 2011.

Spain, Carl. *The Letters of Paul to Timothy and Titus.* The Living Word Commentary. Austin: Sweet, 1970.

Spence, Alan J. *Justification: A Guide for the Perplexed.* London: T. & T. Clark, 2012.

Spicq, Ceslaus. *Saint Paul, Les Epitres Pastorales.* 2 vols. 4th rev. ed. Etudes Bibliques. Paris: Gabalda, 1969.

Sprinkle, Preston M. "The Old Perspective on the New Perspective: A Review of 'Pre-Sanders' Thinkers." *Them* 30 (2005) 21–31.

———. *Paul and Judaism Revisited: A Study of Divine and Human Agency in Salvation*. Downers Grove: Intervarsity, 2013.

Stark, Rodney. *The Rise of Christianity: How the Obscure, Marginal Jesus Movement Became the Dominant Religious Force in the Western World in a Few Centuries*. New York: HarperCollins, 1997.

Stendahl, Krister. "The Apostle Paul and the Introspective Conscience of the West." *HTR* (1963) 199–215.

———. "The Apostle Paul and the Introspective Conscience of the West." In *Paul Among Jews and Gentiles*, 78–96. Philadelphia: Fortress, 1976.

———. "Biblical Theology, Contemporary." In *The Interpreter's Dictionary of the Bible*, 1:418–32. 5 vols. New York: Abingdon, 1962.

———. "Method in the Study of Biblical Theology." In *The Bible in Modern Scholarship*, edited by J. Philip Hyatt, 196–209. London: Carey Kingsgate, 1966.

———. *Paul Among Jews and Gentiles*. London: SCM, 1977.

Stirewalt, M. Luther, Jr. *Paul, the Letter Writer*. Grand Rapids: Eerdmans, 2003.

Stout, Stephen O. *The "Man Christ Jesus": The Humanity of Jesus in the Teaching of the Apostle Paul*. Eugene, OR: Wipf & Stock, 2011.

Stowers, Stanley K. *Letter Writing in Greco-Roman Antiquity*. Philadelphia: Westminster, 1986.

Strecker, Georg. *Theology of the New Testament*. Edited by Friedrich Wilhelm Horn. Translated by M. Eugene Boring. Louisville: Westminster John Knox, 2000. Reprinted from the German original, 1996.

Stuhlmacher, Peter. *Gerechtigkeit Gottes und bei Paulus*. Göttingen: Vandenhoeck und Ruprecht, 1966.

———. *Reconciliation, Law, and Righteousness: Essays in Biblical Theology*. Philadelphia: Fortress, 1986.

———. *Revisiting Paul's Doctrine of Justification: A Challenge to the New Perspective*. Downers Grove: InterVarsity, 2001.

Sumney, Jerry L. "'God Our Savior': The Fundamental Operational Theological Assertion of 1 Timothy." *HBT* 21 (1999) 105–23.

———. "'God Our Savior': The Theology of 1 Timothy." *Lexington Theological Quarterly* 36 (2001) 31–41.

Swaim, Barton. "A New Take on the Apostle Paul." *Wall Street Journal*, May 16, 2019. https://www.wsj.com/articles/a-new-take-on-the-apostle-paul-11558048430.

Thielman, Frank. "The Coherence of Paul's View of the Law: The Evidence of First Corinthians." *NTS* 38.2 (1992) 235–53.

———. *From Plight to Solution: A Jewish Framework for Understanding Paul's View of the Law in Galatians and Romans*. Leiden: Brill, 1989.

———. *Paul and the Law: A Contextual Approach*. Downers Grove: Intervarsity, 1994.

———. *Theology of the New Testament: A Canonical and Synthetic Approach*. Grand Rapids: Zondervan, 2005.

Thiselton, Anthony. "Canon, Community, and Theological Construction: Introduction." In *Canon and Biblical Interpretation*, edited by Craig Bartholomew et al., 1–30. Scripture and Hermeneutics Series 7. Grand Rapids: Zondervan, 2006.

Thomas, Robert L. "Hermeneutics of the New Perspective on Paul." *The Master's Seminary Journal* 29 (2018) 21–43.

Thompson, Michael. *The New Perspective on Paul*. GBS 26. Cambridge: Grove, 2002.

Thorton, Dillon T. "Sin Seizing an Opportunity through the Commandments: The Law in 1 Tim 1:8–11 and Rom 6–8." *HBT* 36 (2014) 142–58.

Thurston, B. "The Theology of Titus." *HBT* 21 (1999) 171–84.

Torrance, T. F. "The Deposit of Faith." *SJT* 36 (1983) 1–28.

Towner, Philip H. "1–2 Timothy and Titus." In *Commentary on the New Testament Use of the Old Testament*, edited by G. K. Beale and D. A. Carson, 894–98. Grand Rapids: Baker, 2007.

———. "Christology in the Letters to Timothy and Titus." In *Contours of Christology in the New Testament*, edited by Richard Longenecker, 219–44. Grand Rapids: Eerdmans, 2005.

———. *The Goal of Our Instruction: The Structure of Theology and Ethics in the Pastoral Epistles*. London: Bloomsbury, 2015.

———. *The Letters to Timothy and Titus*. NICNT. Grand Rapids: Eerdmans, 2006.

———. "The Portrait of Paul and the Theology of 2 Timothy: The Closing Chapter of the Pauline Story." *HBT* (1999) 151–70.

———. "Pauline Theology or Pauline Tradition in the Pastoral Epistles: The Question of Method." *TynBul* 46.2 (1995) 287–314.

Treblico, Paul R. *The Early Christians in Ephesus from Paul to Ignatius*. WUNT 166. Tübingen: Mohr Siebeck, 2004.

Treier, Daniel J. *Introducing Theological Interpretation of Scripture: Recovering a Christian Practice*. Grand Rapids: Baker Academic, 2008.

Trummer, Peter. *Die Paulustradition der Pastoralbriefe*. Beiträge zur biblischen Exegese Theologie 8. Frankfurt: Lang, 1978.

Twomey, Jay. *The Pastoral Epistles Through the Centuries*. BBC. Malden: Wiley-Blackwell, 2009.

Tyson, Joseph B. "'Works of Law' in Galatians." *JBL* 92.3 (1973) 423–31.

Van der Horst, Pieter. "The Jews of Ancient Crete." *JJS* 39.2 (1988) 183–200.

Vanhoozer, Kevin J. *Is There a Meaning in This Text? The Bible, the Reader, and the Morality of Literary Knowledge*. Grand Rapids: Zondervan, 1998.

———. "Wrighting the Wrongs of the Reformation? The State of the Union with Christ in St. Paul and Protestant Soteriology." In *Jesus, Paul and the People of God: A Theological Dialogue with N. T. Wright*, edited by Norman Perrin and Richard Hays, 235–59. Downers Grove: InterVarsity, 2011.

VanLandingham, Christopher. *Judgment and Justification in Early Judaism and the Apostle Paul*. Peabody: Hendrickson, 2006.

Van Neste, Ray. "Cohesion and Structure in the Pastoral Epistles." In *Entrusted with the Gospel: Paul's Theology in the Pastorals*, edited by Andreas J. Köstenberger and Terry L. Wilder, 84–104. Nashville: B&H, 2010.

———. *Cohesion and Structure in the Pastoral Epistles*. JSNTSup 280. New York: T. & T. Clark, 2004.

———. "Structure and Cohesion in Titus: Problems and Method." *The Bible Translator: Technical Papers* 53 (2002) 118–32.

Vaughan, Alton Mark. "An Investigation of the Authenticity of the Pastoral Epistles: A Response to the New Perspective on Paul." PhD diss., Mid-America Baptist Theological Seminary, 1999.

Venema, Cornelius P. *The Gospel of Free Acceptance in Christ: An Assessment of the Reformation and "New Perspectives" of Paul*. Carlisle: Banner of Truth, 2006.

Verner, David C. *The Household of God: The Social World of the Pastorals*. SBLDS 71. Chico: Scholars, 1983.

Visscher, Gerhard H. *Romans 4 and the New Perspective on Paul: Faith Embraces the Promise*. Edited by Hemchand Gossai. SBLit 122. New York: Lang, 2009.

Wall, Robert W. "The Function of the Pastoral Letters within the Pauline Canon of the New Testament: A Canonical Approach." In *The Pauline Canon*, edited by Stanley E. Porter, 27–44. Boston: Brill, 2004.

Wall, Robert W., and Eugene E. Lemcio. *The New Testament as Canon: A Reader in Canonical Criticism*. JSNTSup 76. Sheffield: Sheffield Academic, 1992.

Wall, Robert W., with Richard B. Steele. *1 & 2 Timothy and Titus*. THNTC. Edited by Joel Green and Max Turner. Grand Rapids: Eerdmans, 2012.

Wallace, Daniel B. *Greek Grammar Beyond the Basics: An Exegetical Syntax of the New Testament*. Grand Rapids: Zondervan, 1996.

Ware, James. P. "Law, Christ, and Covenant: Paul's Theology of the Law in Romans 3:19–20." *JTS* 62 (2011) 513–40.

Waters, Guy Prentiss. *Justification and the New Perspectives on Paul: A Review and Response*. Phillipsburg: P&R, 2004.

Watson, Francis. *Paul and the Hermeneutics of Faith*. London: T. & T. Clark, 2004.

———. *Paul, Judaism, and the Gentiles: Beyond the New Perspective*. Grand Rapids: Eerdmans, 2007.

Weber, Max. *Economy and Society: An Outline of Interpretive Sociology*. Edited by G. Roth and C. Wittich. New York: Bedminster, 1968.

Weiser, A. *Der zweite Briefe an Timotheus*. Evangelisch-Katholischer Kommentar zum Neuen Testament. Düsseldorf: Benzinger/Neukirchen-Vluyn: Neukirchener, 2003.

Westerholm, Stephen. *Israel's Law and the Church's Faith: Paul and His Recent Interpreters*. Grand Rapids: Eerdmans, 1988.

———. "Justification by Faith Is the Answer: What Is the Question?" *Concordia Theological Quarterly* 70 (2006) 197–217.

———. *Justification Reconsidered: Rethinking a Pauline Theme*. Grand Rapids: Eerdmans, 2013.

———. "The Law and the 'Just Man' (1 Timothy 1, 3–11)." *ST* 36 (1982) 79–95.

———. "The New Perspective on Paul in Review." *Direction* 44.1 (2015) 4–15.

———. *Perspectives Old and New on Paul: The "Lutheran" Paul and His Critics*. Grand Rapids: Eerdmans, 2004.

Westfall, Cynthia Long. "A Moral Dilemma? The Epistolary Body of 2 Timothy." In *Paul and Ancient Letter Form*, edited by Stanley E. Porter and Sean A. Adams, 213–52. Pauline Studies 6. Leiden: Brill, 2010.

White, L. M. "Urban Development and Social Change in Imperial Ephesos." In *Ephesos: Metropolis of Asia*, edited by H. Koester, 27–79. Harvard Theological Studies 41. Valley Forge: Trinity International, 1995.

Wieland, George M. "The Function of Salvation in the Letters to Timothy and Titus." In *Entrusted with the Gospel: Paul's Theology in the Pastoral Epistles*, edited by Andreas J. Köstenberger and Terry L. Wilder, 153–72. Nashville: B&H, 2010.

———. "Roman Crete and the Letter to Titus." *NTS* 55 (2009) 338–54.

———. *The Significance of Salvation: A Study of Salvation Language in the Pastoral Epistles*. Paternoster Biblical Monographs. Milton Keynes: Paternoster, 2006.

Wiesinger, August. *Biblical Commentary on St. Paul's Epistles*. Translated by J. Fulton. Edinburgh: T. & T. Clark, 1851.

Wilckens, Ulrich. *Der Brief on die Römer*. 3 vols. Cologne: Benzinger, 1978–82.

———. "Die Bekehrung des Paulus als religionsgeschichtliches Problem." *Zeitschrift für Theologie und Kirche* 56.3 (1959) 273–93.

———. "Was heist bei Paulus: 'Aus Werken des Gesetzes wird kein Mensch Gerecht'?" In *Rechtfertigung als Freihei: Paulusstudien*, 77–109. Neukirchen-Vluyn: Neukirchener, 1974.

Wilder, Terry L. "New Testament Pseudonymity and Deception." *TynBul* 50.1 (1999) 156–58.

———. *Pseudonymity, The New Testament, and Deception: Am Inquiry into Intention and Reception*. Lanham: University Press of America, 2004.

———. "Pseudonymity, the New Testament, and the Pastorals." In *Entrusted with the Gospel: Paul's Theology in the Pastorals*, edited by Andreas J. Köstenberger and Terry L. Wilder, 28–51. Nashville: B&H, 2010.

Wilson, S. G. *Luke and the Pastoral Epistles*. London: SPCK, 1979.

Windisch, Hans. "Zur Christologie der Pastoralbriefe." *ZNW* 34 (1935) 213–38.

Witherington, Ben, III. *A Socio-Rhetorical Commentary Titus, 1–2 Timothy and 1–3 John*. In *Letters and Homilies for Hellenized Christians*, 1:23–390. 3 vols. Downers Grove: InterVarsity Academic, 2006.

Wolter, Michael. "The Development of Pauline Christianity from a 'Religion of Conversion' to a 'Religion of Tradition.'" In *Paul and the Heritage of Israel: Luke's Narrative Claim upon Paul and Israel's Legacy*, edited by D. P. Moessner et al., translated by J. M. McConnell and D. P. Moessner, 49–69. The Library of New Testament Studies 452. London: T. & T. Clark, 2012.

———. *Die Pastoralbriefe als Paulustradition*. Göttingen: Vandenhoeck & Ruprecht, 1988.

———. *Paul: An Outline of His Theology*. Translated by Robert L. Brawley. Waco: Baylor University Press, 2015.

Wrede, William. *Paul*. London: Green, 1907.

———. *Paulus*. Tübingen: Mohr Siebeck, 1907.

Wright, N. T. "4QMMT and Paul: Justification, 'Works,' and Eschatology." In *History and Exegesis: New Testament Essays in Honor of Dr E. Earle Ellis for His 80th Birthday*, edited by Aang-Won (Aaron) Son, 104–32. London: T. & T. Clark, 2006.

———. *The Climax of the Covenant: Christ and the Law in Pauline Theology*. Minneapolis: Fortress, 1993.

———. *Justification: God's Plan and Paul's Vision*. Downers Grove: InterVarsity, 2009.

———. *The New Testament and the People of God*. Minneapolis: Fortress, 1992.

———. *Paul: A Biography*. New York: HarperCollins, 2018.

———. *Paul and His Recent Interpreters: Some Contemporary Debates*. Minneapolis: Fortress, 2015.

———. *Paul and the Faithfulness of God*. 2 vols. Minneapolis: Fortress, 2013.

———. *The Paul Debate: Critical Questions for Understanding the Apostle*. London: SPCK, 2016.

———. *Paul for Everyone: The Pastoral Letters: 1 and 2 Timothy and Titus*. 2nd ed. Louisville: Westminster John Knox, 2004.

———. "The Paul of History and the Apostle of Faith." *TynBul* 29 (1978) 61–88.

———. *Pauline Perspectives: Essays on Paul, 1978–2013*. Minneapolis: Fortress, 2013.

———. "Romans." In *The New Interpreter's Bible*, edited by L. E. Keck, 10:393–770. 12 vols. Nashville: Abingdon, 2002.

———. "Romans and the Theology of Paul." In *Pauline Theology: Romans*, edited by David M. Hay and E. Elizabeth Johnson, 3:30–67. 4 vols. Minneapolis: Fortress, 1995–97.

———. *What Saint Paul Really Said: Was Paul of Tarsus the Real Founder of Christianity?* Grand Rapids: Eerdmans, 1997.

Yarbrough, Robert W. *The Letters to Timothy and Titus.* PNTC. Grand Rapids: Eerdmans, 2018.

Yinger, Kent L. *The New Perspective on Paul: An Introduction.* Eugene, OR: Cascade, 2011.

———. *Paul, Judaism, and Judgment According to Deeds.* SNTSMS 105. Cambridge: Cambridge University Press, 1999.

Young, Frances. *The Theology of the Pastoral Epistles.* NTT. Cambridge: Cambridge University Press, 1994.

Zahl, P. F. M. "Mistakes of the New Perspective on Paul." *Them* 27.1 (2001) 5–11.

Zetterholm, Magnus. *Approaches to Paul: A Student's Guide to Recent Scholarship.* Minneapolis: Fortress, 2009.

Ziesler, John. *The Meaning of Righteousness in Paul.* SNTSMS 20. Cambridge: Cambridge University Press, 1994.

———. *Pauline Christianity.* Rev. ed. Oxford: Oxford University Press, 1990.

———. *Paul's Letter to the Romans.* London: SCM, 1989.

Zimmermann, Christiane. "Wiederentstehung und Erneuerung (Tit 3:5): Zu einem erhaltenswerten Aspekt der Soteriologie des Titusbriefs." *NovT* 51.3 (2009) 272–95.

CPSIA information can be obtained
at www.ICGtesting.com
Printed in the USA
BVHW040216171021
618996BV00008B/97